DEAR QUEEN

Janet Anderson

Red Axe Books

ISBN: 978-0993218385

With special thanks to Stephen Doherty without whom this historical record would not have been preserved.

Photo by courtesy of Andrew Miller, MP for Ellesmere Port and Neston
1992-2015

These are to Certify that

Janet Anderson, MP

is, by The Queen's Command, hereby appointed into the Place and Quality of

Vice-Chamberlain to the Household

To have, hold, exercise and enjoy the said Place, together with all Rights, Profits, Privileges and Advantages thereunto belonging.

This Appointment to be during Her Majesty's Pleasure and to become void on the death of the Sovereign.

Given under my Hand and Seal this Second day of May, 1997 in the 46th Year of Her Majesty's Reign

CONTENTS

FOREWORD

BETWEEN 1997 and 1998 Government whip, Janet Anderson MP, Vice Chamberlain to the Royal Household, wrote nightly reports to Her Majesty the Queen on the business in Parliament. The role dates back to Henry VIII. Janet included all the gossip. In a chatty but proper way she referred to Pre-Menstrual Tension, Champagne parties, Christmas shopping, and which woman MPs were pregnant. She was forthright about colleagues on both sides of the House. She told the Queen that: John Bercow, (now Commons Speaker), was "odious" and a 'nasty piece of work' who raised bogus points of order. Twice-Oscar-winner Glenda Jackson missed debates as Transport Minister. The Ulster Unionists were a sour bunch. Former war correspondent and anti-sleaze MP Martin Bell was a pathetic joke figure. One-time Health Secretary Virginia Bottomley objected to the use of the word gay instead of homosexual. And former Tory leader Michael Howard was loathsome. She spoke of the Teletubbies, the risk of the ceiling falling on the heads of MPs and schoolboy behaviour in the House. The reports have never before been published. They make hilarious reading and a colourful diary of an interesting period in British political history.

Ian Hernon, Deputy Editor, Tribune

INTRODUCTION

What are the chances of a Northern lass from good working class stock like me to meeting the Queen and enjoying the hospitality of Buckingham Palace?

Well, I did when I was appointed Vice Chamberlain, the Government whip responsible for writing nightly reports to the Queen, I had no idea it would lead to regular chats with Her Majesty; that I would share gossip and witness at first hand her warmth and humour. . . and even talk about what the public were doing to the carpets in Buckingham Palace.

It was a pleasure and a delight, occasionally livened up by the odd comment from Prince Philip whose sense of humour is legendary. I recall once being introduced to him at a Buckingham Palace reception with my fellow Government whip, Jim Dowd, as a couple (we are now). 'Are you from the same political party?' he enquired with a chuckle, clearly   curious about our relationship.

I kept thinking of both my grandfathers, who were face workers in the pits, my father, who was a Labour agent in Jarrow, and my mum who was a housewife in County Durham . . . if they could see me now.

The first I knew about my new role was when I received a phone call from Nick Brown, then the Chief Whip, after Labour swept to power in the 1997 General Election. FOR those of us on the Labour benches, election night May 1st had been, as Tony Blair said, "a riot of celebration, exhilaration and expectation . . . history was not so much being made as jumping up and down and dancing." After 18 years Conservative government had ended and we had won by a landslide with 418 seats including 101 women MPs. These were heady, euphoric days . . . and for me there was more to come.

Nick said that Tony Blair wanted to make me a minister but he had argued that I would make a fine whip in his office.

A government whip? Wow, I thought, rather fancy the idea of that. But there was more.

'You see,' said Nick, 'there is something we have to do in government which we did not do in opposition, and we think you'd be rather good at it. Someone has to write to the Queen.

'And you get another £20,000 a year,' he added, as an afterthought.

And so I was duly appointed Vice-Chamberlain of the Royal Household, the first woman to officially hold the position.

There are three particular duties: carrying messages from the Commons to Her Majesty and reporting back; acting as the 'hostage' during the ritual for the State Opening of Parliament; and writing to the Queen every day to report events in the Commons.

My first task was to meet the Queen at the Palace to be formally appointed. What would I wear? Men had always worn morning suit and top hat, for which there was an allowance. A woman was uncharted territory. We sought advice from the Palace. A smart suit would be fine and, of course, a hat would be 'de rigueur'. Someone arranged for Browns of Mayfair to deliver a selection of outfits to my home.

Writing to the Queen – goodness, I almost felt like the Queen.

I selected a rather flattering Jill Sander jacket and skirt in a dusky blue (which I still have and which I will never manage to squeeze into again) and trotted off the next day to pay for it.

'What about a hat?' the sales assistant asked. Of course, she had the perfect one to hand, for £350. 'Oh, I couldn't possibly spend that much on a hat,' I said.

'No problem,' she replied, 'we will lend it to you for the trip to the Palace.' Such generosity, how could I refuse? Needless to say, en route back to Westminster, hat box in hand, I fell in love with the hat. I rang back on my mobile. 'Put it on my card,' I said. And so there I was, kitted out for the big day.

The main purpose of that visit to the Palace when you are first appointed Vice Chamberlain is to receive your 'wand of office'. This is a long stick which looks, for all the world, like a snooker cue. It has a silver bit around the middle and unscrews into two parts.

I don't remember much about that first visit to the Palace apart from saying to myself, 'if only my mum could see me now' as I was dropped off by the government car service.

I was pleasantly surprised by the warmth of the Queen. Her Majesty is supremely adept at making you feel at ease in her presence, something I appreciated more and more when I had to report to her.

The real dilemma was should I curtsy or not, and indeed how on earth do you curtsy? It was not something I had ever done before. In the event, I just did a little bob and that seemed to suffice. And when you leave, do you turn your back on the Monarch or walk backwards? I think I did a bit of both.

Having to write the daily message was now a reality. Of course, no one tells you how to do it, apart from being told I could not email it as a special messenger waited every evening at 6pm to take it to the Palace so that the Queen could read it before dinner. The message is hand-written, but that would have taken me forever. I got permission to write it on screen and then it would be transcribed in pen and ink for delivery.

The only instruction I received was that it should be headed 'Janet Anderson MP with humble duty reports' and the greeting should be 'Your Majesty'.

At the outset, I decided I would make it chatty and humorous where I could. I had had sensed from our first meeting that the Queen herself had a pretty good sense of humour. So I tried to intersperse my messages with gossipy bits about what was going on in the Tea Room or the Commons bars.

From the start, the Queen was very interested in how the new women MPs were doing. The election saw the arrival of 101 Labour women MPs. 'It cannot be easy,' she once said to me, 'juggling family responsibilities with Parliamentary and constituency duties, particularly if your constituency is some distance from Westminster.' 'Well,' I said, 'it helps if you have a partner or spouse who is prepared to share the load.' I suspect the Queen understood that only too well for it is clear that Prince Philip has been a great source of support for her.

However, I did tell the Queen that some of the older men were finding it a bit difficult adapting to such an influx of women. I said that once, when a group of us ordered champagne in the Tea Room to celebrate winning a vote, an ageing Tory grandee slammed down his drink and stormed out, complaining loudly about 'the domination of this place by women'. Her Majesty did not seem impressed by this.

In some of my early messages, I mentioned that Glenda Jackson, then a junior Transport Minister, had failed to turn up in the Commons to respond to a debate. Another Minister had to step in at the last minute to deliver the speech she should have made. After that, there were a number of late night debates to which Glenda should also respond. When I next met the Queen, she asked me about this and, displaying a sense of irony I hadn't quite expected, pondered whether Glenda, a double Oscar-winner, had trouble with performing in public.

'Poor Glenda,' she said. A bit like Elizabeth II commenting on Elizabeth I (one of Ms Jackson's most notable roles) I thought.

My first duty, however, was to go to Buckingham Palace as the 'hostage' on the day of the State Opening, in which the Queen outlines the Government's proposed legislation for the coming session.

A Parliamentarian, namely the Vice Chamberlain, is required to stay in the Palace while the Queen is at Westminster, in order to guarantee her safe return. The tradition dates back to the 17th Century. After Parliament cut off the head of Charles I in 1649, his successors were rather apprehensive about visiting Parliament. So a Government car took me to Buckingham Palace on the morning of the State Opening.

As the Royal party was about to leave, a group of us stood in the central courtyard, me with my wand of office, to see the Queen and the Duke of Edinburgh safely off on their journey to Parliament.

Prince Philip did not disappoint. As we were wishing them well, he turned to me: 'Hmm,' he said, 'if we don't come back safely, you get shot or something, don't you?

'But then,' he continued, 'we won't be able to do that now because you are going to ban hand guns.' (Which we were, in the wake of the Dunblane school shooting tragedy). He clearly thought that was very amusing, chuckling to himself as he got into the waiting coach.

I then settled down in front of the television to watch the State Opening (see Appendix). Once it was over, the Queen and Prince Philip returned to the Palace, where there was a little drinks reception, attended by several members of the Royal Family, and only then was I 'released' to make my way back to Westminster.

Another duty was to take Humble Addresses to the Palace for the Queen's signature. I was never quite sure what constituted a Humble Address but they seemed to involve taxation agreements with former colonies.

In any event, they had to be personally conveyed by me to the Palace for the Queen to sign. All of these audiences with her required me to take my wand of office and to be fairly formally dressed (hat of course).

On one occasion the audience took place in the Queen's own study, a really beautiful circular room. Each of the famous corgis had its own feeding and play station dotted around the room. Her desk was piled high with several red boxes, for the paperwork the Head of State has to read is huge.

It was on these occasions that I was able to have a conversation with the Queen. She often remarked on the late night Parliamentary sittings, asking, 'When will they get some sleep?'

After one such marathon session, the Queen remarked that 'My Parliament has been sitting very long hours recently.' She was clearly concerned about the effects on her Parliamentarians. 'I thought Mr Blair looked rather tired when I met him on Tuesday,' she continued. The PM has an audience with the Queen every week, usually on a Tuesday.

Once a Humble Address had been signed, my job was to report it back to the Commons. This involved me standing at the Bar of the House at 2.30pm after Prayers.

Wand of office in hand, I announced 'Madam Speaker,' for it was Betty Boothroyd in those days, 'I have a message from the Queen.' I then had to take six steps forward, bow, six further steps up to the central table, bow again and hand the Humble Address to the clerk who would pass it to the Speaker.

Then came the really tricky bit. I had to do the whole thing in reverse, walking backwards to the Bar of the House. I had practised this in advance, not wanting to make a complete fool of myself. Alas, I did not bargain for the consequences of wearing shoes with heels. These made it very difficult to negotiate my way backwards in a straight line and once I almost fell into the lap of a Labour MP. There was much hilarity right across the Chamber.

Her Majesty was very interested when the Agriculture Minister, Jeff Rooker, planned to ban green top, or raw, milk. She told me she had read about it in my daily messages. 'Is this true?' she asked. I told her I had taken it up with Jeff because the milk was popular in my own constituency. I knew, too, that the Royal Family were devotees of green top milk, especially the late Queen Mother. They get it from their own herds. It has been banned in Scotland and Wales for ages but Jeff never carried out the ban in England. I reckon that, once I had mentioned it in the messages, Her Majesty might have raised it with the Prime Minister.

Every year, the Queen hosts her Royal Garden Parties at Buckingham Palace. These are splendid occasions with hundreds of guests. The Vice Chamberlain is expected to attend all of them.

As ever, hats are de rigeur for the women, though not all the guests observe this convention these days, much to the annoyance of some of the Gentlemen at Arms. These are usually retired military officers who form Her Majesty's Bodyguard of the Honourable Corps of Gentlemen at Arms.

The tradition dates back to Henry VIII. They attend most Royal occasions and act as ushers at the Garden Parties. They wear morning dress and carry large rolled up black umbrellas, which have presumably replaced the spears they carried in Henry VIII's time. Many of the male guests also wear morning dress.

The guests are directed through the Palace, onto the terrace overlooking the gardens, and then assemble on the lawns to await the Queen and other members of the Royal Family.

The Buckingham Palace garden is outstandingly beautiful. It covers 42 acres and has two and a half miles of gravel paths. It has a mulberry tree dating back to the time of James I of England. Notable features include a large 19th century lake, graced by a flock of flamingos and the Waterloo Vase, the great urn commissioned by Napoleon to commemorate his expected victories and presented to the Prince Regent in 1815. There is a summerhouse, a helicopter pad and a tennis court.

A military band plays the National Anthem as the Queen emerges from the Bow Room and slowly processes through the ranks of assembled guests towards her own private tea tent (the Royal Tent). The Gentlemen at Arms divide the guests to make a channel or pathway for the Queen. If other members of the Royal Family were present, as they usually were, they too have their own channel.

The Gentlemen at Arms select guests to be presented to the Queen and they are asked to stand to the front to make sure they were not missed. It was my job to identify any MPs or other parliamentarians present so that they would be selected.

Once the Queen and the Duke of Edinburgh have completed their passage through the crowds, they meet at the end, just in front of the Royal Tea Tent where tea, sandwiches strawberries and all sorts of wonderful goodies are served. I noticed that sometimes the Queen got to the meeting point before Prince Philip, so deep in conversation was he with the guests. It then fell to the Gentlemen at Arms to hurry him along for it was unthinkable that the Monarch could be kept waiting, even by her husband.

Tommy McAvoy, who was the Comptroller of the Royal Household (usually No 3 in the Government Whips office) and I were allowed to take tea in the Royal Tent. We were asked what kind of tea we would like. In those days, in our house, we just had tea – it was all the same. Tommy said he would have Indian and I said China (not having a clue what China tea was like). Tommy was handed his in a large bone china cup, and mine was in a smaller version. 'Oh,' I said, 'I didn't know you served different teas in different sized cups.' 'Oh, no madam,' replied the waiter, 'one doesn't. It's just that he is a gentleman and you are a lady, so he gets the larger cup.' May sound a bit quaint, but not too different from my mum always giving my dad the bigger chop because he was the main breadwinner I suppose.

My conversations with the Gentlemen at Arms were hilarious. What was it like being an MP, they wanted to know. And what was it like being a woman MP? I suppose that was understandable since they had never met a female Vice Chamberlain before (there had not been one).

Most of them were public school, ex military. One told me how his nanny had always sworn by the use of smelling salts and carried them with her everywhere. Lo and behold, he produced a bottle from his pocket, unscrewed the top to show me what they were like. Wow! What a dreadful smell of ammonia, but clearly it was something that gave him comfort because it reminded him of his childhood.

Tommy and I, because of our Palace duties, were allowed to take tea in the Royal tent. But Nick Brown, the Chief Whip and a Cabinet minister, was only allowed in the diplomatic tent, and he was really keen for his mother to meet the Queen.

So we devised a plan. When the Queen and Prince Philip took their leave of us in the Royal tent, they would walk back down the garden and, en route, pass the diplomatic tent, where Nick and his mum would be waiting outside.

It worked like a dream and Her Majesty stopped to talk to Nick's mum. She seemed delighted at the opportunity to make an elderly lady feel valued. Just another example of the Queen's caring sensitivity. It is no wonder her children and grandchildren love her.

The Palace courtiers were clearly very bemused and interested in what Government whips did. So much so that they asked if I would get together a group of my fellow whips to lunch at the Palace.

About six of us went, and we had an hilarious time explaining to them that whips were essentially the Government's business managers; it was our job to make sure the Government's programme was passed, and finally, of course, signed off by the Queen giving her Royal Assent.

But we could not resist also regaling them with a few tales of MPs' misdemeanours with which we had to deal, no names of course.

There were so many of us to go to the Palace that day that the government car service, which has a pool of vehicles for the use of

Government Ministers, could only find a Daimler that was large enough to accommodate us all.

As we were leaving the Palace, Sir Robert Fellowes, then the Queen's Private Secretary and now Lord Robert Fellowes, took us down to the waiting car. As we climbed into the Daimler, he stuck his head through the window and said 'Good Lord, I don't even get one of these.' We all felt terribly grand.

July 1998 was reshuffle time. This is when all Government Ministers, and those who aspire to be, sit by their telephones to make sure they can be contacted 24/7.

There are some very funny stories about politicians who, suspecting they were due to be sacked, actually do the reverse. They disappear so they cannot be reached. This creates a problem because the Prime Minister cannot appoint someone new to a post until the sitting incumbent is either moved or sacked.

There have also allegedly been occasions when surnames have been muddled up and the wrong person has been appointed. If you are to be sacked, No 10 will try to warn you and will arrange for you to see the Prime Minister in his room at the Commons rather than subject you to the walk up Downing Street in front of the cameras.

So, when I was asked to report to No 10, I knew I was not to be sacked, although I had no idea where I was to be moved. I was soon to know.

Well,' said Mr Blair, 'the Queen has loved your daily messages, you know.' I assumed that Her Majesty had mentioned this when she met the Prime Minister.

'Oh, good,' I said, 'I expect that's because I used to give her all the gossip.'

'You mean, who's seeing who?' he asked, with a rather impish smile. 'Certainly not,' I said, 'I wasn't going to tell her that.'

Alas, my days of writing the daily message, which I had enjoyed so much, were at an end.

'I would like you to take on Tourism, Film and Broadcasting as one of Chris Smith's junior Ministers at the Department of Culture, Media and Sport,' Mr Blair said.

What a terrific job! How could I refuse, but I should certainly be sad to relinquish my Royal role.

Before I could do that, I had to return to the Palace to hand over my wand of office to the Queen, whereupon she 'broke' it in two (which is to say she unscrewed it). It was then inscribed with my name and later returned to me. I have it still.

I cannot deny there was a certain sadness about bidding farewell to the Queen. I had found her such a warm and understanding person and someone who truly cares about others.

Our final meeting was just before the summer opening of Buckingham Palace to the public. I decided to be a bit cheeky and ask her what it was like to open your home like this.

'Do you know, everyone shuffles along in a line,' she said, while giving a little demonstration of the public shuffle.

'This means,' she continued, 'that they push all the carpet pile in one direction, so the following year, we have to turn all the carpets round so they can push it back the other way.'

A lovely person, and practical too.

Now it was someone else's turn to write the Queen's Daily Message. I am reliably informed though that I was the last one who wrote it personally and that it is now largely penned by the whips office assistants.

That's a shame because I certainly got the impression that it was a tradition the Queen valued, a more personal and informal way of linking her with her parliament and her government. A sort of daily parliamentary sketch that would entertain her. And frankly, if you want the title of Vice Chamberlain, you should do the job properly. The Conservative MP, Nick Soames, once told me his grandfather, Winston Churchill, had had the job for a time, and had enjoyed it so much he carried on doing it while he was in the Cabinet. Nick also told me that the Palace had enojoyed mine too. I must say I was flattered that someone as grand as Nick Soames should say that to me.

'You're awfully friendly to some of us on our side of the House these days,' I said to him, 'but then maybe you have more friends on our side than on yours?' 'Hm,' he said, 'that may be true, but cannot say I relish the thought of an afternoon with Glenda.'

Oh dear, poor Glenda again, I wonder what the Queen would have said if I had told her that.

THE DAILY MESSAGES

Janet Anderson MP, with humble duty reports Monday 3 November, 1997

Your Majesty,

It was clear from the daily 2.15pm Whips' meeting today that the timing of the day's business was difficult to predict. It's possible we could whiz through everything very quickly or be here until the early hours.

Questions were to Your Secretary of State for Defence. There was much laughter when Nicholas Soames, a former Defence Minister, was reprimanded by the Speaker for speaking to a civil servant in the box. They are, of course, there to back up the Government front bench and not the Opposition though Mr Soames will presumably have known the young lady in question from his time as a Minister. Madam Speaker said she didn't care how pretty the young lady was, this was no excuse for Mr Soames to speak to her.

There was a lengthy discussion about the Eurofighter project, initiated by Preston MP, David Borrow. This project is very important for Lancashire and all Lancashire MPs, including me, welcomed Your Government's decision to exempt the Eurofighter from the spending review.

We then progressed to questions to the Church Commissioners, which concentrated on celebrations for the Millennium. Dennis Skinner voiced concern about hundreds of thousands of people descending on the Millennium Dome with lighted candles. Did this not put the Dome in danger of catching fire, he asked. Mr Stuart Bell, the MP for Middlesborough, who answers for the Church Commissioners, replied that the Dome was the responsibility of Your Minister without Portfolio, Mr Mandelson. He did, however, remind the House that all church bells would be rung for 5 minutes at 12 noon on 1st January 2000, followed by a period of prayer, and that there would also be a chapel inside the Dome to ensure that the churches were as closely involved as possible with the celebrations.

Your Health Secretary, Mr Dobson, made a statement about breast cancer screening. This followed the discovery in June that 12 women in Devon, who had not been referred for treatment after being screened for breast cancer, had subsequently developed cancer and two of them had died. At the time, Mr Dobson asked the Chief Medical Officer, Sir Kenneth Calman, to establish the facts and his report has been published today. The report covers three aspects:

1. the independent assessment of the technical competence of breast screening in Exeter based on the audit of mammograms;

2. the examination of the organisational, managerial and quality control arrangements in the Exeter breast cancer unit; and

3. the review of national and regional arrangements for quality assurance of the breast cancer screening service.

The report concludes there were serious faults in all three and Your Health Secretary said he was already taking action to implement the main recommendations. Mr Dobson also referred to the problems with cervical cancer screening which had arisen in Canterbury. He said that many of the problems, both at Exeter and Canterbury, sprang from the shortcomings of the internal market. These included the absence of arrangements to secure high and uniform standards even for cancer screening systems which were supposed to be national; legal obstacles to intervening in the affairs of Trusts which are falling down on the job and staff not being able to speak their minds.

Mr Dobson said that all of this must be changed and Your Government intended to make the necessary changes starting with a White Paper on the future of the National Health Service, but he urged women to continue to be screened. He said, despite what had gone wrong, screening remains the best way of identifying breast and cervical cancers and pre-cancers in time to make possible early and therefore more effective treatment.

Business proceeded with consideration of the Lords Amendments to the Firearms Bill during which there will be votes to overturn Lords amendments which sought to permit people with disabilities and Olympic competitors to continue to own handguns. There will then be a debate on the Education (Student Loans) Bill and various other bits and pieces. The adjournment debate is from Caroline Flint, a new Yorkshire MP, on the subject of unadopted roads. Some of my Southern colleagues questioned what this was about. I assured them it was a big problem in the Pennines as I knew only too well from my own constituency where we not only have a surfeit of unadopted roads, but walls and bridges too, so I shall listen to Caroline's debate with interest.

Janet Anderson MP, with humble duty reports Tuesday 4 November, 1997

Your Majesty,

Everyone has been trying this morning to find out what happened to Your Minister for Transport last night, Glenda Jackson, who failed to show up to respond to Caroline Flint's debate about unadopted roads. Not unnaturally, the Opposition seized the chance to move in the bully boys in order to maximise Your Government's embarrassment. In the end, a speech had to be faxed across from Miss Jackson's office at the Department, and then Your Minister for Local Government, Hilary Armstrong, was dragged out of her office and into the Chamber to read the speech. She performed brilliantly. What a trooper. However, at the time of writing, we still do not know what happened to Miss Jackson. I understand it is the subject of some discussion 'at the highest level'.

First for Questions today was Your Secretary of State for Scotland. This particular question time was rather dull, I am afraid. It didn't even liven up when Ann Winterton got onto law and order and the need to keep people locked up for longer. And Desmond Swayne, a new Tory MP, who tried to get in during the early part of the question time, eventually gave up. That was a shame because it denied Labour MPs the opportunity to shout 'barking' as they normally do when Mr Swayne rises to speak. I believe this is a rather unkind reference to Mr Swayne's alleged state of mind.

However, the questions covered a wide range of subjects, as usual. A great deal about Your Government' s Welfare to Work proposals. Mr Andrew Rowe suggested that some young people who were more 'backward' might need longer to lever themselves back into the job market. Mr Brian Wilson, a junior Scottish Minister, told him quite firmly that in Scotland people were never referred to as backward. Mr Dennis Canavan wanted to know exactly what the Scottish Parliament would be able to do. Luckily for him, Madam Speaker recognised him today. He recently shaved off his beard and immediately afterwards, the Speaker did not recognise him. It seems to be a growing practice for Members of Parliament to shave off their facial hair.

Mr Canavan has now been joined by Alastair Darling, Keith Bradley and Kevin Hughes. Contrary to popular belief, this has not been done on the instructions of Your Minister without Portfolio, Mr Peter Mandelson.

There were then questions to Your Lord President of the Council, Mrs Ann Taylor. She referred to Your Government's continuing attempts to modernise the proceedings of Parliament and more effectively to scrutinise legislation and undertook that as many Bills as possible would first be produced in draft form.

Mr Richard Spring then introduced a Ten Minute Rule Bill to prohibit bull bars from motor vehicles, something which has widespread support in the House and which was previously the subject of a Private Member's Bill by Labour backbencher, Mr Paul Flynn.

The rest of the day is filled up by two Opposition debates. The first on your Government's proposals for student finance. We anticipate some sniping from one or two of our own backbenchers, as well as the Opposition, on the subject of tuition fees. And than a further debate on 'Threats to Rural Life and the Rural Economy', with votes at 7pm and 10 pm.

And, can you believe it, Miss Glenda Jackson is down again this evening to respond to the adjournment debate on the subject of 'roads in East Sussex'. Let us hope she turns up tonight or the Chief Whip will certainly want to know why.

Janet Anderson MP, with humble duty reports Wednesday 5 November, 1997

Your Majesty,

The Wednesday morning adjournment debates today were dominated by Minister for Transport, Glenda Jackson and, thankfully, she turned up for all of them. Subjects covered were road safety, agriculture in rural Wales, the Sand-Kite Incident and safety on the Thames, the A5 trunk road and Government proposals for legal aid. The House then adjourned until 2.30 pm.

You can always rely on Welsh Questions being lively, and today was no exception. It certainly helped to gee up the troops for Prime Minister's Question Time. There were questions about the beef ban, the use of capital receipts, the Welsh Assembly and much else besides.

But, of course, everyone was waiting for questions to Your Prime Minister.

For some inexplicable reason, the Opposition had decided they would question Your Prime Minister on Europe. This was viewed with incredulity on the government benches since the official Opposition seem to be increasingly divided on Europe with every day which passes. They were, of course, referring to a Commission proposal to extend the Social Chapter to smaller firms. Mr Blair made it plain that this was simply a proposal which Your Government would not support. But it all rather fell flat for the other side when Mrs Cheryl Gillan tried to raise the issue again and referred to Your Prime Minister as her 'Honourable Friend'. Naturally, the Chamber hooted with laughter whereupon Mrs Gillan pleaded that 'it's tough on this side'. Your Prime Minister suggested that she might therefore consider joining our side and that, for one moment, he had thought she was going to.

Clare Ward, who at 24 is, I think, the youngest Labour MP, and a member of the Select Committee on Culture, Media and Sport asked about an addictive gambling game called Keno which is threatening to enter our public houses. This apparently is a numbers game with a draw every 15 minutes and is seriously compulsive. Mr Blair said that Your Home Secretary was considering this and that there was also concern that the introduction of such a game would reduce the takings of the National Lottery. I suspect we may see something about this in the forthcoming Lottery Reform Bill, for which I shall be the responsible Whip.

This was followed by a Statement from Your Secretary of State for International Development on the White Paper she has published today 'Eliminating World Poverty: A challenge for the 21st Century'. The White Paper basically sets out Your Government's policies for the sustainable development of the planet, recognising that nearly one in four of the people of the world live on the margins of human existence. It is the first White Paper on Development for over 20 years, and has been warmly welcomed. The business which follows this is extremely boring, pretty non contentious and I think we are in for an early night though the evening adjournment debate sounds interesting - Freedom of speech in the NHS.

Janet Anderson MP, with humble duty reports Thursday 6 November, 1997

Your Majesty,

A very quiet day in the House today, I am afraid. In fact, I suspect many Honourable Members have already left for their constituencies as the House rose at around 8 pm last night, and it looks as though tonight will be about the same.

First order for questions was to Your Secretary of State for Agriculture, Dr Jack Cunningham. Not surprisingly there was much discussion about BSE.

Dr Cunningham has done rather well on this issue. When the Government Whips Office paid a visit to Brussels during the summer recess, we were told that there was the greatest admiration for Dr Cunningham for his virtuoso performance before the BSE Committee of the European Parliament, for the fact that he had volunteered to appear before the Committee and that, by his performance, had gone some way to pacifying the German members.

And so, BSE and the situation of beef farmers generally was very much on the agenda for questions today. Dr Cunningham said he was aware of the particular problems facing hill beef farmers. They were not only facing the fallout from the BSE crisis, but also had to contend with Your Government's inability to raise the hill livestock compensatory allowance, as we had said that, for two years, we would stick to the previous government's spending limits. Dr Cunningham did point out, however, that £450 million of direct support would go to farmers in the beef sector this year, and that he had succeeded in getting the Council of Ministers to agree a uniform position on beef imports, to operate from 1st January 1998. He said that he had had to threaten to take unilateral action if necessary in order to get this agreement.

Then, to howls from the Opposition benches, he said that the solution to the problems in the beef sector was not more subsidy but to solve the BSE problem, which had been created by the previous government, and to deal with the overcapacity of beef in Europe.

There followed a brief period of questions to Your Attorney General, for which I am afraid many Members left the Chamber. The performance of the Crown Prosecution Service was raised. Your Government recognises that there are difficulties, such as lack of local accountability and the need for better liaison with the Chief Constable.

Your President of the Council then announced that the business for next week will include the Greater London Authority (Referendum) Bill, the Bank of England Bill, the Local Government (Contracts) Bill (which is concerned with the Private Finance Initiative), a debate on modernisation of the House (long overdue in my view) and on the policing of London.

Various Members raised constituency issues, as they can do during Business Questions, but nothing of any great significance. There then promises to be a 15 minute debate on all stages of the Supreme Court (Offices) Bill, something called the

Nuclear Explosions (Prohibition and Inspections) Bill and an adjournment debate on the London Fire Service.

So all in all a rather dull day and my apologies, Your Majesty, for a correspondingly dull message. Hopefully next week will be more lively.

Janet Anderson MP, with humble duty reports Monday 10 November, 1997

Your Majesty,

The journalists in the Commons lobby had a hard choice today over what to do at 3 pm. Should they tune in for the Louise Woodward*verdict or make sure they were in the gallery for the first outing at the dispatch box for Your Minister without Portfolio answering questions on the Millennium Experience and the Dome. But more of that later.

First Order for Questions was Your Secretary of State for Culture, Media and Sport, Mr Chris Smith. Opposition Members were determined to turn just about every question they could round to donations to the Labour party and the minimum wage and how the latter would mean the destruction of the tourist industry. Thankfully, they did not score many, if any hits. Nigel Evans, the Conservative Member for Ribble Valley (who receives a disproportionately huge amount of air time in Lancashire where Tories are something of a dying breed) tried to allege that Your Government was neglecting the pensioners by not giving them free television licences. Sadly for him, he had written to Your Secretary of State on this very subject on the 6th July and had managed to misspell the word licence not once, but twice. Possibly the result of 18 years of Conservative education policy came the retort from Mr Smith, who made it clear this would cost millions of pounds and Your Government was not going to do it. However, he did point out that the whole question of the licence was up for review in two years time in any event.

There were other questions about Millennium projects in the regions. Peter Pike, the MP for Burnley welcomed the £1.7m which was to be used to create 500 hectares of new woodland in the Forest of Burnley. Michael Fabricant wanted to know if there would be funding to repair church bell frames, as well as church bells. There was a question about disabled people who wanted to shoot and even one about children's radio. This was followed by references to too many cartoons on television. When the Minister, Mr Fisher, pointed out that there was only one cartoon a day during prime time on each of the major channels, his fellow Minister, Mr Banks, (who once famously described himself as a bar room sage) suggested 'they should come here'. I suppose proceedings in the Chamber could sometimes be likened to a cartoon.

Certainly, when the time came for Your Minister without Portfolio to answer questions, the Chamber did become very animated - especially on the Opposition benches who behaved in an extremely childish fashion. I have known Mr Peter Mandelson for nearly a quarter of a century now, and I cannot, for the life of me, understand why he should provoke such fury among Tory MPs. In the event, he was well supported by the Labour benches and he handled it all extremely well. The Tories cannot wait for the whole Dome Experience to fail, but I fear they will be sadly disappointed. As Peter said, we expect the Experience to be the most original and inspiring Millennium event in the world with a national programme of events and activities that will extend right across the country.

Questions to the Parliamentary Secretary in Your Lord Chancellor's Department followed. Predictably the main questions were about the reform of legal aid and the future structure of the Courts.

And then the Speaker had selected a Private Notice Question from Mr David Winnick about Iraq. Michael Howard, the Shadow Foreign Secretary, can never resist cheap jibes when he is at the dispatch box. Today was no exception. He said he hoped Your Minister, Mr Fatchett, would not allow his decisions to be influenced by his past views on income tax and defence. Presumably Mr Howard has dug out an obscure reference from Mr Fatchett in the dim and distant past to hypothecated taxes. But it really was not on for Mr Howard to behave in this way during a discussion in the Chamber about something of such great concern to us all. Your Minister, I am pleased to say, rose to the occasion with dignity and aplomb so I think the score was probably 10 - 0 to Your Government.

Now the House is debating the Second Reading of the Greater London Authority (Referendum) Bill and 10 of our London colleagues have put in to speak. So the votes will certainly not happen before 10 pm I dare say there will be much talk of London mayors and no doubt Mr Livingstone will feature in the debate.

One or two other bits of inconsequential business will follow and then on to the Adjournment debate, when new MP, Bob Russell, will speak about the closure of courts in Essex. That's when we whips will allow the troops to go home. They even get a little message on their electronic pagers 'We are now on the Adjournment and you may go home. Thank you.' Just to show that Government whips are the warmest and cuddliest of people.

* Louise Woodward, a nineteen year old British nanny, was sentenced to life imprisonment by a court in Massachusetts for the murder of a baby, Matthew Eappen. On appeal, the judge reduced the second degree murder verdict to manslaughter and sentenced Woodward to time served, equivalent to the 279 days she had already spent in jail.

Janet Anderson MP, with humble duty reports Thursday 13 November, 1997

Your Majesty,

I must apologise for I am afraid today's message is likely to be fairly brief. After a pretty turbulent Wednesday, today is fairly quiet.

First Order for Questions was Your Secretary of State for Education and Employment, Mr David Blunkett. There was much talk about Your Government's proposals for the New Deal to get people off benefit and into work. There are several stages to this. The young unemployed will be the first group to benefit, followed by the long term unemployed, single parents and then eventually the intention is to try to provide work opportunities for the disabled. All the evidence is that this is working. Real partnerships are being established around the country. Naturally Conservative Members are not happy with this and lose no opportunity to criticise Your Government's policy.

Other subjects covered included the prevention of fraud against Training and Enterprise Councils and the admissions procedure to secondary schools in Hertfordshire. There was also a rather heated exchange about funding for higher education, where, inevitably, Conservative MPs raised the question of tuition fees. Your Minister, Dr Kim Howells, who represents a mining area in Wales rose magnificently to the occasion. He said that, on taking up his duties as a Minister, he had been appalled to find that 4 out of 5 children from the professional classes went on to university, whereas only 1 in 10 of those from unskilled families did so and that it had to be a top priority of Your Government to make it possible to achieve a better balance. As the mother of a son at Glasgow University, I could not agree more. Far too many of my son's friends were unable to go to university because their parents could not afford it.

This was followed by the Business Statement where the Leader of the House, Ann Taylor, announces the business for the following week. Next week, we can look forward to an Opposition debate from the

Liberal Democrats, Second Reading of the Northern Ireland (Emergency Provisions) Bill, committee consideration of the Greater London Authority (Referendum) Bill and business of the Public Accounts Committee. As usual, several members took the opportunity to raise constituency matters. However, as we are on a one line whip, I suspect many are already constituency bound as I write this.

There followed some fairly mundane Commons business to do with the Parliamentary Contributory Pension Fund and the House of Commons Members' Fund and there will later be a debate on Modernisation of the House of Commons. This is something which greatly exercises many of the new members, who find some of the procedures rather strange and confusing, so I expect we shall have some interesting contributions.

The recent report of the Modernisation Committee, set up by Your Government immediately following the election, suggested a number of ways of improving the scrutiny of legislation. It suggested that some Bills should be timetabled with an agreement that they would not be guillotined and that some Bills should be published in draft form first to provide a chance for better consultation with interested parties.

The Adjournment debate is in the name of Mr Martin Linton on the subject of government support for young people from under-privileged families. And that will be that, with Members leaving for their constituencies to do their advice surgeries. A rather tedious day, Your Majesty, for which again my apologies.

Janet Anderson MP, with humble duty reports Monday 17 November, 1997

Your Majesty,

Surprisingly, after a rather turbulent week for Your Government last week, the House today is the very picture of peace and tranquility. Well, so far, that is. But jokes about Marlborough are strictly forbidden! *

First Order for Questions today was to Your Secretary of State for Social Security, Harriet Harman. You can always guarantee that Honourable Members will have a host of questions relating to problems their constituents are having with the benefit system.

Today was no exception. There were particular concerns about the operation of the Child Support Agency which were acknowledged by Ministers. Your Government plans to bring forward a review of the Agency in the early part of next year. So far as pensions are concerned, Your Government also plans to publish an initial framework for change in the first part of 1998. Ministers said their aim was to ensure that pensioners have security and dignity in retirement; that they should share fairly in rising national prosperity, and that public finances should be both sustainable and affordable.

As ever, Dennis Skinner could not resist a dig at the Government front bench. Recognising that Your Government was committed to remaining within the spending guidelines of Your previous Government for the first two years, he wanted to know whether any cuts in benefit would be restored after that. This drew a chuckle from Madam Speaker. But there are rumblings within the Parliamentary Labour Party about Your Government's plans in respect of lone parent benefit. This was to be cut by Your previous Government (for new lone parents) and Your new Government has reluctantly had to accept that there is no money available within the budget to reverse this. Your Secretary of State for Social Security is to address the Parliamentary Labour Party meeting this Wednesday morning on this very subject. I am sure she will remind colleagues that the whole emphasis of our New Deal for Lone Parents is to get them off benefit and into work. As she pointed out during Questions today, Your Government has also allocated £12.5m for training and childcare for lone parents over the lifetime of this Parliament.

Following questions, the Conservative MP, John Bercow, attempted to raise a bogus point of order on the subject of Your Prime Minister's television interview yesterday. Madam Speaker told him that he could always try to catch her eye during Prime Minister's Questions on Wednesday. Someone else complained about the closure of the coastguards' station in his constituency. Madam Speaker said she would look favourably upon an application for an adjournment debate.

Simon Hughes then opened the first Opposition debate for the Liberal Democrats in this Parliament on the subject of 'Public Service'. Mr Hughes concentrated mainly on the Health Service, education, the police and fire service, and seemed to say they all needed more money. Where, asked new Labour MP, Bob Blizzard, was the money going to come from. Did the Liberals really believe it could all be funded out of an extra 1p on income tax. Mr Hughes responded by saying Liberal Democrat policy was to spend that extra 1p on education, and the rest they would fund out of other taxes. Dennis Skinner then waded in and attacked the Liberal Democrats for misleading people. Spindoctoring, he said, had been invented in Liberal 'Focus' leaflets.

So, all in all, this looks like a fairly lively debate. You can always be sure that the only thing which will ever unite Labour and Conservatives in the Chamber is when they have the chance to attack the Liberals.

This debate should go up till 7 pm but I doubt if it will, as the Liberals only have two speakers. So much for their concern for the public service. And then we are on to debate the Report of the Standards and Privileges Committee on Mr Neil Hamilton and others. I predict this will certainly be lively with attempts to raise Formula 1 matters. But I think this is very much a Westminster thing. I am told no-one on the doorsteps of Beckenham is raising it and our latest poll puts us one point ahead.

But oh dear, Glenda Jackson has to respond to the adjournment debate tonight, yet again. This time on the subject of the British Merchant Fleet.

* Following the Government's decision to exempt Formula 1 from the ban on tobacco advertising, it transpired that the head of Formula 1, Bernie Ecclestone, had donated £1m to the Labour Party.

Janet Anderson MP, with humble duty reports Tuesday 18 November, 1997

Your Majesty,

Questions today were to Your Secretary of State for the super ministry of the Environment, Transport and the Regions, and Deputy Prime Minister, Mr John Prescott. Ministers reasserted that there would be no directly elected regional assemblies until after the next election. There is, of course, great interest in this subject particularly in the North and the North West where there is pressure for Your Government to act sooner. However, these Honourable Members will just have to accept that Your Government has a heavy legislative timetable and it will simply not be possible to do everything in the first parliament. This is something which Government Whips discussed with Your Prime Minister this morning and is, of course, why Your Government cannot guarantee time for Mr Foster's Bill to ban foxhunting.

As you will know, Your Government is anxious to persuade more people to use public transport and to cut down on the use of cars. This policy was challenged by Opposition spokesman, Richard Ottaway, who suggested that, particularly in London, there were many people for whom use of the car was essential. This may be true, but something has to be done. Traffic in the capital was virtually at a standstill this morning.

Other questions covered the manufacture and repair of railway engines, raised by Mrs Gwyneth Dunwoody, in whose Crewe constituency, she claimed, were made the best railway engines in the world. Sir Sidney Chapman, who is incidentally Chair of the Accommodation and Works Committee on which I serve, and who was, of course, Your Majesty's Vice Chamberlain under the previous administration, wanted to know if Your Government would put pressure on President Clinton to show a greater commitment on global warming. This was also raised by Helen Brinton, the new Labour MP for Peterborough. Your Minister, Michael Meacher, confirmed that Your Government would be bringing forward a White Paper on this. Mrs Anne Campbell, who is a keen cyclist, suggested that more people should be encouraged to cycle.

There was an amusing interlude when one Honourable Member spoke about the problems caused by leaves on railway lines, which prompted a Labour wag to shout 'New Labour, new leaves'. Laughter also ensued when Mr Patrick Hall asked a question about concessionary travel and Your Minister for transport, Glenda Jackson, asked 'Do you miss me?' Miss Jackson, who celebrated her 60th birthday recently, is presumably referring to the fact that she does not use concessionary travel as she has a government car.

Questions were followed by a PNQ on the terrible tragedy in Egypt* yesterday and a statement on the mis-selling of personal pensions. During the first, Ministers confirmed that they had advised British visitors to exercise extreme caution when visiting upper Egypt. Chris McCafferty, one of the new Labour women, spoke movingly about a grandmother, mother and five year old child, all from the same family in her constituency who had died. It really does beggar belief.

Helen Liddell, the very forceful (and undoubtedly future Cabinet material in my view) Treasury Minister then made a statement on the mis-selling of personal pensions. Helen has, of course, got very tough with the companies who, through vigorous marketing, sold over 5 million personal pensions between 1988 and 1994.

Many nurses, teachers and other professional were persuaded to abandon the safety of their occupational schemes and lost out as a result. 600,000 cases are now being reviewed and the cost of compensation to these people is likely to be at least £2 billion. Helen outlined a package of sanctions aimed at maintaining the pressure on pension firms to meet their targets for resolving the cases of pensions mis-selling.

There followed a Ten Minute Rule Bill seeking to establish equity of funding across the country in the National Health Service, and then a debate on the Second Reading of the Northern Ireland (Emergency

Provisions) Bill which we hope will be non controversial. Your Government is hopeful that we can maintain the bi-partisan approach to Northern Ireland - it is, after all, the only way we shall make progress.

Votes on this at 10 pm and then lots of Government business to be moved without debate. The duty Whip will have to do a lot of bobbing up and down -let's hope they do it at the right time. One false move and government business could be lost. And then the adjournment debate on the National Health Service in North Essex. A pretty varied day and another late night!

*More than 60 people were killed after an attack on a group of foreign tourists visiting a temple in Luxor.

Janet Anderson MP, with humble duty reports Monday 8 December, 1997

Your Majesty,

Questions to Your Secretary of State for Culture, Media and Sport, Mr Chris Smith, began with a tribute to Billy Bremner, the much loved, former Leeds footballer whose death from cancer was announced yesterday. There was certainly an air of sadness about the House of Commons Chamber.

Mr Adrian Sanders, who had the first question, had, unfortunately withdrawn it. This was a pity since it denied Mr Smith the opportunity to reveal that charities had received £ 1. 8 billion from the lottery over the period of the current licence. (The Lottery is, of course, extremely topical at the moment as Your Government published the Lottery Bill last week, which aims to divert more funding into health and education.) However, things livened up with the second question from Mr Dennis Skinner (Beast of Bolsover as he is affectionately known). He wanted to know what was being done to promote more sporting activities for young people and said it was about time we got rid of the 'blazer, bag and twinset brigade' from sport, especially tennis.

Mr Tim Loughton, the new Tory Member for East Worthing, asked a question about admission charges to museums. Again this has been topical over the weekend, as the British Museum has been forced by Your Secretary of State to abandon any plans for admission charges. Mr Smith feels very strongly that there should be the widest possible access to our museums and is fervently opposed to charges. He announced that he had produced a consultation paper on the development of a code of practice and that adherence to this code would be a condition of future grant in aid.

On the back of this, Mr Brian Iddon (one of the new Labour members from Bolton who has been making worrying noises about possible decriminalisation of soft drugs) wanted an assurance that there would be free access to museums and galleries for Bolton schools.

Of course, the Tories could not resist the urge to raise sport sponsorship but it fell rather flat, despite the best attempts of their oafish contingent - Mr Nicholas Soames and company. However, it was clear they were retaining their fire for the next Minister at the Dispatch Box, Your Minister without Portfolio, Mr Peter Mandelson.

Peter rose to take five minutes of questions on the subject of the Millennium Experience at 3.10 pm. They shouted, they jeered, they heckled relentlessly from the Opposition benches, but I am afraid to say that they simply exposed themselves for the uncouth, unruly and loutish bunch they are. I really do not think this is the kind of behaviour the public expect of their Members of Parliament. However, Peter dealt coolly and calmly with them and we could not resist pointing out that they were unlikely to be aware of any progress on the Millennium Dome since few of them were left with London constituencies. London has almost joined Scotland and Wales as a Tory free zone, but not quite.

There followed the customary bogus points of order which Madam Speaker took with her usual good humour. Though she became quite strident when a Conservative backbencher took his life in his hands (or at least his future opportunities to speak in the Chamber) by suggesting how she might deal with them. 'Enough,' shouted Madam Speaker, 'I know exactly what I'm doing on this one'.

Angela Smith, the new Labour MP for Basildon, then moved a presentation Bill on Waste Minimisation, to be followed by the Second Reading debate on the Government of Wales Bill. Debate on this will be continued tomorrow, so we have to make sure a Labour backbencher is on his or her feet at 10 pm, preferably someone who is unlikely to give way to an Opposition speaker, to avoid any pitfalls. So no votes tonight and a fairly quiet House of Commons, which gives me the opportunity to have dinner with the Vice Chair of my constituency party - an important man to keep sweet.

Janet Anderson MP, with humble duty reports Tuesday 9 December, 1997

Your Majesty,

Questions today were to Your Secretary of State for Health, Mr Frank Dobson. Sadly, he was just about the unhealthiest person in the Chamber and had difficulty in speaking. His PPS, Hugh Bayley, came to the rescue with a glass of Lemsip and Madam Speaker offered him some Nigroids, small tablets which apparently help to tighten up the throat. He drank the former but declined the latter.

Sally Keeble, the new Labour MP for Northampton North, spoke about a constituent of hers who had changed her role as a secretary in the NHS to serve in the front line of patient care as a nurse. Ministers said this was just an example of what needed to happen everywhere in the NHS and that Your Government would continue to strive to reduce bureaucracy. Mr David Hanson, who is PPS to the Chief Secretary to the Treasury, probably qualified for the sycophant of the week award (though there is a lot of competition) when he praised Ministers for what they were doing to reduce bureaucracy. Mr Dobson rose to say that he agreed with every word His Honourable Friend had said.

Things livened up a bit when junior Minister, Alan Milburn (who, in my view is destined for the Cabinet) reprimanded the Liberal Democrats for refusing to acknowledge the extra money Your Government had injected into the NHS. 'A little bit of gratitude would not come amiss,' he said.

There was a rather bawdy exchange around the subject of the Salford Health Action Group and acronyms. Mr Dobson said that while he was known for his vulgarity (Frank is at his best entertaining us all with the latest risque joke in the tea room), he had no intention of being vulgar in the Chamber or, at least, he continued 'not in this Chamber'.

After Questions, Madam Speaker read a letter from the retiring Clerk of the House, Sir Donald Limon and Mrs Ann Taylor, as Leader of the House, paid a warm tribute to him. The Clerk is the person who runs the House. There are many who feel the job would be far better done by a Chief Executive, but they were keeping quiet today.

Poor Mr Dobson then had to get to his feet again to deliver a statement on the Health Service which Your Government intends to make modern and dependable by way of a ten year plan which will see the end of the internal market and GP fundholding which, as Frank said, have set doctor against doctor and hospital against hospital. The official Opposition did not like this very much, but then they did have 18 years to get it right and failed.

And so on to the main business, a continuation of the debate on the Government of Wales Bill which began yesterday. Someone unkindly suggested that the reason we had to allocate two days for this debate was because the Welsh were so verbose. I think, however, it's probably because this is a major constitutional issue which merits serious consideration. Whether that will happen or not is another matter, as most Honourable Members of all parties will be off to the Irish Embassy Christmas

Reception at 6.30 pm. Let us hope we can manage to get them into the right voting lobby on their return!

Janet Anderson MP, with humble duty reports Monday 15 December, 1997

Your Majesty,

Your Secretary of State for Social Security, who has been very much in the news of late, Harriet Harman, was first for questions today. The Opposition were determined to make the most of the occasion.

There were a number of questions about the future of additional benefits for lone parents, following Your Government's announcement that, from April of next year, new lone parents will receive the same in benefit as two parent families. However, they will, at the same time, be given every encouragement to find work if they wish.

Opposition Members wanted an assurance that there would not be an element of compulsion in the New Deal for lone parents to find work. Ministers said there would not. Ministers also emphasised that there was no question of benefits being removed from those who were genuinely in need. This, of course, referred to the news coverage over the weekend where it was alleged that Your Government was intending to cut or tax benefits to the disabled. That is not, of course, Your Government's intention, but the comprehensive spending review will leave no stone unturned. And we have to remember that expenditure on disability benefits has risen by 400% in the last six years.

Mr Norman Baker, the Liberal Democrat from Lewes, somehow managed to turn his question about lone parent benefit into one about our complaint over the BBC's treatment of Your Secretary of State for Social Security, Harriet Harman, on the Today programme the other morning. Ministers replied that the BBC could well look after themselves without the help of the Hon. Member for Lewes.

There were a number of questions about the Child Support Agency where Members complained that it was difficult for constituents to get through to the various telephone numbers for the Agency. One MP referred particularly to the Dudley office, whereupon Madam Speaker was heard to mutter 'hear, hear'.

Question 8 from the new Member for Don Valley, Caroline Flint, referred to women's issues. This meant that Joan Ruddock, for the first time, rose to the dispatch box in her capacity as Minister for Women.

Questions were followed by Your Prime Minister's Statement about the European Council which he attended in Luxembourg on 12 –13 December. This meeting was mainly concerned with the enlargement of the Community to include Cyprus and the countries of Central and Eastern Europe. Mr Blair confirmed that agreement had been reached to establish a European Conference for the 15 EU Member States and those European countries aspiring to join. He also referred particularly to Turkey and said that Turkey herself recognised that time and changes are needed before actual accession negotiations can be envisaged. But he said that full recognition of her eligibility for accession is a marked step forward for Turkey.

The Statement was followed by the usual, fairly bogus points of order, during which Madam Speaker got rather cross with some Honourable Members. Mr Norman Godman certainly stretched a point of order when he said he had been unable to get to his constituency surgery on Friday because of the fire at Heathrow and so he had been unable to receive in person a gift left for him by a constituent, namely a bottle of Campbelltown 15 year old malt. Should he register this gift, he asked. Madam Speaker retorted that someone had given her a box of throat tablets the other day and she knew exactly what to do with them – she would give them to some Honourable Members who had quite a lot to say for themselves.

And so it rumbled on; more about Formula One, tobacco advertising, the conduct of Your Financial Secretary etc. Dennis Skinner wanted to know if Madam Speaker would exercise her powers under the Mental Health Act to deal with the amnesia clearly being suffered by Opposition

Members who appeared to have forgotten all their misdemeanours in government.

At last, the House progressed to the main business which concerns the Police (Northern Ireland) Bill Second Reading which Ministers said was essential for the better policing of Northern Ireland. We do not anticipate this will run too late and so we may get an early night after all. Although there may be some interest in Mr Bob Blizzard's Adjournment debate on the subject of Illegal imports of beer. A topical issue as we approach Christmas, I suspect.

Janet Anderson MP, with humble duty reports Tuesday 16 December, 1997

Your Majesty,

It was Your Deputy Prime Minister, Mr John Prescott, who was to hog most of the time in the Commons Chamber. He was first for Questions. This question time is always interesting and varied, since his is a Department which covers Environment, Transport and the Regions - the superministry as it has become known.

Hilary Armstrong, Your Minister for Local Government and Housing, could have done without the question from her neighbouring and fellow Labour MP, Ronnie Campbell, who wanted to know why Northumberland County Council had done better in terms of funding out of previous Tory governments than it had under this Labour government. Not a terribly helpful question from a colleague. Hilary disputed this but said she was always ready to meet local authorities to discuss their allocations.

There was much hilarity in the House when she revealed that she was experimenting with the idea of video conferencing between herself and local authorities around the country. That way, she said, it would save local councillors timely and costly visits to London. The reason for the laughter was that we all know only too well, on all sides of the House, that there is nothing our local comrades like better than an 'overnight' in London. They get to stay in a smart hotel and expenses to boot.

There was warm praise for Mr Prescott for his performance at the Kyoto conference. Without him, said Mr Hugh Bayley, there would have been no agreement at all. How apt, therefore, that Questions to Your Deputy Prime Minister should be followed by a Statement from Your Deputy Prime Minister about the outcome of the United Nations Conference on Climate Change in Kyoto. Mr Prescott said that the conference had demonstrated beyond doubt that genuine political will did exist between all the participating countries to set legally binding targets for reducing greenhouse gas emissions between the years 1990 and 2010. The outcome was that all countries had suggested a larger cut than previously - America most notably had moved from zero to a cut of 7% and that the agreement will produce a cut of more than 5% in total emissions.

There followed a Statement by Your Scottish Secretary, Mr Donald Dewar, on the Scottish Water Industry Review which Your Government set up to consider how best to return the Water Authorities in Scotland to local democratic control. Mr Dewar pointed out that, since the review was launched, the Scottish people had given a resounding endorsement to the establishment of a Scottish Parliament and that Parliament would be able to bring the Water Authorities under the proper level of scrutiny that a modern democracy demands, through its oversight of the Scottish Executive. Mr Dewar also said he wanted the water authorities to become more responsive at a local level, and he would be asking water authorities to build further on local links which would be helped by the community planning system he would shortly be proposing. Mr Dewar made it plain that Your Government was determined to improve democratic accountability, facilitate investment, promote efficiency, ensure continuity of public water supplies, protect public health and minimise disruption to the industry. He further announced that he had asked Mr Robert Fraser, a distinguished figure in the water industry, to lead an exhaustive enquiry into the circumstances surrounding recent events in the West of Scotland.

The main business of the day is the Second Reading of the National Minimum Wage Bill. Alas, so lengthy have been the statements, that the debate has not commenced at the time this message has to be despatched. But a lively debate it is sure to be. 19 Labour Members have put in to speak. There is much speculation in the Whips office as to how many of these are now members of the 'Lone Parents and Benefits' party! One of my colleagues expressed surprise at so many speakers since they were presumably in favour of the policy. Ah, said I, but they can always argue about the level at which the minimum wage is likely to be set. And, said another colleague, whatever it is, it will not be enough. How right he is. Thankfully we are talking about a very small minority and one which Your Prime Minister is more than capable of dealing with.

So, Your Majesty, I am off now to the Safeways Christmas reception, and then I must, in my capacity as social whip, continue the collection for the whips' party at 12 Downing Street on Thursday night. Oh, and Glenda has the adjournment debate again - this time on the gripping subject of by-passes for North East Hertfordshire.

Janet Anderson MP, with humble duty reports Wednesday 17 December, 1997

Your Majesty,

The usual Wednesday morning adjournment debates covered the diverse subjects which Honourable Members choose to raise including Mediation services, Regulation for the provision of funeral services and the proposed closure of Burnley valuation office.

The House then adjourned until 2.30 pm when we reassembled for Questions to Your Chancellor of the Duchy of Lancaster, Dr David Clark. Dr Clark confirmed Your Government's determination to establish a Food Standards Agency and said that his proposals for a Freedom of Information Act, set out in the White Paper 'Your Right to Know', would transform government in this country from a culture of secrecy to a culture of openness. This democratic theme continued throughout Question Time. Gerry Steinberg, the MP for Durham, claimed that Your previous government had packed unelected quangos with Tory appointees. In his county of Durham, he said, the quangos were full of Tories while there was not one single Tory councillor elected to a local authority.

As ever, the House filled up for Questions to Your Prime Minister at 3 pm. There was much debate about party funding and Members' interests as the Consultation document on party funding has been published today. Mr Blair said the document called for all political parties to publish information on donations going back to 1992; confirmed that the Labour party would do this, and called upon Mr Hague to make sure his party did the same.

The general mood of the House was jolly, even Christmassy. Everyone congratulated Mr William Hague on his forthcoming marriage though, sadly Mr Hague could not resist the urge to make a political point. He referred to the honeymoon period Your Government had enjoyed since the election which was 'coming to an end' while his honeymoon 'was about to begin. Mr Blair retorted that Your Government's marriage with the electorate was set to continue up to the next general election and beyond. Your Prime Minister was even gentle with the Leader of the Liberal Democrats today and, when chastised for doing so by Labour backbenchers, said 'Look, it's Christmas'. Mr Donald Anderson called for the Welsh Assembly to be placed in Swansea and

Mr Eric Clarke called for a national integrated fuel policy in order to save our coal mines. Mr Blair said he was glad that the generators and RJB Mining had come to a short term agreement which would sustain jobs until next summer, but acknowledged that an overall review was needed.

Conservative MPs persistently tried to raise the matter of Your Financial Secretary to the Treasury and his offshore trusts. Your Prime Minister repeatedly emphasised that the Minister had done nothing wrong and had adhered to the Ministerial Code of Conduct. He was then challenged by Mr Bob Wareing, recently returned from a period of suspension and still feeling bitter, who asked whether the money to be spent on the Millennium Dome would not be better spent on the disabled and severe weather payments. This was Old Labour at its worst and Mr Blair swiftly dismissed him, pointing out that the Culture, Media and Sport Select Committee had only today published a report saying that the Dome had been 'magnificent in its conception' and would be 'breathtaking in execution'. So that was Mr Wareing dealt with as firmly as he deserved to be.

The new member for Swindon, Julia Drown, introduced a 10 Minute Rule Bill to improve the gathering and provision of information on the energy efficiency of homes, and we were then in to the first piece of main business on Fisheries concerning Your Government's intentions to negotiate the best possible fishing opportunities for British fishermen.

There was much debate in the daily Whips meeting about whether the vote on this should be at 7 pm or 8 pm, bearing in mind that many Honourable Members would be keen to attend the various Christmas receptions taking place around the House. We opted for 7 pm in the end so that we could move quickly on to the European Communities (Amendment) Bill (Allocation of Time) where the only speaker on the Government side will be Your Foreign Secretary. This will ensure plenty of time for Opposition Members to use the debate to expose, yet again, how deeply divided they are on Europe.

But the real stars of the day have been the Teletubbies - Guests of Honour at the Commons Children's Christmas Party this afternoon, at the specific request of John Birt. I am reliably informed that this is the first time they have ventured out of Teletubbyland so we are honoured indeed.

Janet Anderson MP, with humble duty reports Thursday 18 December, 1997

Your Majesty,

I fear today's Message will be necessarily brief. The House of Commons distinctly resembles the Marie Celeste today, and many Honourable Members are already on their way home to their constituencies - laden, as ever at this time of year, with the usual House of Commons whisky and mints for constituents and local party members - reselection boxes, as they are sometimes known. *

First for questions today was Your President of the Board of Trade, Margaret Beckett, who told me the other day that she was responsible for writing the Daily Messages for a period during the Labour governments of the 1970s. Once again, the House was in a pretty light mood, as everyone gets ready for Christmas. Mr Nick Palmer (one of three Members who is a member of MENSA) said it was no wonder the Conservatives were confused about the single currency, given the extent to which they apparently relied on foreign donations. Steve Pound, who really is one of the new members to whom it is always worth listening in the Chamber, had a convoluted question about third generation telephone technology and the number of Queens Park Rangers supporters to the West and East of his constituency. (Steve also does a wonderful impersonation of the Prime Minister which we hope he might repeat at the Whips Christmas Party tonight at 12 Downing Street.)

More serious questions were concerned with the export competitiveness of British industry, science policy, renewable energy sources, inward investment and much else. The Minimum Wage featured prominently in the exchanges following on the news that Michael Fallon, the MP for

Sevenoaks and Opposition Spokesperson on the minimum wage, had been moved to the Opposition Treasury Team. This was largely the result of the efforts of Labour MP, Denis McShane, who kept raising the matter of Mr Fallon's business interests because he was a director of companies which were notorious for paying low wages and therefore should have declared an interest in any debates on the subject of the minimum wage. H was also forced to apologise to the House. Good for Denis.

Tributes then followed to Sir Donald Limon, the Clerk of the H use, who is retiring. Everyone spoke warmly of Sir Donald and said they would miss him. He first came to the House in 1956 when 100 of our existing Members were not even born and will be remembered particularly for introducing induction for new Members. There were several bogus points of order (life in the Chamber really wouldn't be the same without them) and Dennis Skinner always has one. He said it was a bit rich of the Tories to complain that there was no Business Statement today, since Members usually asked during that Statement for something to be raised in the House the following week, and William Hague had made it plain that he didn't think we should be sitting next week. (The House is coming back for one last day on Monday).

And then the main business - The Public Processions (Northern Ireland) Bill Second Reading - on which there is unlikely to be a vote mainly because the Tories are getting ready for William Hague's wedding tomorrow, and we are getting ready for our Whips' Party.

There is no doubt that the House will be empty for Mr Eric Pickles' adjournment debate on Hospital services in Brentwood and Ongar.

* Labour MPs are required to go through a 'reselection procedure' with their local constituency parties once every parliament where party members have to vote in favour of the incumbent if he or she is to be allowed to stand for election again.

Janet Anderson, with humble duty reports Monday 22 December, 1997

Your Majesty,

Today is the last sitting day before Christmas and, even though everyone is concentrating on their various celebrations (yet another at Downing Street tonight), there was a surprisingly good attendance in the Chamber for Questions to Your Home Secretary.

Dennis Skinner hoped there was not going to be a privacy law which would merely protect the great and the good. The Shadow Home Secretary tried as hard as he could to provoke Your Home Secretary by implying there was a rift between him and Your Lord Chancellor over the incorporation of the European Convention of Human Rights into domestic law and also the treatment of witnesses in rape cases. In the latter, Your Government is looking at ways in which women victims can be protected from the ordeal of being cross examined in the witness box by their alleged attacker. Thankfully, Mr Straw did not rise to the bait.

Mr Bob Laxton caused much amusement when he produced a small Christmas stocking which had been made for Madam Speaker by volunteers in his constituency. Normally, Madam Speaker would have frowned on such behaviour, as visual aids are forbidden in the Chamber. However, even she could not resist a smile on this occasion. This broadened into a positive beam when Home Office Minister, Alun Michael, said he hoped that, given the size of the stocking, it was to be filled by Father Christmas rather than Madam Speaker's legs.

Madam Speaker's legs came up again later in Question Time, at least indirectly. During a question on the opening hours of public houses and clubs, reference was made to the nightclub industry, of which Madam Speaker allegedly had some experience. This was, of course, a reference to Miss Boothroyd's days as a Tiller girl.

A mystery was also solved for me at Question Time. On Saturday, after a heavy day's Christmas shopping in Manchester with my teenage daughter, we were seriously delayed on the way home because the main A666 road to Bolton had been blocked off. All was revealed by Bolton MP, Dr Brian Iddon, who explained that a minicab driver in his constituency, Mr Hussain, had experienced problems with some passengers, one of whom had then pursued him across the A666 whereupon he had been struck by a car and killed.

As if that wasn't depresssing enough, Maria Eagle then wanted to know what Your Government was going to do about crime on the Dymchurch Estate in Speke where she said young people were running riot with hammers and pickaxes. We'll stop all the repeat cautions, explained Minister Alun Michael, and make sure they get final warnings in future. Getting them jobs might help too, so let's hope the welfare to work New Deal for young people is a success.

We were then supposed to have a Statement from Your Secretary of State for Agriculture, Dr Jack Cunningham. Unfortunately, Jack had to rise to the dispatch box at 3.30 pm to explain that he couldn't make the statement because the computers in his office had broken down.

Ideally, we should have been able to revert to the main business on the School Standards and Framework Bill, but, as Mr David Blunkett could not be found immediately, there was no alternative but to suspend the sitting for 15 minutes until David could continue with the education debate.

The statement then finally followed at 4.30 pm. This was on the beef industry and on BSE and its consequences - something I understand only too well since my farmers in Rossendale are very exercised about it.

Your Secretary of State for Agriculture said Your Government was convinced of the need for substantial restructuring of the European industry and believed that the restructuring should start now. Early consultations with the farming industry would now take place and an inquiry is to be instituted into the whole BSE affair, to be conducted by Lord Justice Phillips. Dr Cunningham also announced an increase in the

Hill Livestock Compensatory Allowance for this year only, which will certainly please my farmers. However, he made it plain that Your Government would support moves to replace these allowances, which are production linked payments, with instruments better designed to deliver environmental benefits.

Dr Cunningham confirmed that Your Government's aim for agriculture policy was to change fundamentally the narrow producer focus of the present Common Agricultural Policy, to decouple support from production, to work for sustainable farming and to give consumers, taxpayers and the environment greater priority.

And then we were back on to the Education Bill which will finish at 10 pm and thankfully we will all get away for our Christmas break, to return on 12 January.

Janet Anderson MP, with humble duty reports Monday 12 January, 1998

Your Majesty,

First day back and we're not expecting a huge turnout today. The main business is the Second Reading of the Scotland Bill. We are only on a one line Whip as the business will continue tomorrow.

However, there was a reasonable attendance for Question Time. First Order for Questions today was Your Secretary of State for Defence, George Robertson. As we had all expected, this particular Question Time was dominated by messages of sympathy, from all parts of the House, for Your Minister for the Armed Forces, Dr John Reid, who tragically lost his wife Cathy last week following a heart attack. John is such a popular Member and he and Cathy were clearly such a happy couple, there was a real depth of feeling for him and his two sons in the Chamber.

The first Question concerned research into illnesses possibly related to Gulf War service. (This was from new Labour Member for Warrington North, Helen Jones, who made one of the best maiden speeches ever when she first came in, entirely without notes and has certainly gained respect as a result.) Several Members came in with supplementary questions on this one, mostly concerned with their own constituents who were allegedly suffering from such illnesses, including civilians as well as service personnel.

Mr Robertson confirmed that his Department was undertaking a major programme of research into the possible health effects of the combination of vaccines and tablets which British troops were given during the Gulf War. He said that consideration would also be given to the effect on civilians.

As ever, Members chose to raise varied constituency issues. Gerald Howarth, the Conservative Member for Aldershot) wanted to know what was happening over the sale of the Farnborough aerodrome to the

Geneva based TAG Finances SA, and said he was particularly concerned that the historic buildings on the site would be protected.

Malcolm Savidge (Labour, Aberdeen North) asked what was being done to ensure that Sadam Hussain complied with UN Resolutions in Iraq and Jim Fitzpatrick (Labour, Poplar and Canning Town) inquired about the recruitment of ethnic minorities into the United Kingdom's armed forces.

Questions followed to the Chairman of the Public Accounts Committee, Mr Bob Sheldon, who said he thought Your Government should look at the need to amend legislation to enable the National Audit Office to ensure that the spending of lottery reserve monies gave proper value for money. There was then a brief period for Questions to Mr Stuart Bell, who answers for the Church Commissioners.

Mr Norman Baker (Lib Dem, Lewes) questioned the expenses paid to bishops and said could not the Church of England take a leaf out of the Church of Scotland's and do more instead to help the poor and house the homeless. Mr Bell pointed out that the best part of bishops' expenses went towards staff salaries.

The House then moved on to the main business of the day - the Second Reading of the Scotland Bill. Your Secretary of State for Scotland, Donald Dewar, had hardly begun his speech before Honourable Members opposite were bobbing up and down to challenge him with the 'Midlothian Question' which is of course whether and why Scottish Members should have a say over English matters once the Scottish Parliament has been established. Donald dealt with them superbly and deftly, as ever. It is a question which unites some rather strange bedfellows. As Donald said to one, 'the Honourable Gentleman, in pursuit of truth cannot be particular about the company he seeks' .

And so the debate labours on, with some embarrassment on the Opposition Benches for, of course, there is not one single Conservative MP in Scotland. It will, I fear, run right up to 10 pm, and then Mr Phil

Woolas, new Labour Member for Oldham East and Saddleworth, has the adjournment debate on the subject of 'A national radio channel for children'.

Janet Anderson MP, with humble duty reports Tuesday 13 January, 1998

Your Majesty,

Government Whips made sure the Chamber was well attended at 2.30 pm today as First Order for Questions was to Your Foreign Secretary. Since Robin has been rather in the news just recently, we thought it essential to show him some solidarity and support. In the event, the Opposition got the message and chose to concentrate on Foreign Affairs.

Mr Harry Cohen, the Labour Member for Leyton and Wanstead had Question No 1 asking for sanctions against Iraq to be removed since he alleged these were harming children and the sick. This is, of course, a propaganda ploy Sadam Hussain is fond of using. When I was in Saudi Arabia recently, there was much coverage of a demonstration against sanctions by mothers in the streets of Baghdad.

All the usual suspects bobbed up to get in the act – Tam Dalyell, David Winnick, Tony Benn. Your Foreign Secretary made it quite plain that Iraq had an appalling record of oppression and that Your Government would not give consideration to the lifting of sanctions. Moreover, he emphasised that Iraq continued to refuse to adhere to UN Resolutions. He also referred to the fact that Sadam Hussain had no fewer than 45 presidential palaces, more than any other country in the world.

Shadow Foreign Secretary, Michael Howard, rose to the dispatch box to express concern about the recent news that Sadam Hussain had halted the work of the UN inspection team within the last 24 hours. Mr Cook said he shared this concern and he would be having discussions about it with Madeleine Albright when he visited Washington on Thursday.

At the end of this particular exchange, Mr Cohen (who had asked the original question) said he was not satisfied with the answers, and gave notice, on a Point of Order, that he would seek to raise the matter on the adjournment.

Other questions concerned enlargement of the European Union during the UK presidency, particularly in respect of Cyprus. This was raised by Robin Corbett, a Labour Member who has long had an interest in Cyprus.

The Conservative, James Paice, asked what the government was going to do about the reform of the Common Agricultural Policy. This caused much amusement and Your Foreign Secretary pointed out that the Opposition had had 18 years to do something about it. There was even louder laughter when Mr Paice alleged that your previous Government had in fact obtained reform in 1992 – I cannot say that my farmers in Rossendale noticed!

Mr Tony Benn then presented a Bill at the back of the Chair to provide for a new Declaration to be made by Members of Parliament upon their election to the House of Commons. We shall have to wait and see what that is about since Presentation Bills are given no time for debate or explanation.

There was then a fairly tedious 10 Minute Rule Bill moved by the Liberal Democrat, Mr Ronnie Feam, to subject local government boundary changes to referendums. I think we've probably got quite enough of those in the pipeline as it is.

And so on to the main business – continuation of the Second Reading of the Scotland Bill. There will be two votes on this at 10 pm as the Opposition have tabled a reasoned amendment which 'accepts the clear decision of the Scottish people in favour of a devolved Scottish Parliament' but goes on to say that they are unhappy with the way in which Your Government is going about it. I suppose that was to be expected, but it does unfortunately mean the troops will need to be here longer than they would otherwise. The votes will also be followed by several Orders, so we shall still have to keep them here for them. Oh dear, it could be late, I fear. Ah well, what else can they expect after three weeks' holiday!

Janet Anderson MP, with humble duty reports Wednesday 14 January, 1998

Your Majesty,

The House certainly livened up today - presumably because it was the first Prime Minister's Question Time since the break. More of that later.

The morning sitting witnessed the usual backbench adjournment debates which are not often well attended but it does give Honourable Members a chance to raise something which is usually of burning importance in their own constituencies, however obscure it might seem to the rest of us. Today's covered Welsh agriculture, the registration of persons sailing on board passenger ships and the national hunt racing industry. The one on fuel poverty and energy efficiency surprisingly provided a more amusing interlude when the Opposition spokesman suggested that if Your Government had not provided £85 million in compensation to beef farmers, then more could have been spent on energy efficiency. Let us hope someone draws that to the attention of the National Farmers' Union!

One other morning debate attracted all the usual suspects. This was initiated by Mr Austin Mitchell who, in his wisdom, wanted to talk about prescribing cannabis something noted by the Whips who are already not too happy with Mr Mitchell's wife, Linda McDougall who has produced the TV series on Westminster Women and who chose to publish private conversations she had with Mrs Robin Cook. We now look forward to a period of silence from the pair of them.

The House then adjourned until 2.30 when we reassembled for Questions to Your Secretary of State for Northern Ireland, Dr Marjorie Mowlam (or Mo, as she is known to us). Everyone loves Mo and there was a huge cheer as she rose to her feet.

Dr David Winnick, the Labour Member for Walsall North, is not always helpful to Your Government but, on this occasion, he praised Dr

Mowlam's determination to keep the peace process going. And so say all of us. Mo chose to refer particularly to her recent visit to the Maze Prison. It had not, she said, been an easy decision to make but, in her view, anything which kept the talks moving was worth doing. And so it has proved. She had, she said, received numerous calls from relatives of many of those who had suffered an untimely death at the hands of prisoners in the Maze, thanking her for what she had done and expressing the view that, if it meant that others would not suffer as they had done, then it certainly was worth it.

By this time, the Chamber was full in anticipation of Your Prime Minister's entry. In he came looking relaxed and confident, obviously rested from his family break in the Seychelles. Of course the Opposition could not resist suggesting that he had spent more time in the Seychelles than he had in the House of Commons. This was not only cheap, it is untrue and he dealt with it in his usual competent fashion.

There was a great deal of anger on the Government benches when Opposition Members tried to raise the question of travel for Your Foreign Secretary's new partner.* It really is so tasteless. So when it happened the second time, with an attempt by Mr John Bercow (a rather nasty piece of work who is so short that when he rises there are always shouts of 'stand up'). This time, Your Prime Minister decided to go for the jugular. Mr Bercow, he said, reminded him of a Conservative Member in the last Parliament, Mr David Shaw, who would long be remembered for being both nasty and ineffectual in equal proportions. And Labour's Jim Murphy, one of the several former National Union of Students' Presidents in the House, was prompted to remark that perhaps we were all wishing that someone else spent less time in the House.

Much of the debate was about Your Government's Welfare to Work and benefit reform proposals, with which Leader of the Opposition, Mr Hague, appeared to suggest that the Opposition would cooperate. Well, we shall see. The not very clever Liberal Democrat, Vince Cable (cabled not wired as one wag described him) asked about the future of pensions

- as if Your Prime Minister would be likely to pre-empt the current consultation in the Chamber. And one of our new Labour stars, Steve Pound from Ealing North, pointed out that, as it was the 50th birthday of the National Health Service this year, so too was it his own 50th birthday. He would, he said, however, be more than content with a modest card from Your Prime Minister.

It was certainly a lively occasion. So rowdy were the Conservatives that Madam Speaker was forced to rise to her feet and pronounce that Members on their side of the House had been 'impossibly badly behaved'.

Your Secretary of State for Agriculture then delivered a Statement about Your Government's plans for a Food Standards Agency, something which is long overdue in view of the widespread support for the principle of separating responsibility for promoting food safety from responsibility for sponsoring the food and farming industries.

And then the main business with the Second Reading debate on the Regional Development Agencies Bill. There are 31 speakers down on the Government benches alone. Oh dear. They will not all get in. However, it does mean some of them could be persuaded to stay to speak on Friday when there is a Teresa Gorman Bill on a similar subject which, alas, will have to be stopped if we are to avoid blocking Your Government's legislative timetable. That will certainly cheer the heart of Parliamentary business whip, Jim Dowd, who has the unenviable task of getting sufficient speakers on Fridays to carry out this not always very pleasant duty. But it has to be done and such is the lot of we whips. Never be a whip if you want to be popular.

There will, I suspect, be two votes at 10 pm and then home soon afterwards, unless, of course, this evening's receptions at 12 Downing Street (for women MPs) and

11 Downing Street (for a contingent from the North West) are still going on. And well they might be.

* The late Robin Cook had left his wife, Margaret, in order to continue his relationship with Gaynor Regan, a member of his staff.

Janet Anderson MP, with humble duty reports Thursday 15 January, 1998

Your Majesty,

I promise to make today's message relatively brief to make up for yesterday's, for which again my apologies.

Again today the Whips had a job to do to make sure the Chamber was as full as possible. This was because First Order for Questions was Your Chancellor of the Exchequer and we were anxious to provide support for Your Financial Secretary to the Treasury, Geoffrey Robinson, in case the Opposition decided to give him a hard time over his offshore trusts. True to form, they tried.

When Your Chief Secretary, Alistair Darling, rose to answer a question about individual savings accounts, there were cries of 'Ah' from Nicholas Soames and his friends. They had, of course, expected Mr Robinson to do it and were ready to ambush him if he did. However, as Alistair pointed out, Chief Secretaries take an interest in all Treasury matters, in fact they take an interest in the activities of other Government departments too. I dare say most of his Cabinet colleagues think he takes too much interest in their affairs!

Your Chancellor of the Exchequer, Gordon Brown took great delight in poking fun at the Opposition over their disagreements about European Monetary Union - something which will, no doubt, receive a further airing later in the day when the House continues the debate on the Committee stage of the European Communities (Amendment) Bill. Fiona MacTaggart, who is reputedly one of the richest Labour MPs and has a castle in Scotland, but who represents Slough, wanted to know what Your Government was going to do to protect jobs in the event of the abolition of duty free (which is, of course, set to happen). I assume Fiona's interest stems from Heathrow, which must be either in or near her constituency. Ministers pointed out that, to a large extent, this was a

European initiative. This is certainly true but Fiona's point about jobs is a valid one.

Jacqui Smith, one of the new Labour women, stood to congratulate Your Government on keeping its promises on V AT. This was a reference to the reduction in VAT on fuel from eight and a half per cent to five, a pre-election promise delivered as soon as we could after the election, which contrasted with Your previous government's increases in VAT despite what they had promised at election time. Good old Jacqui. She is one of two of our women who are expecting babies - the other is Deborah Shipley.

Peter Lilley, Shadow Chancellor, tried again to raise Geoffrey Robinson's tax payments (or lack of them) but we're all rather tired of that now. So, it was with some relief that we were all given a chance to hoot with laughter when Virginia Bottomley accused Your Government of being 'bossy and authoritarian'. I suspect the reason for the amusement is that Virginia often herself adopts a kind of schoolteacher, jolly hockey sticks approach in the Chamber.

Your President of the Council, Ann Taylor, then delivered the usual Business statement announcing the business for next week - oh dear, running three line whips almost every day. Honourable Members used the occasion to raise all sorts of diverse issues from whether or not Dame Shirley Porter should have her title removed to whether new Members of Parliament should have to swear allegiance to the Queen. Your Majesty will be unsurprised to know that the latter came from Mr Dennis Skinner with reference to the Presentation Bill introduced by his Honourable Friend, Tony Benn, earlier in the week.

We shall then move on to the European Bill which will continue to 10 pm. However, the Foreign Affairs Whip, Greg Pope (who is convinced he owes his victory in his Catholic dominated Hyndburn constituency to the fact that he was down as POPE Gregory on the ballot paper) has kindly ensured that there are unlikely to be any votes after 9 pm. So, a relatively early night for us - at last.

Janet Anderson MP, with humble duty reports Monday 19 January 1998

Your Majesty,

Everyone seems to be in very good spirits today, despite the scurrilous weekend press reports about alleged rifts between Your Prime Minister and Your Chancellor of the Exchequer. No doubt it will all blow over in due course when the press find something else to divert them.

First Order for Questions today was Your Secretary of State for Culture, Media and Sport. These particular sessions are always lively - Your Minister for Sport, Tony Banks, is always good for a laugh and then the Opposition can never resist having a dig at Your Minister without Portfolio (Peter Mandelson). Today was no exception.

Andrew MacKinlay, the Labour MP for Thurrock, may be small but you can be sure he will make his presence felt. As someone, he said, who had seen his first ballet at the age of 46 in Brataslava, he welcomed the action Your Government was taking to improve access to the arts for young children. When Tory MP, John Greenway, remarked that there was no need for anyone to wait that long to see a ballet, Your Minister for Sport, true to form, shouted 'have you seen the queues at Sadlers Wells?' Surprisingly there was no reference to the comment from Sir Richard Eyres, who is conducting the inquiry into the Royal Opera House, when he said that he would not want to sit next to anyone at the opera who was wearing 'a singlet, shorts and smelly trainers'. (Seems pretty self evident to me that none of us would.)

Other questions concerned the choice of Sheffield for the UK Sports Institute, sport in primary schools, the principle of additionality for lottery money, the comparative price of restaurant meals in New York and London (I thought they were about the same) and how the New Deal was going to work in Blackpool.

There was great hilarity when Your Secretary of State responded to a question from Mr Michael Fallon, now the Conservative MP for

Sevenoaks. He was previously the MP for Darlington but was defeated by rising star, Alan Milburn in 1992.

Chris Smith couldn't resist referring to Mr Fallon's search for a safe Conservative seat and listed the 15 constituencies for which he had tried before he finally landed up in Sevenoaks. Poor Mr Fallon looked very embarrassed.

Tony McNulty, the new Labour MP for Harrow West (who is really good news, always willing to be helpful to the whips) asked a pertinent question about school playing fields. In recent years, of course, too many schools have sold off their playing fields. In fact they were encouraged to do so by Your last Government. As I am sure Your Majesty saw last week, Your Government has announced that any further sales will require the express approval of Your Secretary of State. Quite right too. My three did so little sport at school, it really was a disgrace.

At 3.10 pm we were on to questions to Your Minister without Portfolio, Mr Mandelson, who answers specifically on The Dome. The Tories are always up for this and desperate to score a hit on Peter. As ever, they failed. And Your Minister without Portfolio has asked me to tell Your Majesty that the Dome is going to be the most enormous success. I am sure it will be a) because we cannot afford it not to be; and b) because Peter is in charge.

A brief slot for questions to the Parliamentary Secretary in the Lord Chancellor's department followed. Mr Harry Barnes raised a distressing example of how someone who is disabled had been refused the use of an alphabet board in court and there was much discussion about equal rights for solicitors and barristers in court. And then panic set in.

It was twenty nine minutes past three. Business on the European Communities (Amendment) Bill (we were continuing to debate the committee stage) was due to continue at 3.30 pm and there was no Foreign Office Minister in sight. Oh dear, what was I to do. There was no way I could stand up at the dispatch box and talk about the European

Communities Bill, but it looked as though I might have to. In came Greg Pope, the Foreign Affairs Whip. A look of horror crossed his face as he looked at the front bench and out he dashed to find a Minister - any Minister would do. In the meantime, I ran up to the backbenches and instructed them to raise Points of Order if the Minister did not appear. What on, they asked? Anything I said, anything at all. Just stand up and make a fuss.

And would you believe it Your Majesty, with seconds to spare, Your Minister for Europe, Douglas Henderson (or wee Doogie as we call him) strolled in. 'Don't you ever do that to me again,' I said. Madam Speaker and I both heaved a big sigh of relief. And Mr Pope kindly agreed to cover the rest of my bench note so I could get off to pen this Daily Message.

And so we are now on to the remaining stages of the European Bill which should receive its third reading tonight and we'll be on our way home at 10.30 pm. But, oh dear, Glenda has got the Adjournment debate again. This time on the Hindhead A3 tunnel initiated by Virginia Bottomley. I predict there will be no more than two people in the Chamber for that one.

Janet Anderson MP, with humble duty reports Tuesday 20 January, 1998

Your Majesty,

After a busy morning for the whips, making sure our Honourable Friends on the Government benches remember to vote in the elections to our National Policy Forum (and, most importantly, vote for the right candidates), the House assembled at 2.30 pm for Questions to Your Secretary of State for Scotland. There was a warm welcome for Dr John Reid, the Scottish MP whose wife tragically died recently at the early age of 49. As he said to me, sometimes the House can be the friendliest place in the world

I think: the emphasis should be placed on 'sometimes'!

So we began what the Deputy Chief Whip described as an 'ethnic' day. Scottish questions first, and then the continuing debate on the Government of Wales Bill, to establish a Welsh Assembly. The proceedings on this will span eight days and it may be of great interest to Welsh Members, but not really to the rest of us.

Scottish questions were dominated by discussion about the plight of beef farmers in Scotland. Your new Scottish Minister, Calum McDonald, made his debut at the Dispatch Box. Calum, who has to travel between surgeries in his Western Isles constituency by rowing boat, replaced Malcolm Chisholm who was sacked when he voted against Your Government over the issue of benefits to lone parents. Opposition Members were demanding better compensation for Scottish farmers. However, as Calum pointed out, they have already received £85 million this year, compared with £60 million in the last year of Your previous Government.

There was also much concern about the number of hospital beds in Scotland where Honourable Members chose to highlight the position in their own constituencies.

Dr Sam Galbraith replied for Your Government and confirmed that the highest quality service would be provided in Scotland. He told the House that he was himself a locum surgeon on the Isle of Sky so he well understood the kind of service which was required. This reminded me of a very funny story about Sam. He was once stopped by a opinion pollster on Skye. When asked what he was doing there, he said he had been 'climbing mountains and chasing women'. The pollster then enquired about his occupation. 'I am a brain surgeon,' replied Sam. Whereupon the woman threw her notes to the ground and said 'will you be serious, I'm only doing my job'.

Questions to the House of Commons Commission followed. Your President of the Council referred to the work of the Modernisation Committee and confirmed that the Committee was looking at ways of improving scrutiny of legislation. She told the House that some Bills would be published in draft form and could be considered by the appropriate Select Committee before they commenced their passage through Parliament. This will be a very radical improvement to the way we do our business.

The Conservative Member, Richard Page, then moved a 10 Minute Rule Bill to amend the Parliamentary Constituencies Act 1986. His motives in doing so are not clear. Perhaps he wants to change all the constituency boundaries in the hope that his party may return to power at the next election.

And then on to Wales - again. With an Adjournment debate to look forward to on the gripping subject of the Inclusion of Test Match Cricket as a listed sporting event.

Janet Anderson MP, with humble duty reports Wednesday 21 January, 1998

Your Majesty,

The traditional Wednesday morning Adjournment debates today were more lively than usual as most of them covered what are currently fairly controversial subjects. Labour MP, Andrew Dismore (formerly at Westminster City Council) had the first on Probity in local government. Not surprisingly this was about the Dame Shirley Porter affair. This was followed by a debate initiated by the formidable Tory and former Minister for Home Affairs, David Maclean on tax avoidance and offshore trusts, which was really about the Geoffrey Robinson affair. Two other debates concentrated on recent incidents at the Maze Prison and sanctions against Iraq affecting children and the sick. The latter was from Labour MP, Harry Cohen, one of a handful of MPs who consider that sanctions should be lifted.

The House then adjourned until 2.30 pm when we reassembled for Questions to Your Secretary of State for Wales. Oh dear, today is truly an 'ethnic' day. Welsh Questions, followed by the continuing debate on the Government of Wales Bill. Even the Adjournment debate this evening is about power cuts in North Wales over Christmas.

There were lots of questions about the New Deal, Welfare to Work plans and the benefits it would bring to the unemployed in the individual constituencies of Honourable Members. Others covered the location and cost of the Welsh Assembly, extra cash for the Health Service in Wales and the economic viability of hill farming.

As ever, the House quickly filled up towards 3pm in readiness for Questions to Your Prime Minister. We had been expecting a rough ride, particularly over the recent publicity relating to the financial affairs of Your Paymaster General.* In the event, Your Prime Minister was ready for them. He skillfully got the Government troops off on the right foot by revealing that this morning he had received a hoax call from someone at Capital Radio who had managed to convince the No 10 switchboard that he was Leader of the Opposition. This ensured several cracks about hoax callers during the next half hour.

I have to admit that Your Leader of the Opposition is certainly improving at Prime Minister's Question Time though he did fail to score a direct hit with his questions about the recent reference by Your Secretary of State for Social Security to affluence testing. The feisty, former Prisons Minister, Ann Widdecombe, came up with a typically witty (or sarcastic would probably be a more apt adjective) question asking Your Prime Minister whether he attributed recent disputes over affluence testing, lone parents, individual savings accounts and the Paymaster General to the 'psychological flaws of Your Chancellor the Exchequer'. There was, said Your Prime Minister 'something of the night about that question' referring, of course, to what Miss Widdecome had said about Your former Home Secretary, Michael Howard.

And so the banter continued. Madam Speaker was forced to rise to her feet to demand that Honourable Members should 'keep quiet and listen to the questions'. New Labour MP, Barbara Follett (wife of the best selling author, Ken) welcomed Your Government's proposals to improve literacy and numeracy. Seemingly we are anxious to see more concentration on mental arithmetic - does this mean we might be considering banning calculators, I wonder? And a Labour MP, announced, to hoots of laughter, that he had received a letter from Your Leader of the Opposition inviting him to a meeting today to discuss his supplementary question. As he said, there are few enough Conservative MPs, you'd think the Leader's office would know who they all are.

But everything calmed down for Dr Nick Palmer to introduce his 10 Minute Rule Bill to amend the Firearms Act 1968 to restrict the acquisition and possession of air weapons. This passed without a vote and now we are on again to the Committee Stage ofthe Government of Wales Bill. We are only on Clause 2 and there are 44 clauses in the Bill. Goodness knows when we shall finish it all, but we will adjourn the debate with a vote just before 10 pm. The Whips have a tough job on their hands to get this lot through in good time, but get it through they will have to do.

*Geoffrey Robinson, the Paymaster General, had been criticised by the Parliamentary Standards Commissioner after failing to record a £12.5m offshore trust in the Register of MPs' Interests.

Janet Anderson MP, with humble duty reports Thursday 22 January, 1998

Your Majesty,

First Order for Questions today was to Your Minister of Agriculture, Fisheries and Food. Having received a delegation of farmers from Rossendale earlier this week (their annual visit to the Commons), it was important for me to pay attention. What I was particularly looking for was a question about green top (raw) milk. This is very popular in my constituency and if Your Government does decide to ban it (they are currently undertaking a consultation) there will be a public outcry in my part of Lancashire.

In the event, green top milk was not mentioned, but a great deal else was. We even had one question about dead sheep carcasses which, complained one Honourable Member, deterred tourists from visiting his constituency.

There were lots of questions about hill farmers, who are often among the very poorest of farmers. They rely heavily on the Hill Livestock Compensatory Allowance which has now been frozen for several years. Your Minister, Dr Jack Cunningham (he's a doctor of chemistry) said that hill farmers would benefit especially from the £85 million aid package for the livestock industry which he had announced just before Christmas.

More questions about beef - of course; one on banning hunting with hounds (that Private Members' Bill is, I gather, pretty bogged down in committee upstairs at the moment) and Andrew Mackinlay, the Labour MP for Thurrock wanted to know what Your Government was doing to prevent the flooding of Tilbury if there should be a North sea surge and the Thames barrier was used. Where would the water go, he wanted to know? Clearly, Andrew thinks there is a good chance it would end up in Tilbury.

Questions to Your Attorney General followed. Dennis Skinner wanted action taken against a training company in his constituency which he alleged received £3.2 million of taxpayers' money and made fraudulent claims which would have required one tutor to work for 94 hours in 14 different locations in one day. Dale Campbell-Savours raised the questioning of a woman's past sexual experience in rape cases in court. Your Attorney General said it was a matter for the judge but it was something Your Government was looking at. We are, incidentally, also looking at the way in which it has been possible for rape victims to be cross examined by the defendant in court. It is something which greatly exercises women's groups around the country.

The usual Business Statement covered the business for next week. Monday will be Wales - again! Tuesday, Opposition debates on the Green Belt and London Underground. Wednesday and Thursday will be Scotland - again! And then the usual Private Members' Bills on Friday, the vast majority of which will have to be blocked by my good friend and fellow Whip, Jim Dowd, in order to protect Your Government's legislative programme.

And then on to the Bank of England Bill. Sadly for a Thursday, this is likely to go quite late.

(2)

Your Minister for Defence, Dr John Reid, has the Adjournment Debate. He is replying to Ms Diane Abbott on the subject of Racism in the Armed Forces. By then, I am sure, most Honourable Members will have left for their constituencies, like me, for a round of advice surgeries, school and factory visits and all those other things MPs do at weekends in an attempt to secure their future livelihood at the next general election.

Janet Anderson MP, with humble duty reports Monday 26 January, 1998

Your Majesty,

First Order for Questions today was to Your Secretary of State for Social Security, Harriet Harman. It was, I am afraid, rather dull though Madam Speaker did her best to liven it up. She cut short rather a lengthy answer from Harriet complaining that she had two other people to call on that particular question so would Harriet get a move on.

The Conservative MP, David Amess, alleged that Your Government was causing great anxiety to the disabled as a result of the benefits review. Harriet assured him that anyone in genuine need would not lose out but that those disabled people who wanted the opportunity of a job would be helped into work.

There were Conservative cheers when Minister for Women, Joan Ruddock, rose to the dispatch box for the first time since she was appointed. She gave a very competent reply about what Your Government was doing to tackle the problem of domestic violence and said that an additional £30,000 had already been given to the national helpline.

Mr Tam Dalyell then had a Private Notice Question on relations with Iraq. Your Minister, Tony Lloyd, said Your Government was keeping the situation under review and that nothing was ruled out, but that there were no plans to deploy additional forces at the moment. Tam Dalyell was not happy, however. He said there was not one Arab country in favour of military action and he felt that such action would merely strengthen the position of Saddam Hussain. He is clearly worried that the United States might seek to take action simply to deflect the present media coverage relating to the President. Your Foreign Minister replied that Your Government would continue to explore every diplomatic possibility, but that if this did not work, then the military option could not be ruled out.

And so on to the continuing debate on the Government of Wales Bill Clauses 22 - 79. There is no chance whatsoever that we will finish that little lot and indeed the Welsh Whip was unable to guarantee significant progress - anything could happen, he said. Indeed, it could. For Opposition MPs could, if they chose to be difficult, force votes on every single clause. I sincerely hope they do not or we'll still be here for breakfast.

My apologies, Your Majesty, for this report of what turned out to be a rather tedious day.

Janet Anderson MP, with humble duty reports Wednesday 28 January, 1998

Your Majesty,

This week's regular Wednesday morning debates covered The Millennium Dome, Road safety, Policing in Devon and Cornwall, The A650 Bingley relief road scheme and Railway noise (and poor old Glenda had to deal with the last three - hers is obviously a job to avoid in Government).

The House reassembled at 2.30 pm for Questions to Your Secretary of State for International Development. There was concern about land distribution in Zimbabwe, the plight of small farmers in Tibet, the need for a sustainable development plan for Montserrat and access to clean water in developing nations.

Your Prime Minister was certainly in top form for Prime Minister's Questions today at 3 pm. In fact, I think it was probably the first time he scored several direct hits on the Leader of the Opposition. Mr Hague tried hard to press Your Prime Minister on the difference between a spouse and a partner, questioning Your Government's interpretation of the Code of Conduct for Ministers, and asking whether Your Prime Minister could be sure that the public purse was not paying for both at the same time. Your Prime Minister confirmed that Your Government was behaving today in exactly the same way as Your previous Government had and dismissed the Leader of the Opposition's questions with short, sharp answers - usually simply the word 'no'. This tactic was quite simply brilliant for, when Mr Hague rose for the fourth time, Your Prime Minister went in for the kill. There was, said Mr Blair, a crucial difference; that what the public had disliked about Your previous Government was cash for questions, cash in brown envelopes, and parliamentary reports on individual members deliberately suppressed before the general election. This was terrific stuff. Mr Hague was well and truly flattened and the Labour benches cheered Your Prime Minister to the rooftops. But he was not finished. Moreover, he said, Mr

Hague had never so far asked one question about schools, or health or crime, and that (he rose to a crescendo) was why he was Leader of the Opposition and would remain so.

Game, set and match I think. The Labour benches screamed for more, and everything else after that paled into insignificance. However, I must mention, as did Linda Gilroy in PMQS, that the Standing Committee on the Minimum Wage Bill sat for a marathon 26 and a half hours last night, and only finished at 1 pm today. They did get a break for breakfast, which is why, when I arrived in the Tea Room at 8.30 am today, the armchairs were littered with bodies trying to get a quick snooze. What a bunch of heroes. I gather the Opposition Chief Whip is now threatening to withdraw all cooperation. Well, let him try. I'm pretty sure our new boys and girls will be on for that, and will take them through every night if necessary. So much, Your Majesty, for modernisation!

Dr Phyllis Starkey then introduced a Door Supervisors (Registration) Bill to establish national standards for door supervisors and to establish a national register of door supervisors. This is such an important Bill, but I don't know whether we can find time for it this session. It concerns those private security guards who act as bouncers on the doors of nightclubs. There have been a number of incidents where people have been badly injured, or even killed, in scuffles with these people. I remember the former Tory Chair of the Home Affairs Select Committee, Sir Ivan Lawrence QC (who sadly lost his seat at the last election) remarking, when we were taking evidence on this issue, that 'you virtually needed a conviction for grievous bodily harm to become a door supervisor'. I imagine if we cannot find time for Phyllis's Bill, then something will be done at a later date.

Edward Garnier QC, who used to be my pair in the days when we had pairing,* rose to complain about the tactics in committee of the supporters of the Foxhunting Bill, or Wild Mammals Hunting with Hounds Bill, to give it its correct title. Apparently the Committee has sat for 4 days and is only on line 2 of the Bill. Oh dear. Goodness knows what is going to happen to this. Let us just hope, privately, that it does not get into the Lords to hold up all our manifesto legislation. Anyway, as Your Majesty will know, Your Government is neutral on this one.

And, alas, it's further proceedings on the committee stages of the Scotland Bill. The reading of Hansard covering the Scotland and Wales Bills is highly recommended for all who suffer from insomnia.

* The pairing system enables an MP to 'pair' with another on the opposite side of the House for particular votes so they can both absent themselves from the vote in order to carry out constituency or other business. It ceased in 1997 because the Labour government had such a large majority.

Janet Anderson MP, with humble duty reports Thursday 29 January, 1998

Your Majesty,

Following prayers today, Madam Speaker had a rather different statement to make. This was to reassure Honourable Members that they were safe in the Chamber. Apparently, during the night a piece of the ceiling fell onto the benches in the Chamber, not too far from where Your Prime Minister would have been sitting had the House been in session. It could, at the very least, perhaps have meant a couple of byelections. Let's hope they've got the rest of the ceiling firmly and securely in place.

First Order for Questions was Your Secretary of State for Education and Employment, David Blunkett. New Labour MP, Dr Alan Whitehead (formerly the leader of Southampton Council) wanted to know about progress on the University for Industry. Just as a previous Labour government had introduced the Open University, so, he said, would this one equal that achievement with the University for Industry. Opposition MPs, who could not resist shouting 'reading' at Dr Whitehead, were firmly put in their place by a shout of 'oh grow up'.

Liberal Democrat MPs had the cheek to criticise Your Government's plans for student finance. They really do have a nerve. All the evidence is that, now people are beginning to understand how it will work, the number of applications for undergraduate places is actually increasing. This was, of course, our intention. Your Education Minister, Dr Kim Howells, retorted that at least we had had the guts to make a decision, not a characteristic for which the Liberal Democrats were renowned.

Another Liberal Democrat, David Rendel wanted consolidation of qualifications for 14 to 19 year olds into a single framework. Dennis Skinner, as ever, brought the House down with the comment 'well, he'd know, wouldn't he, he went to Eton. At last, your Minister, Stephen Byers (definitely one of our rising stars) had a chance to answer a question. He was the one who, when asked recently what 7 x 8 equalled, he said 54, and got some flack for it. Naturally Honourable Members Opposite milked this for all it was worth. However, Steve, just as you would expect, was able to make a joke of it himself. Your Government, he said, was making an extra £22m available this year to improve security in schools. That is, he said 11 x 2 .... 'I think'.

Your Prime Minister then made a Statement on 'The Events of 30th January 1972' or Bloody Sunday as it is more commonly known. To a hushed House of Commons, he announced that Your Government had decided that there were grounds for a further Inquiry; that the Law Lord, Lord Saville, had agreed to chair a tribunal of three, and that the other two members were likely to be from the Commonwealth.

The announcement was welcomed with 'scepticism' by the Leader of the Opposition although he did say that if Your Prime Minister thought it was right to have a further Inquiry, then he would accept that. Generally, it received an extremely warm welcome from all sides of the House, until we got to the Ulster Unionist David Trimble. To shouts of 'disgraceful' he said he thought the statement had been 'mealy mouthed'. Thankfully he is in the minority. Almost everyone else agreed with Your Prime Minister that it is in the interests of everyone that the truth is established, and told.

The usual Business statement followed covering next week's business. At least it's not all Scotland and Wales; we only have Wales on Monday and Tuesday but there are all sorts of other diverse subjects coming up: the Public Processions (Northern Ireland) Bill, the Police Grant Report and the English Revenue Support Grant Reports. Opposition Members tried to raise short term contracts for women, and asked if Your Foreign Secretary could reply to such a debate (very droll).

Dennis Skinner stepped in to say he thought there should be a debate on William Hague's short term contract, entitled 'Waiting for Portillo'!

We'll never change, Your Majesty. No wonder my constituents in the gallery this afternoon remarked that this place was 'just like school'.

Janet Anderson MP, with humble duty reports Monday 2 February, 1998

Your Majesty,

The word on everyone's lips today is Iraq and, indeed, there is a Private Notice Question on that very subject (of which more later). However, first we had to deal with Questions to Your Home Secretary, Mr Jack Straw. Mr Straw, it has been revealed, will be accompanying Your Prime Minister on his forthcoming visit to the United States, which has prompted some to speculate that Mr Straw's star is in the ascendant. Mr Robin Corbett wanted to know what Your Government was doing about drug related crime. Ministers said that it was precisely because Your Prime Minister recognised the extent and seriousness of the problem of drugs that he had established a high powered committee under Your Lord President of the Council,

Mrs Ann Taylor. Labour MP, Diane Abbott, to shouts of 'very good' from Opposition Members, specifically referred to the problem of drugs in Holloway Prison, where women often went in drug free only to become addicted by the time of their release.

A question from David Winnick about the voting system for general elections caused some amusement. It is, of course, well known that Your Home Secretary has long been a supporter of 'first past the post' although he supported the setting up of a Commission under Lord Jenkins to look at the whole electoral system. It was for that reason that Conservative Members shouted 'be honest Jack', as he rose to the dispatch box to respond for Your Government. It was something the Commission was considering, he said, and drew laughter from all sides of the House when, in answer to a supplementary about New Zealand (a country which apparently now regrets moving to a system of proportional representation) he referred to the number of trips being undertaken by the Commission to examine other systems, though he did not know whether New Zealand would be included. 'With wives or partners?' came the questions. Mr Straw replied that he had no idea whether they were taking their wives or partners. (I do wish this issue would go away, but seemingly it will not, thanks to our wonderful media).

Your Foreign Secretary then responded to a Private Notice Question from the Shadow Foreign Secretary on the latest developments relating to Iraq. Mr Cook reaffirmed that Your Government was pursuing a diplomatic solution but that the use of force could not be ruled out and all means necessary would be deployed to ensure that Saddam Hussein complied with his international obligations. There was overwhelming support for Your Government from all sides of the Chamber. When Tam Dalyell asked what would happen if a bomb hit an anthrax installation, Your Foreign Secretary replied that, by his very question, Mr Dalyell had acknowledged that Saddam Hussein was indeed in possession of weapons of mass destruction,

Your Foreign Secretary made it plain that we had no quarrel with the Iraqi people and that, if force became necessary, then steps would be taken to keep any civilian damage to a minimum. The Labour MP, Ernie Ross, who has long taken an interest in the Middle East, pointed out that it was difficult for countries in the Middle East to publicly state the position which they privately held. This was certainly confirmed for me on my recent visit to Saudi Arabia. The Saudis certainly want Saddam Hussein dealt with, not least because their defences would be easily and quickly overwhelmed should he decide to attack them, but it is obviously difficult for them to say this publicly.

The Chief Whip asked us all to sound out Members of the Parliamentary Labour Party on the subject. It is clear that the vast majority feel that if force has to be used, then so be it and agree with Your Foreign Secretary that Saddam Hussein has to be stopped, and that he should not underestimate our resolve to see that he is stopped.

Sir Sidney Chapman, formerly Your Majesty's Vice Chamberlain, then rose on a point of order in his capacity as Chairman of the Accommodation and Works Select Committee. He wished to thank all those craftsmen who had toiled every hour over the weekend to repair the ceiling of the Commons Chamber. I think we all agree with that. Thanks to them, our safety is ensured and we can be confident in the knowledge that there is unlikely to be any further bits falling into the Chamber. Let's hope so anyway.

And so on to Wales. The Government of Wales Bill continues in committee and goodness knows what time the votes will be, if any. I fear, Your Majesty, with the greatest of respect, that Honourable Members from Wales are not renowned for the brevity of their contributions! But we shall finish at 10 pm and then

Mr Keith Simpson has an adjournment debate on 'Big cats in Norfolk'. I think I might just look in on that.

Janet Anderson MP, with humble duty reports Wednesday 5 February, 1998

Your Majesty,

This particular Wednesday morning was a great deal more interesting than most. In fact, I think it is fair to say that the Parliamentary Labour Party has been through a pretty intensive, and most helpful 'bonding session'.

The occasion was Conservative MP, Mr Oliver Letwin's adjournment debate on The termination of the employment of Anne Bullen at the Foreign and Commonwealth Office. Anne Bullen was, of course, the Diary Secretary to Your former Foreign Secretary, Douglas Hurd, but what Opposition Members really wanted to raise was the allegation that Your Foreign Secretary had considered his current partner, Gaynor Regan, for the job after Anne Bullen was relieved of her post. Well, I have to tell you, Your Majesty, Government Members were on for this and determined to give Opposition Members a hard time, most particularly Your former Home Secretary, Michael Howard, who is regarded by many on the Labour benches as particularly loathsome. I think we pretty well succeeded. Your Minister pointed out that Mr Howard had failed to ask any question of substance on the vast majority of foreign affairs issues, so wasn't it about time he got on with his job, instead of bothering with trivia. Or was he, asked Mr Fatchett, merely taking a sabbatical between his former job as Home Secretary and his future job in the City.

So, all in all, Labour MPs were pretty pleased with themselves after that. This bode well for Prime Minister's Question Time, and we were not disappointed. At one point Madam Speaker had to scream at Honourable Members to 'stop shouting' and Your Prime Minister referred to one contribution from William Hague as 'a load of rubbish'. Actually it was. He said something like the only thing Your Government was doing for farmers was as a result of Labour Party members buying eggs to throw at Your Chancellor of the Exchequer, which was pretty poor really.

Conservative Members were very exercised (again) about building on greenbelt, so Your Prime Minister patiently pointed out that Your Government was planning more greenbelt not less. Rhodri Morgan (whose wife Julie, is also an MP) wanted the House of Lords reformed to make it more democratic and Joan Ryan talked about the links between ill health and poverty, poor housing and unemployment.

Brian Sedgemore, a Labour MP not generally known for his support for Your Government, surprised us yet again today by saying that there could be no better way of celebrating the 50th Anniversary ofthe National Health Service than be saving St Bartholomew's Hospital. Yes, said Mr. Blair, and he knew all about Barts because his two eldest children were born there.

So all in all a very exciting day which was a bonus really, because we were just relieved we didn't have to listen to any more about the Government of Wales Bill.

There was also some discussion on the Police Grant Report for England and Wales and then the remaining stages ofthe Public Processions (Northern Ireland) Bill, which may go beyond 10 pm, but we have our fingers crossed.

Janet Anderson MP, with humble duty reports Tuesday 3 February, 1998

Your Majesty,

First Order for Questions today was to Your Deputy Prime Minister, John Prescott, whose Department of Environment, Transport and the Regions is often dubbed the 'Super Ministry' and covers a wide range of subjects.

There was a great deal of hilarity when Labour MP, Anne Campbell, raised the question of a walking strategy. Anne is a tireless campaigner for the encouragement of walking and cycling as opposed to the use of the car. Your Minister, Glenda Jackson, referred to the work of the Walking Steering Group, to laughter from the Opposition benches. (In fact the Group was set up in 1996 under your previous Conservative administration.) The Minister was also forced to congratulate Virginia Bottomley, who even managed to introduce the subject of the Hindhead Tunnel into the discussion about walking. That certainly took some doing.

The future of the greenbelt has received a lot of publicity in recent days, and today's Question Time was no exception. The Hon Nicholas Soames, as ever, got in on the subject of the West Sussex Structure Plan, which has been rejected by Your Government and is now the subject of a judicial review. In the face of some heckling, Your Deputy Prime Minister repeatedly pointed out that, despite recent assertions to the contrary, there were actually more areas now designated as green belt than had been the case before the general election.

Labour MP, John Hepple (who is Parliamentary Private Secretary to the Leader of the Lords) wanted to know what Your Government was doing to reduce the numbers sleeping rough in towns and cities outside London. Your Minister for Local Government, Hilary Armstrong (who, like me, is a member of the Parliamentary Methodist Fellowship) said Your Government had already allocated over £20 million for rough sleepers projects and that there was to be a further £1.5 million pump priming funding for the next 12 months. When tackled about the number of empty local authority houses (in my own Borough there are 500), she said Your Government was working with local authorities to resolve this difficult problem and that what Your Government wanted was to make sure that every single house in this country was a home.

There then followed a Statement from Your Health Secretary, Mr Dobson, on the future of London Health Services. Your Government, Your Majesty, has decided to accept the recommendations of the Turnberg report which will mean a £1 billion boost for London's health services (£880 million capital investment, and at least £140 million on extra primary care, mental health and community services).

Mr Dobson reaffirmed that Your Government wants to make sure that every Londoner has access to top quality health care. The Turnberg Report recognises that, in many parts of London, particularly in the most deprived areas, primary care, mental health, intermediate care and community services are simply not up to the standard to which everyone in our country is entitled.

To cheers, Mr Dobson announced that Barts Hospital would not be closed - a hospital which has served London for 875 years. He said that Barts would continue in its present role while the new Royal London Hospital is being built and other hospital developments are taking place in the East End of London. Afterwards, Barts will concentrate its renowned specialist expertise with a focus on cancer and cardiac services.

Mr Michael Fabricant then introduced a 10 Minute Rule Bill on the subject of a Parliamentary Currency Commission, which appears to be concerned with the European Single Currency.

And so on to Wales - again. Still we can console ourselves with the thought that we only have a further 6 days on the Government of Wales Bill. Whether our loyal backbenchers will stay the course with enthusiasm is another matter.

We shall end the day with an Adjournment Debate on Breast cancer screening and, hopefully Your Majesty, be heading for our beds before midnight at the very least.

Janet Anderson MP, with humble duty reports Thursday 5 February, 1998

Your Majesty,

I am afraid this Daily Message, Your Majesty, is likely to be even more lacklustre than usual. This is because business on the Public Processions (Northern Ireland) Bill continued, thanks to the Ulster Unionists, until the early hours of this morning. In fact, the House did not rise until 2.40 am. This meant it was bed for me at 4 am and out again at 8 am so I hope Your Majesty will forgive me if I do not entirely rise to the occasion.

Actually, I think everyone is feeling the same as we all seem to be rather subdued today. It was most of the payroll vote (ie. Government Ministers) who had to stay to vote. The Chief Whip takes the view that if you get paid you have to vote, but several of the backbenchers hung around just for the fun of it. I suspect this was because a lot of them were still on a high after yesterday morning's mauling of Oliver Letwin, the Conservative MP who dared to raise the question of the appointment of Your Foreign Secretary's diary secretary. I see the Daily Telegraph parliamentary sketch has today described our behaviour as the 'visceral slaughter of fair play'. But isn't that precisely how Parliament has operated for years?

And so on to Questions to Your President of the Board of Trade. There were lots of questions about small businesses, the competitiveness of British companies, support for rural areas under Objective 2, the future of the coal industry and, of course, the minimum wage. John Redwood, the Opposition spokesperson, was particularly obnoxious today, accusing Mrs Beckett of wearing an 'old Labour outfit'.

Your Health Secretary, Mr Dobson (hero of the week for saving St Batholomew's Hospital) then made a Statement on Public Health, flanked by Public Health Minister, Tessa Jowell. Mr Dobson said he was today announcing proposals to do more to stop people falling ill. He said that 187 million working 5 days were lost to the economy every year through ill health. He said it was the job of Your Government to identify risks to health, to assess them and where appropriate either for the Government itself to take action to reduce the risks or to ensure that people who might be affected are aware of the risks and know what the odds are.

The Green Paper which was published today shows how Your Government intends to tackle the root causes of bad health, how we intend to concentrate on the major killers - heart disease and stroke, cancer, accidents - and how we will be taking major initiatives to promote healthy schools, healthy workplaces and healthy neighbourhoods.

The Lord President, Mrs Ann Taylor, then announced the business for next week, and there were the usual questions from backbenchers covering all sorts of things. Probably the most important concerned Iraq. It was, said Mrs Taylor, clear that the vast majority of Honourable Members supported Your Government's position. That is certainly true from the soundings we Whips have taken. If Saddam Hussein has to be bombed, then so be it, say most of them.

And then we are on to a debate on Local Government Finance with a vote at 10 pm. However, sadly, Your Majesty, I shall miss this as I have to go to my son's open evening and then to a leaving party at 12 Downing Street. But I might just be in time for the Adjournment debate on the closure of the South Crafty tin mine in Cornwall.

Janet Anderson MP, with humble duty reports Monday 9 February, 1998

Your Majesty,

Questions to Your Secretary of State for Defence were, as might be expected, dominated by questions about Iraq and possible military action.

Dr Brian Iddon, the new Labour Member for Bolton South East, even managed to insert a constituency link into his question. He understood that the codename for the operation in Iraq was Operation Bolton. Would it not be better, he asked to stick to codenames like Desert Storm. Your Secretary of State replied that if it had been codenamed Operation Hamilton (the name of his constituency) then he was sure his constituents would have been proud to have been associated with action to deal with Saddam Hussein.

Ann Clwyd said she thought that military action was hardly likely to remove the main problem, ie Saddam Hussein, and could consideration therefore be given to bringing him before an international court to be tried for crimes against humanity Your Secretary of State confirmed that was certainly a suggestion which was 'in the air'.

Other questions concerned the level of educational attainment by armed forces personnel. This from Conservative, Tim Boswell. One of the Ulster Unionists (who we have not yet forgiven for keeping us up half the night last Wednesday) asked if soldiers in the Royal Irish Regiment, who had been on operational duty, could not be encouraged to take up educational opportunities instead.

Your Secretary of State also confirmed that the first Eurofighter aircraft would be delivered to the Royal Air Force in June 2002. As David Borrow, the new Labour Member for Preston (and one of a handful of new Members who have made no secret of their homosexuality) pointed out, this made the Conservatives look rather foolish as they had claimed, during the election, that a Labour Government would not go ahead with

Eurofighter. I am so glad we did. It is really important for aerospace jobs in Lancashire, many of which are held by constituents of mine.

Questions then followed to Your President of the Council. Virginia Bottomley tried to allege that Your Prime Minister was hardly ever in the House and why didn't he spend more time in Parliament. It turned out, said Mrs Ann Taylor, that in fact Your Prime Minister had already answered more questions in the time available under the new arrangements than his predecessor. This was largely because, so far, Mr Blair had not missed any Prime Minister's Question Time, whereas his predecessor often did. This latter point was forcibly made by Dennis Skinner, who can never resist the opportunity to have a go at Virginia (or Golden Virginia, as he calls her).

There was also a question to the Chairman of the Finance and Services Committee, Dr Lewis Moonie, about the cost of the new parliamentary building, Portcullis House.

It is certainly going to be expensive - £250 million at the latest estimate. However, as Dr Moonie pointed out, supported by veteran Labour MP, Gwyneth Dunwoody, we are just about the only Parliament in the world where every Member does not have his or her individual office. Yes, he said, the building was going to be expensive, but wasn't better to ensure a high quality building, rather than seek to emulate some of the 'monstrosities' which had appeared in the area recently.

And now, Your Majesty, we are on to a debate about the Child Support Agency, initiated by the Liberal Democrats. This is such a tricky area. Your Minister,

Frank Field, said that Your Government was not yet ready to come up with the final plans for reform but would do so by the summer and the House would have an opportunity to debate them. I think everyone is agreed that absent parents must take responsibility for their children, but it is also clear that the present system is a mess. Let us hope we can come up with a workable and fair solution.

Another Opposition debate on Railway Services will follow after the 7 pm vote, but will finish at 10 pm, whereafter Dr Ian Gibson will introduce an Adjournment Debate on the subject of The future of cancer research.

Janet Anderson MP, with humble duty reports Tuesday 10 February, 1998

Your Majesty,

Your Foreign Secretary, Robin Cook, had a tough afternoon today, though he handled it well. First there were Questions to Your Foreign Secretary, followed by a Statement on Iraq.

Sadly, too much time, in my view, was devoted during questions to the subject of Mr Cook's partner, Gaynor Regan, and whether or not he had or hadn't considered her for the post of his diary secretary. You really wouldn't think we might be on the verge of war with Iraq, Your Majesty, when this is all Your Official Opposition can think about. As Mr Cook at one point said, it appeared that Honourable Members opposite have done nothing else but think about his diary secretary for the last 19 days.

However, some questions at least were concerned with more serious issues. These included Your Government's review of the Dependent Territories (which is apparently, if the media is to be believed, the subject of a turf war between two particular Ministers); loopholes in the EU code of conduct on arms sales; and a request for Your Foreign Secretary to visit Brazil. There would have been a question on Your Government's ethical foreign policy on British exports, but sadly

Mr Richard Spring (whose question it was) was not present to ask it. Oh dear, Madam Speaker will not call him to speak for a while. *

Mr Cook then delivered the Statement on Iraq. It was basically a statement repeating the reasons why it was necessary not to rule out military action, should it prove impossible to reach an accommodation with Saddam Hussein by diplomatic means. Probably the most shocking statistic revealed by Your Foreign Secretary was the fact that Saddam Hussein holds 8,400 litres of anthrax (he had admitted only 650 litres), and that he has the capability to manufacture enough extra anthrax to fill two more warheads every week. One such warhead could depopulate an entire city.

There was much support for Your Government's position. Your former Prime Minister, John Major, nodded vigorously as Gerald Kaufman said there should be no concessions to Saddam Hussein and no lifting of sanctions - that his total compliance with UN resolutions was not negotiable. I had wondered why John Major was in the Chamber, since we don't see him very often now. We soon understand why. He was determined to contribute to this debate and the House received him in silence. Saddam Hussein was, he said, a psychopath without conscience and there must be no concessions to him. Moreover, Mr Major called on his side of the House to support Your Government's position.

David Maclean, formerly a Home Office Minister, then introduced a 10 Minute Rule Bill to provide for the preservation of war memorials; and to ensure their proper transfer to a suitable location if their present site is redeveloped. This enabled him to make lots of emotive references to the need for proper remembrance and so on. I have no doubt this is a Bill which will command wide public support and that we can expect a campaign from the Honourable Gentleman. No wonder he was objecting to other Private Members' Bills last Friday for, of course, the fewer that move up the legislative ladder, the more time for his Bill. Yes, David Maclean, is one of only a handful of Conservatives who is settling down into Opposition and exploiting it for all he's worth.

And now, Your Majesty, we're back on to the Scotland Bill - again - and it looks as though we shall be here until gone midnight.

Ah well, it gives me plenty of time to embark upon some sleuthing. The press are running stories that there are five Labour women MPs who are either pregnant, or have had babies since the election. We know who four of them are, but who is the fifth? And, more importantly, is she married, or at the very least in a stable relationship? I certainly hope so.

* The Speaker usually takes a dim view of any MP who does not turn up to ask a question they have tabled.

Janet Anderson MP, with humble duty reports Wednesday 11 February, 1998

Your Majesty,

This morning's Adjournment debates covered Hospital services in Kent, Maternity services in the NHS, The A21, Home Zones (which I think have something to do with bicycles), and the case of Scots Guardsmen Fisher and Wright. This latter was from the Independent, sleaze-free, Martin Bell, who always wears a white suit. Actually, I think it makes him look just silly but presumably he doesn't care!

The House then reassembled at 2.30 pm for Questions to Your Secretary of State for Northern Ireland, Dr Marjorie (Mo) Mowlam. Everyone loves Mo, even Madam Speaker it seems. For Mo twice chose to directly address Honourable Members when she should, of course, have been addressing the Speaker. Anyone else would certainly have been hauled up by Betty for that.

There was further evidence of Mo's popularity when Jeremy Corbyn (not known for his loyal support for Your Government) praised Your Secretary of State for her commitment and integrity. Others were not quite so complimentary, and the Ulster Unionists were as pessimistic and unhelpful as they usually are. They really are a sour bunch. Apart from discussion of the peace process, there was one about nursery education when Mo revealed that 2,200 new pre-school education places would be created in Northern Ireland from September.

There was only half an hour for Northern Ireland Questions as today was the day for Questions to Your Prime Minister. Madam Speaker has been trying for some time to prevent both sides from shouting and cheering as their respective leaders enter the Chamber. Sadly, Labour MPs were having none of it, which prompted Madam Speaker to say she had 'won the battle over here' (pointing to the Opposition benches) and she was determined to 'win the war over here' (pointing to Your Government benches). I suspect the comparative silence of the Tories has more to do with their views on William Hague than any directives from the Speaker, but there you are.

The Opposition obviously thought their best chance of embarrassing Your Prime Minister was by raising the question of the Bill to incorporate the European Convention on Human Rights into British law (the Human Rights Bill).

Did Your Prime Minister, asked Mr Hague, agree with Your Lord Chancellor that this would introduce a privacy law by the back door. No, it would not, said Mr Blair without referring to whether or not he agreed with the Lord Chancellor, who has been a little tricky just lately. Lord Irvine had, alleged Mr Hague, made enough comments about the matter to paper his apartment. Your Home Secretary had even laughed at that, he went on. Whereupon Your Prime Minister retorted that he was pretty sure Your Home Secretary was laughing at the Right Honourable Gentleman (ie.

Mr Hague) rather than with him. Mr Hague persisted with his questioning on a privacy law, finally forcing Mr Blair to remark that 'frankly it wasn't that great a question the first time he asked it'.

Paddy Ashdown asked if Your Prime Minister would take action to strengthen the Competition Bill, which a Liberal Democrat amendment in the Lords succeeded in amending the other night, supposedly to make sure that Rupert Murdoch could not engage in predatory pricing policies. There was no need, said Mr Blair, as the Bill was already strengthening existing powers to bring us into line with the rest of Europe. In any event, he said, newspapers were perfectly entitled to compete and where there was any abuse the Office of Fair Trading could investigate. Quite right too, but there will be a job of work for we whips to do to get the amendment overturned when the Bill returns to the Commons.

Additional work for the whips was also signalled by Madam Speaker at the end of Prime Minister's Questions. I think we all saw this coming for Ministers in particular have often been unnecessarily verbose when responding to questions in the Chamber. Questions and answers had to be shorted, she said, in order for more Honourable Members to participate. And would the whips, she asked, make sure that this message was conveyed to all Honourable Members. Actually Betty is right about this. Some Ministers are so long-winded, I'm surprised anyone bothers tabling questions to them.

There was then a Private Notice Question from Sir Alistair Goodlad to Your Secretary of State for International Development to ask what Your Government was doing to alleviate the suffering of the victims of the earthquakes in Northern Afghanistan. Clare said we were doing all we could and emergency relief was getting through to the victims, though the weather was not helping. However, the ceasefire in the civil war was. She also said there was an international review under way into how emergency and humanitarian aid was provided in such situations with an emphasis on reconstruction and development in order to avoid future dependency.

Mr Desmond Turner then moved a 10 Minute Rule Bill to provide for compensation for victims of motor accidents, after which we moved on to the Local Government Finance (Wales) Bill and the Greater London Authority (Referendum) Bill.

Mr Ken Livingstone graciously informed us last night that he had difficulty with one clause of the above Bill and would not therefore be supporting Your Government (no change there!) However, he said he would abstain rather than vote against, while pointing out that, had it been a month ago, he would most certainly have voted against. This is, of course, because Mr Livingstone, above all else, wants to be Mayor of London and is therefore moderating his rebellions. I think he'll need to do better than that. Rumour has it that Glenda is to put her hat into the ring.

And then, Your Majesty, several Orders, some of which could be debatable. Could be 1.00 am and I have no doubt that Miss Geraldine Smith will be on her own for her Adjournment Debate on the Heysham M6link road. Apart, of course, for the Minister - Glenda Jackson!

Janet Anderson MP, with humble duty reports Thursday 12 February, 1998

Your Majesty,

I fear that Honourable Members are looking rather tired today as the House did not rise until the early hours of this morning. However, by the time it came to Questions to Your Chancellor of the Exchequer, they had perked up, ready for the fray.

There were questions about IMF rescue plans for the South East Asian economies when Your Chancellor revealed that the Philippines were to receive $1 billion, Thailand $6.7 billion, Indonesia $18 billion and South Korea $35 billion.

Mr Chris Pond, Labour Member for Gravesham (and husband of Euro MP, Carole Tongue) wanted a statement on expenditure plans for the windfall levy. The Conservatives, of course, opposed the windfall levy but, as Your Chancellor pointed out, the money was being put to excellent use to provide new work and training opportunities for young people, the long-term unemployed, lone parents and the sick and disabled. It would also be used to fund new capital projects for schools, and expanding out of school childcare. There were other questions about the taxation of lawyers' fees and progress on the mis-selling of pensions. Your Government takes the latter issue very seriously indeed. About 60% of the cases requiring review are now completed but Ministers made it plain that no corners will be cut at the expense of investors. Fines have already been imposed on some of the guilty companies and we are hopeful that this will serve as a warning to others.

There were no statements today so Business Questions to Your President of the Council, Mrs Ann Taylor, followed. Mrs Taylor, who now announces the business two weeks in advance instead of one (which has done much to make the lives of Honourable Members more tolerable) said that next week we would be discussing the Human Rights Bill which has come back to us from the Lords. On Tuesday there will be a debate on Iraq in Government time which promises to be lively. I have no doubt that there will be overwhelming support on all sides of the House for Your Government's position.

On Wednesday of next week we shall debate the Social Security Benefits Up-rating and Pensions Increase Order and on Thursday we shall move on to the Scottish Revenue Support Grant Reports. On Friday (Hurrah!) we shall have our first constituency Friday of this year, which means the House will not be sitting so we can all depart for our constituencies to undertake the usual round of advice surgeries etc.

And now, Your Majesty, we are yet again continuing to debate the Scotland Bill, or at least Honourable Members from Scotland are. Hopefully we shall finish at 10 pm, or soon after and then poor old Glenda has the adjournment debate again - this time on the gripping subject of the A3 and Kingston By-pass.

Janet Anderson MP, with humble duty reports Monday 16 February, 1998

Your Majesty,

The day commenced with what became a rather complicated and confusing Question Time. First Order for Questions was to Your Secretary of State for Culture, Media and Sport, who was followed by Your Minister without Portfolio (in respect of the Millennium Experience), then the Member representing the Church Commissioners and, because there were relatively few Questions to him, we went back to the Minister without Portfolio.

That in itself was confusing but, to make matters worse, Madam Speaker (after her call last week for brevity in question time) was determined to romp through the questions as quickly as possible, in order to call as many Honourable Members as possible. Sadly, this meant that no fewer than 9 Members on the Government benches were not present for their questions. A stern warning is winging its way towards the Members Letter Board for each of them.

However, those questions which were taken covered a broad spectrum. The Member for Bolton North East, Mr David Crausby, rather unhelpfully asked if we could not make the granting of concessionary television licences for pensioners on a more equitable basis. This is, of course, because some pensioners in sheltered housing still benefit from the 5p licence, while others have to pay the full rate. The problem about making it fairer, as Your Ministers pointed out, is that it would cost Your Government around £450 million to do that. Others asked about the distribution of lottery money and whether it could not be distributed more evenly around the country.

Mr Phil Woolas somehow managed to mention the Oldham Childminders Association and Mr Colin Pickthall was concerned that Your Government should ensure the widest possible television coverage for test cricket.

New Labour Member, Margaret Moran, presumably one of our women

Mr Brian Sedgemore chose to describe as Stepford Wives, was bang on message with a question about public libraries and the National Grid for Learning.

There were no statements or PNQs, but there were a few Points of Order.

Mr Tam Dalyell again raised Iraq (of which more tomorrow as we have a full debate on that issue), but then we moved swiftly on to the Second Reading debate on the Human Rights Bill (Lords). Dr Brian Mawhinney used the occasion to direct much criticism at Your Lord Chancellor and the alleged rift between him and Your Home Secretary. Opposition Members are becoming very fond of accusing Your Government, Your Majesty, of doing one thing and saying another. This was, of course, a slogan we developed against the Conservatives in the run up to the General Election. You would think, wouldn't you Your Majesty, that they could be a tad more original.

The debate will undoubtedly continue up to 10 pm when we can expect two votes. There are plenty of speakers and, while Opposition Members may complain about giving more power to the judges, I believe this to be a popular measure. It quite simply incorporates the European Convention of Human Rights into domestic law.

We promised to do this at the election, and now we are doing it. Hardly a case of saying one thing and doing another.

And, for once, the Adjournment debate has nothing to do with transport. Tonight's is concerned with Education funding for Rutland. A relatively early night for us all and I assure Your Majesty we will make the most of it.

Janet Anderson MP, with humble duty reports Tuesday 17 February, 1998

Your Majesty,

Your Secretary of State for Scotland was first up for Questions today. Mr Dewar can never resist having fun at the expense of the Conservative benches, none of whom, of course, represent Scottish constituencies. He mocked one who stood up to question him by referring to his Scottish antecedents which, were, said Mr Dewar, 'well buried'.

The questions were indeed varied. Subjects ranged from the Scottish agricultural industry, the financing of local government in Scotland and relations between the Scottish Parliament and the European Union to the number of primary schools in Scotland offering foreign language tuition (74%) and the electronic tagging of offenders under Restriction of Liberty Orders.

Questions to the Parliamentary Secretary in Your Lord Chancellor's Department, Mr Geoff Hoon, were rather more lively as Honourable Members lost no opportunity to raise the cost of refurbishing Your Lord Chancellor's residence. Dennis Skinner complained about the reform of the legal aid system at a time when Your Lord Chancellor was apparently spending £8,000 on beds (actually it's £16,000 allegedly for the Pugin beds in question) and £69,000 on wallpaper. Mr Hoon replied that the refurbishment was nothing to do with him, but was a matter for the House of Lords.

Mr Chris Mullin, Chair of the influential, all party Select Committee on Home Affairs, caused some amusement when he asked what was the purpose of QCs, except as a device for perpetuating restrictive practises and artificially inflating fees. Mr Mullin is a tireless campaigner against what he perceives as the exclusivity of the legal profession. Possibly the only subject which exercises him to a greater extent is what Freemasons get up to.

But, of course, what everyone was waiting for was the debate on Iraq. No fewer than 40 Honourable Members have put in to speak. As the Foreign Affairs Whip pointed out to us in the Whips meeting, 23 of these were members of the Labour Party but only 11 of those were expected to support Your Government's position. The job of the Whips today is quite clear. We have to make sure we restrict the number of Labour MPs voting against Your Government to what we affectionately refer to as 'the usual suspects'. Let us hope we are successful. We shall know the worst at 10 pm when there will be two votes - one on the Conservative amendment (which was written with Government help through the usual channels) and one on the Government's substantive motion. Both will be supported by Your Government so a resounding majority is, in any event, a certainty.

I think we were all reassured to hear Your Foreign Secretary confirm that the door to peace would be held open as long as possible. Let us just hope that a diplomatic solution is still within reach.

Janet Anderson MP, with humble duty reports Wednesday 18 February 1998

Your Majesty,

This morning saw the usual round of backbenchers' Adjournment debates. One of the most interesting was that on the recruitment of teachers, initiated by

Mrs Margaret Hodge, the Labour MP for Barking (and former leader of Islington Council). Mrs Hodge is the Chair of the Select Committee on Education and Employment which has produced a report on the need to recruit more teachers. Sadly, Mrs Hodge was disappointed with Your Government's response to her committee's report, which she described as 'lukewarm'. There were some entertaining contributions to the debate, including one from Labour's Charlotte Atkins who bemoaned the fact that there were not more male teachers in primary schools, and

Mr Bob Blizzard who refreshingly, for a former teacher, complained about teachers who 'whined' instead of getting on with the job.

There were other debates on Montserrat, the availability of 'flu vaccinations from the NHS, the livestock industry, and errors of diagnosis and treatment by the NHS. The House then adjourned until 2.30 pm.

First Order for Questions was Your Secretary of State for Wales. Many of the questions were concerned with education in Wales. Your Ministers said that standards of literacy and numeracy in Welsh schools were not high enough, and

Your Government has therefore set very clear targets for further improvement. There was a broad welcome for the increased funding to reduce class sizes in many areas, in line with Your Government's manifesto commitment at the general election.

Desmond Swayne, the colourful Conservative Member for New Forest West, again asked for an inquiry into the counting of votes in the Welsh referendum. This really is old hat now. By whatever majority, the people of Wales voted for a Welsh Assembly and I am afraid Conservative Members will just have to live with that reality. Of course, they do not have any MPs in Wales, so I guess they are a little out of touch. That is presumably why they continue to field Mr Nigel Evans, the Conservative Member for the Ribble Valley in Lancashire, at Welsh Questions. So far as I can ascertain, Nigel's only connection with Wales is that he owns a newsagent's business in the Welsh Valleys.

Questions to Your Prime Minister followed and the Parliamentary Labour Party was in good form. This was probably due to the fact that the House last night overwhelmingly supported Your Government's policy towards Iraq. Only 21 Labour MPs chose to vote against Your Government and, as predicted by the Whips, these were, as ever, the 'usual suspects'.

It was noticeable that a number of Labour's new women MPs bobbed up to ask good questions, with a confidence I certainly never enjoyed as a new Member. Your Prime Minister was also on top form. Your Leader of the Opposition, Mr William Hague, for once (at least to start with) opted for a more consensual approach and thanked Your Government for supporting the Opposition amendment to the motion on Iraq last night. This was not surprising as the amendment was written for the Opposition by Your Government!

Mr Blair said he hoped very much that the mission of the UN Secretary General to Baghdad would be successful, and confirmed that Your Government would continue to press Saddam Hussein for full compliance with the UN resolutions. He emphasised that our quarrel was not with the Iraqi people but with Saddam Hussein.

MPs welcomed the additional money announced by Your Government to reduce class sizes. 100,000 more children, said Mr Blair, would now find themselves in classes of under 30 than would otherwise have been the case. The mood of the House lightened up even more when the ebullient Chairman of the Catering Committee,

Mr Dennis Turner, asked Your Prime Minister to join with him in celebrating a week of British beef, whether it be braised, boiled or whatever. They are, Your Majesty, serving beef in many forms in all the dining rooms of the House today, and we have all signed a book to record our support for British beef.

Charlotte Atkins berated the Liberal Democrats for supporting the New Deal, while opposing the windfall levy which is funding it. Could they find her, she asked, a Liberal Democrat bank manager. Beverley Hughes welcomed the National Minimum Wage and highlighted how this would help many women in her North West region who often had to endure poverty pay. Mr William Hague then returned to the Human Rights Bill and whether or not this constituted a privacy law. What did Your Lord Chancellor think, he asked, when he was not looking through furniture catalogues.

Oh dear, these jokes about Your Lord Chancellor's official residence are beginning to wear a bit thin. And then, 1o and behold, a Liberal Democrat popped up to say that he was in fact a former Liberal Democrat bank manager.

And so on to what was a very difficult statement indeed for Your Home Secretary to make. This was to announce Your Government's acceptance of the independent report from Lord Justice Stuart-Smith who, at Your Government's request, had reconsidered all the evidence on the Hillsborough Disaster. Lord Justice Stuart-Smith concluded that there was no basis on which there should be a further public inquiry. As Mr Straw conceded, this decision was a great disappointment to the bereaved families. He referred to 'all of us who have lost children in any circumstances' and spoke with great feeling. He does himself, of course, have direct experience of this having lost an infant daughter many years ago.

The House continued, Your Majesty, with the Annual Benefits Uprating Order which we expect to finish reasonably early. At last, the promise of an early night.

Janet Anderson MP, with humble duty reports Thursday 19 February, 1998

Your Majesty,

I am afraid today has proved singularly uneventful, for which my apologies. Despite the strong feelings about the ban on beef on the bone, and the future of green top milk, Questions to Your Secretary of State for Agriculture were fairly calm.

There was one exception when the Conservative Member for Ludlow, Mr Christopher Gill, asked how many farmers had committed suicide in each of the past five years. Your Ministers did not have the statistics to hand, but said the high rate was of particular concern to Your Government and was adopting policies to reduce this rate.

Questions about green top milk revealed that 800 responses have already been received (including one from me!) during the consultation period and more are expected before the closing date of 24 February. I know from conversations with the Minister, Jeff Rooker, that he is very concerned about the bugs found in raw milk and he told me there are allegedly links with BSE. However, I also happen to know, Your Majesty, that Your Prime Minister has anxieties about any more bans so we shall keep our fingers crossed. I have suggested we merely go for a stricter health warning on the bottles.

The ban which continues to be controversial is, of course, the ban on beef on the bone. But Labour MP, Robin Corbett, leapt to Your Government's defence, said they were right not to take risks with public health and that he had not had one single complaint from his constituents about the non-availability of T bone steaks and oxtail.

Other questions concerned the amount of imported beef fed to British armed forces, the likely effect of a minimum wage on the agricultural industry and the Food Standards Agency White Paper.

Questions to Your Attorney General (for which there is only 15 minutes) were about the Glidewell Report on the future of the Crown Prosecution Service (which is expected in March). There were so many questions on this that no other subject was covered.

Your President of the Council, Mrs Ann Taylor, then made the usual Business Statement. We shall next week be discussing the Scotland Bill (again), the European Parliamentary Elections Bill, the Government of Wales Bill (again) and, on Friday, there is to be a debate on the Government's Priorities for Women. I am sure many of our new Labour women will wish to participate in that.

Honourable Members chose to use the Business Statement to raise the usual wide range of subjects. Today we had NHS waiting lists, delays over the Lottery Bill, requests for a further debate on Iraq before any military action is taken and, once again, the cost of refurbishing Your Lord Chancellor's residence. Dennis Skinner rose magnificently to the occasion on the latter subject. Was the House aware, he asked, that the decisions about the refurbishment had been taken by a Committee in the Lords which was dominated by Conservatives. Well that certainly took the Opposition by surprise. Good old Dennis! And then on to what promises to be a rather dry debate about Local Government Finance in Scotland. Few speakers are expected, so I predict we shall be on our way home to our constituencies by 7.30 pm at the latest.

Janet Anderson MP, with humble duty reports Monday 23 February, 1998

Your Majesty,

First Order for Questions today was to Your Secretary of State for Social Security and Women, Harriet Harman. There were questions about Your Government's pensions review. Harriet confirmed that Your Government is determined to ensure that the next generation of pensioners retire not on means tested benefits, but on the basic State pension and a good second pension.

Following recent press reports that Your Government was considering making television licences free for all pensioners, this too was raised. Goodness knows where the leaks have come from. We had thought in the Department of Culture, Media and Sport that this was unlikely as it would cost approximately £500 million to implement. Ms Harman said she would bring the matter to the attention of Your Secretary of State for Culture, Media and Sport.

Housing benefit fraud was again on the agenda. This is something on which Your Government is pledged to crack down. It is a huge problem of which all Honourable Members will have their own experience. There is a particular problem of partners living separately in order to attract two lots of housing benefit, something which is made easier by the number of council houses lying empty. There are around 500 in my constituency alone.

Your Minister for Women, Joan Ruddock, got a fair crack of the whip for the first time at Question Time. Rosie Winterton, one of the new Labour women, welcomed Your Government's proposal to introduce a Working Family Tax Credit, and said this would be a great help to low paid women who had difficulty meeting the cost of childcare. Ms Ruddock also referred to the intention of Your Government to use our Presidency of the European Union to highlight the problem of violence against women. Other questions concerned the Child Support Agency, which works very unfairly at the moment, and is under review (Labour Members called upon Opposition Members to apologise for the mess); the Minimum Wage; the New Deal for Lone Parents and the way in which the Benefit Integrity Project is working. This particular project involves people on Disability Living Allowance where they are called in to ensure they still qualify for it. Unfortunately, some people appear to have been taken off this particular benefit when they should not have been. Ministers confirmed that, in order to avoid this, further safeguards would be introduced into the system.

There was then a Statement from Your Deputy Prime Minister and Secretary of State for Environment, Transport and the Regions on Planning for the Communities of the Future. Essentially this statement was about household growth and what Your Government will do to accommodate it. The proposals are to replace the top-down 'predict and provide' mentality of the past with a more decentralised and flexible system targeted on maximising the proportion of homes to be built on urban sites.

Mr Prescott also pointed out that Your Government is committed to protecting the countryside and revitalising our towns and cities, and that the two objectives are inter related for by making urban areas more attractive places to live and work, we will relieve the pressure on the countryside. Your Government will develop regional targets for the building of new homes on previously developed (brown field) sites and these targets will draw on local knowledge.

Your previous Government achieved an average of 42% building on brown field sites, which was below their aspirational target of 50%. Under the new system Your new Government expects to raise the proportion of new housing on all brown field sites from 50% to at least 60% over the next ten years. This statement should help to reassure people that Your Government is serious, Your Majesty, about protecting the green belt.

And now we are (yet again) on to business on the Scotland Bill. Surely we must be nearing the end of this by now! At least we know we shall finish by 11 pm tonight, which is one hour later than it might have been - but the quid pro quo is an early finish on Thursday. Hurrah.

Janet Anderson MP, with humble duty report Tuesday 24 February, 1998

Your Majesty,

Questions today were to Your Secretary of State for Health, Mr Frank Dobson, and were pretty much dominated by questions about smoking, particularly the worrying increase in the number of young women who smoke. Your Minister, Tessa Jowell, said that she would soon be meeting with editors of teenage magazines to see what could be done to discourage young women from smoking. There are, of course, rumours that Your Chancellor of the Exchequer intends to put the price of a packet of cigarettes up by 25p in the Budget, but we shall have to wait and see. Certainly something needs to be done to halt this upward trend.

The Liberal Democrats wanted to know when hospital waiting lists were likely to come down. Your Secretary of State acknowledged that waiting lists were still too high but gave a commitment that they would be well below the numbers we inherited over the course of this Parliament. There was an interesting question about telemedicine where we learned that all general practitioners will be connected to the NHS net by 2002.

Questions were followed by a Statement from Your Prime Minister on Iraq for which the Chamber quickly filled up. Mr Blair was received in absolute silence as he first set out the background to the current dispute and then outlined what had been achieved by Kofi Annan, the UN Secretary General, in Baghdad. Your Prime Minister referred specifically to the special group which is to be established to inspect eight clearly defined Presidential sites and said Your Government was awaiting clarification of the details of the special group. Three things were essential, he said. The Commissioner in charge of this group must be properly qualified for the task; the details of the inspection regime must preserve in full the professional and technical nature of the inspections and the inspectors; and there can be no question of negotiating with Saddam Hussein over the integrity of the weapons inspection process.

Your Prime Minister emphasised again that our quarrel was not with the Iraqi people, and that we would, if possible, increase the direct bilateral help we give to them. He also said that there would be no change in the readiness of British or US armed forces in the Gulf until all the requirements of the agreement brokered by Kofi Annan had been met. His Statement was widely welcomed by the House - on all sides.

And so on to the Committee Stages of the European Parliamentary Elections Bill where a Labour backbencher, Andrew Mackinlay, is seeking by his amendment to get Gibraltar included. I don't know why on earth Madam Speaker has selected this amendment for debate, as it appears to have nothing to do with the Bill, and can only serve to ensure we make little progress this evening. Sadly, this means we shall have to bring the business back on Thursday night, and the promise we had held out for an early night then will, once again, bite the dust. So much for the Jopling Reforms and sensible hours.

Oh, and Your Majesty may be interested to know that tonight's Adjournment debate has been allocated to the feisty Miss Ann Widdecombe on the subject of farmers' incomes. The Minister responding will be Mr Jeff Rooker. He's the one who wants to ban green top milk - but we are working on him.

Janet Anderson MP, with humble duty reports Wednesday 25 February, 1998

Your Majesty,

This morning's Adjournment debates were on the subjects of Health inequality, The Strategic Defence Review, Special Needs Education in Croydon, Foreign ownership of utilities and the Destruction of Security Service files - so a pretty broad spectrum was covered, as usual.

The House reassembled at 2.30 pm for Questions to Your Secretary of State for International Development, Clare Short, who announced that her Department has provided more than £400 million humanitarian and reconstruction assistance to Bosnia Herzegovina since 1992. There were several questions about progress on land mine clearance. Ministers said that Your Government had doubled expenditure on demining and was working for greater international cooperation in order to speed up demining worldwide.

One question concerned Voluntary Service Overseas and there was reference to a report in Sunday's Observer newspaper which claimed that fewer young people were signing up for this. David Hanson wanted to know what was being done to help refugees in Sudan. He particularly praised his own constituents for the work they were doing to raise funds for the refugees.

As the time approached 3 pm - and Questions to Your Prime Minister - the House, as ever, became busier and noisier. 'The House must come to order,' shouted Madam Speaker and Your Prime Minister and Leader of the Opposition entered the arena.

Opposition Members were clearly intent on highlighting the proposed march this coming weekend by the Countryside Alliance. However, as Your Prime Minister pointed out, there are 30,000 more hectares of greenbelt than there were under Your last government and farmers had received £85 million more in aid. He hoped, continued Your Prime

Minister, that Tory MP, Mr Nigel Evans, would remember that as he lit his beacon in his Ribble Valley constituency tomorrow night.

Mr William Hague chose to ask a question about the Guardian article by Polly Toynbee this morning which implied that Your Government was going to change its policy on benefits for lone parents. The article was quite simply wrong, said Mr Blair. Unfortunately, Mr Hague continued with his planned supplementary which had not anticipated Your Prime Minister's answer and it all rather fell apart.

Mr Denis McShane asked Your Prime Minister to welcome the survey from Income Data Services which showed that many employers were already adjusting the wages they paid to their employees to ensure they would not fall foul of the National Minimum Wage when it was set. Sally Keeble spoke in glowing terms of Your Chancellor's proposals to introduce a tax credit for working families on low incomes which, she said, would greatly help many families in her constituency; and Jenny Jones pointed out that two thirds of women pensioners were forced to rely on income support so she hoped Your Government would bear that in mind in their pensions review. I must say there certainly seems to be more debate about such matters in the House since we have greatly increased the number of women MPs.

Your Majesty's Official Opposition then asked a Private Notice Question about the Ramblers Association who had apparently received a copy of Your Government's proposals on the 'Right to Roam' before its publication. Your Minister, Mr Michael Meacher, admitted that this had been given to the Association in advance, for their private perusal and gave an unreserved apology to the House.

And so on to the last day on the Government of Wales Bill, for which we are all truly grateful.

Janet Anderson MP, with humble duty reports Thursday 27 February, 1998

Your Majesty,

There is much disenchantment around the House today as there are dark rumours that the House may sit until at least 10 pm on the European Parliamentary Elections Bill (committee stages). This is the Bill which introduces a form of proportional representation for the European elections. Discussions are continuing through the usual channels to see whether agreement can be reached for a 7 pm finish, which would enable Northern Members to get their last train home, and Scots Members to catch their last flight home.

The Parliamentary day began, however, with Questions to Your Secretary of State for Education and Employment. The questions concentrated very much on Your Government's proposals to get particularly young people off benefit and into work. Ministers referred to the fact that hundreds of companies had now signed up to cooperate with the New Deal, including major concerns like W H Smith, Dixons, Tesco and Sainsburys. The Conservative MP, Gerald Howarth, drew laughter when he asked why it was taking so long for Your Government to improve school standards. This was rather rich from someone whose party was in government for 18 years, and at the end of whose period of office almost half of 11 year olds could not read or write properly. Ministers referred to the structured daily literacy hour which will happen in all primary schools from September and to Your Government's target of 80% of 11 year olds to reach the expected standard for their age in English by the year 2002. Labour MPs could not resist pointing out that, for the duration of these questions, there were a mere 17 Conservative :MPs in the Chamber.

The usual Business Questions followed when Your President of the Council announced the business for the following two weeks. Her Shadow, Mrs Gillian Shephard, complained bitterly that there were far too many announcements made by Your Government outside the

Chamber when she felt that Parliament should be the first to know. Mrs Taylor then told us what to expect next week.

My apologies, Your Majesty, I mistakenly informed you that we had endured the last day of business on the Government of Wales Bill this week. Lo and behold, I find we have another day on this on Monday. Let us pray it is the last. We also have a 10 Minute Rule Bill on the Welfare of Broiler Chickens, further business on the Scotland Bill and the remaining stages of the European Parliamentary Elections Bill.

Mr Harry Cohen requested a debate on what Your Government is doing to help the people of Iraq, rather than a debate on whether or not we should bomb Iraq. Mrs Taylor said that while she could not promise a debate she did think that information should 'see the light of day'. The Liberal Democrat Chief Whip, Mr Paul Tyler, complained that official police photographers had been taking photographs of students participating in a lobby of Parliament yesterday. Was this to be come the norm, he wanted to know. Others wanted something done about the decision to restrict Yesterday and Today in Parliament to the long wave band. Mrs Taylor referred to the Select Committee on Culture, Media and Sport, which met this morning and asked that no decision be taken on this until the Committee had had an opportunity to report.

And so on to more debate of the European Parliamentary Elections Bill. Let us hope we are not too late, because some of us have to be in at 9.30 am tomorrow for an all day debate on Your Government's Priorities for Women. I suspect that particular debate will be rather dominated by the Labour women.

Janet Anderson MP, with humble duty reports Monday 2 March, 1998

Your Majesty,

A relatively dull day today I am afraid. Even Questions to Your Home Secretary was rather uneventful, although Conservative, Alan Clark, caused some amusement when he claimed that the best way to reduce the prison population was not to prosecute wrongdoing.

Several Conservative Members complained that Your Government was not spending enough on law and order. It was gently pointed out that, since Your Government was committed to their projected spending plans for the first two years, this was an argument which really didn't wash. It is quite extraordinary how positions have been reversed. Now we have Conservative Members calling for increased spending, and Labour Members arguing for restraint and prudence.

Chris Mullin wanted to know if Your Home Secretary would do something about youths with air rifles who were out of control. Mindful of criticisms that Your Government is banning too many things, Your Home Secretary paused before responding. 'Careful' shouted the Hon Nicholas Soames. Question Times really wouldn't be the same without him. 'Well done Brinton,' he called, when new Labour MP, Helen Brinton, who is always on message, praised Your Government for its action to help the voluntary sector which did so much, she said, to tackle the problems of social exclusion in her Peterborough constituency. For the first time, of course, Your Majesty's Minister of State at the Home Office, also has responsibility for the voluntary sector.

Reference was made to last week's Victim Support Week and the launch of the new national telephone helpline for victims - the 'Victim Suppportline'. Bruce Grocott, one of Your Prime Minister's Parliamentary Private Secretaries, urged Your Home Secretary to continue to blame Your last Government for problems on law and order up to the year 2008. This was on the basis that Margaret Thatcher had persistently blamed Your previous Labour Government for anything she could from 1979 right up to 1990 when she was deposed as leader of her party.

Gerry Bermingham wanted to know if better use could be made of suspended sentences. Gerry is a practising barrister who is always present for Home Office questions. There were also questions about different electoral systems. A new system is to be introduced for elections to the Scottish Parliament and Welsh Assembly; Members of the European Parliament are to be elected using a regional list system and proposals for electing the Greater London Assembly will be announced shortly. General elections are, of course, still carried out on a 'first past the post' basis, though a new Parliamentary group has just been set up to argue the case for the Alternative Vote system, which would introduce an element of proportionality, while retaining the constituency link.

But that was just about it. Nothing terribly exciting, and now we are, at last, on to what promises to be the very last day for discussion of the Government of Wales Bill. At least the Chamber is a bit more colourful than usual, with Honourable Members sporting yellow daffodils in recognition that yesterday was St David's Day.

We should get on to the Adjournment shortly after 10 pm when Sir Michael Spicer will raise the subject of The future of community hospitals, with rising star and Minister at the Department of Health, Alan Milburn. Poor Alan gets very fed up with being described as a 'rising star'. But he certainly is one of Your most competent and likeable junior Ministers. I suspect he will indeed go far.

Janet Anderson MP, with humble duty reports Tuesday 3 March, 1998

Your Majesty,

First Order for Questions was Your Deputy Prime Minister and Secretary of State for the Environment, Transport and the Regions, Mr John Prescott.

Mr Prescott announced that Your Minister for Local Government, Hilary Armstrong, had today launched a consultation paper on best value in local services. This, he said, would take forward Your Government's commitment to introduce a comprehensive regime, which will empower local people, and ensure continuous improvement in the performance of local services.

Other questions concerned the accountability of Regional Development Agencies, something which exercises many local authorities. Ministers pointed out that the agencies will be non-departmental public bodies and, as such, will be accountable to Ministers, though they will be required to consult the designated regional chamber and account for their activities to the chamber.

Tim Boswell wanted to know what was being done about improving air quality and Ministers referred to Your Government's National Air Quality Strategy and Dr Vincent Cable (a Liberal Democrat) asked what plans Your Government has to reduce local authorities' reliance on central government funding. (Labour MP,

Phil Woolas, has calculated that if the Liberals' policy on this were to be adopted and all local services funded locally, the average Band D Council Tax would be around £3,000!). Hilary Armstrong replied that Your Government was consulting on possible changes to the system of local government financing.

We were then on to transport questions. As ever, Honourable Members wanted to know about particular roads in or around their own constituencies. Ian Bruce asked about the Dorchester Relief Road and

Simon Bums about the future of the Driving Test Centre in Buchan Road, Chelmsford, which is apparently to be moved to a different site in Chelmsford. Chris Mullin wanted to know how many miles of new road had been approved since the election - 36 miles of road on new alignments as it turned out.

John Austin (he used to be John Austin Walker, but following a split with his partner, who was named Walker, he is now just plain John Austin) then introduced a 10 Minute Rule Bill to render unlawful religious discrimination in employment and in the provision of certain types of goods, to create new offences relating to incitement to religious hatred. A worthy Bill, but alas it is unlikely to be allocated time to become law, such is the pressure of Parliamentary business.

The main business today is Opposition business. The Conservatives have decided to divide the day into two debates: the first on the subject of ISAs, PEPs and TESSAs, and the second on the subject of the Countryside. I suspect the second will be somewhat livelier than the first, though the first is clearly designed to embarrass Your Paymaster General, Geoffrey Robinson. All the old hoary chestnuts came out about offshore trusts and Your Lord Chancellor's wallpaper. Conservative Members claim that the limit on ISAs of £50,000 is too low. I have to say I've had no complaints from my constituency of Rossendale and Darwen. But then, when you're working in a shoe factory for £2.50 an hour, you're not likely to be able to save anywhere near that figure. If only they had the chance.

Janet Anderson MP, with humble duty reports Wednesday 4 March, 1998

Your Majesty,

This morning's Adjournment debates managed to cover a number of fairly controversial topics including the Benefits Integrity Project. This is the system under which benefit recipients are called in to see whether they are still eligible for the benefit they are currently receiving. It has resulted in a number of people with disabilities having their benefits removed unjustly, which is why Your Secretary of State recently announced that a new independent element would be introduced into these reviews in order to make sure they were fair. Other Members raised the treatment of Irish born people in Britain, the Channel Tunnel rail link, Driving restrictions for insulin-dependent diabetics and Housing in the green belt at Silsden in Ann Cryer's Keighley constituency (Ann is part of a mother and son team in the House as her son, John, is also a Member, as indeed was her late husband, Bob, who was tragically killed in a car accident).

The House then adjourned until 2.30 pm when we all reassembled for half an hour of Questions to Your Chancellor of the Duchy of Lancaster. Members raised Your Government's Freedom of Information White Paper' Your Right to Know', on which there have apparently been 500 responses during the consultation period, the great majority in support of Your Government's policy. Labour Members welcomed the new openness of Your Government's approach which, they said, contrasted starkly with the lack of information available from Your previous Government. Other questions concerned the need to reduce bureaucratic requirements imposed on business by the European Commission and the possible problems with computers as we move into the year 2000.

As ever, the Chamber filled up for Questions to Your Prime Minister. It's really quite extraordinary, Your Majesty, how Your Official Opposition have adopted many of the accusations we levelled at them in the run up to the General Election. Today's was on allegedly broken promises and, more specifically, Your Government's policy on student funding. Why, asked Mr Hague and others, had Your Prime Minister not accepted the Dearing Report in full. The answer was quite simple, responded Mr Blair. Your Government had decided there was a better way of helping students from poorer families than protecting the maintenance grant and making all students pay tuition fees. In short, under the new arrangements, one third of students would pay no tuition fees at all and one third would pay reduced fees.

The Liberal Democrat, Nicholas Baker, asked (again) if Your Prime Minister would visit his constituency. Mr Blair replied that he was sorry he had no plans to do so at the moment. Ann McGuire (who is Parliamentary Private Secretary to Your Secretary of State for Scotland) made a feisty contribution when she pointed out some Scottish Office statistics which revealed that GDP and incomes in Scotland had gone down under Your last Government while homelessness had increased. She went on to accuse Conservative Members of 'donning their Barbours and plunging headlong into collective denial'. Labour Members liked that one.

Paddy Ashdown chose to ask about hospital waiting lists, on which Your Government has admitted we have to do better; and Ken Livingstone (no surprise here) wanted to know if Your Prime Minister was going to adopt the CBI preference on trade union recognition which would require more that 50% of the total workforce to vote for it. Well, he will have to wait for the answer - we are still consulting.

Maria Fyfe sought confirmation that there would be equal numbers of men and women in the Scottish Parliament. Chris Mullin asked if Your Prime Minister, when he came to publish his memoirs, would give Harper Collins a wide berth. Mr Blair, to loud cheers, expressed the hope that the Agriculture Council would next week endorse the European Commission's majority recommendation this morning that the export certified herd scheme is now through. A pretty wide-ranging Question Time altogether today.

As ever, the Chamber began to empty as Mr Geoff Hoon, Your Parliamentary Secretary to the Lord Chancellor, rose to make a statement about the future of legal aid and access to justice. Your Government's proposals, he said, were about controlling expenditure, better targeting legal aid and getting value for money. Moreoever, he announced that Your Government would be establishing a Community Legal Service to help those who are effectively excluded from legal redress. And no one mentioned Your Lord Chancellor's wallpaper, which certainly makes a welcome change.

Mr Bill Etherington then introduced a 10 Minute Rule Bill to protect the health and welfare of broiler chickens kept in indoor husbandry systems, after which we continued the debate on the Scotland Bill. Surely we must be reaching the end of our deliberations on this by now! Still, at least we have been told by the Scottish whip that there is only likely to be one vote at 8 pm, so we can all go off to the GJW party at the Reform Club, which is always a good do.

Janet Anderson MP, with humble duty reports Thursday 5 March, 1998

Your Majesty,

Your President of the Board of Trade, Mrs Margaret Beckett, was first up for Questions today.

Christine Butler asked if the women's unit at the Department of Trade and Industry (I did not know we had one) could work more closely with the women's unit at the Department of Social Security in order to encourage more women into science. Conservative Ann Winterton, while she did not say she disagreed with this, was clearly more interested in encouraging boys who, she said, were lagging behind the girls.

Conservative Members spent some time concentrating on Mrs Beckett's Blind Trust, which helps to fund her office; there was general condemnation of the director of United Utilities who recently received a £3 million payout and everyone bemoaned the closure of the last tin mine in Europe in Cornwall. Julian Brazier, the Euro sceptic, tried to raise a supplementary about economic convergence for the Single European Currency, but it really wasn't relevant to the question which had been asked. 'Has the Honourable Gentleman read the question?' boomed Madam Speaker. He sat down, suitably admonished.

Mrs Ann Taylor, Leader of the House, then announced the business for next week, which will include the remaining stages of the National Minimum Wage Bill, Opposition debates on 'Labour's Hidden Taxes' and 'the Government's Damage to Pensioner Incomes', further deliberations on the Schools Standards Bill and European Parliamentary Elections Bill and, on Friday, yet another day on the foxhunting bill. Somehow, I suspect that may be the end of the road for this particular bill.

And so, Your Majesty, a rather tedious day, for which my apologies. We are just hoping that votes will be kept to a minimum tonight as one of our colleagues, the Northern Ireland and Friday Whip, Jim Dowd, is holding his birthday party at No 12 Downing Street. But I might just pop back for the Adjournment debate which is in the name of Mr Dale Campbell Savours and concerns the preparation and presentation of evidence in the trial of Owen Oyston. This particular gentlemen, who is detained in one of Your Majesty's prisons after having been convicted of rape, is of great interest to us in the North West. I think the kindest way of putting it is to say that he is a man who has led a full and colourful life!

Janet Anderson MP, with humble duty reports Monday 9 March, 1998

Your Majesty,

Questions to Your Secretary of State for Defence were pretty much dominated today by the leak in weekend newspapers that Your Government's Strategic Defence Review was allegedly considering axing the parachute regiment and the marines or changing their traditions in some way. Ministers confirmed that this was not the case, and also that the leak had not come from them. (Well, they would say that, wouldn't they.)

John Hutton, the Labour MP for Barrow (a constituency which depends on Trident for its survival) wanted to know about Your Government's 'Smart Procurement' which is a ruthless examination of our procurement programme to ensure value for money. No doubt former Conservative MP, Jonathan Aitken, will be taking a keen interest in this!

Jane Griffiths from Reading (one of a number of new MPs who holds advice surgeries in the local supermarket) wanted to know what was being done to increase the number of people from ethnic minorities in the armed forces. Your Minister, Dr John Reid (who so tragically lost his lovely wife Kathy recently) replied that, starting in April, the goal for each Service will be that 2% of new recruits should be from ethnic minorities, with the figure rising annually by 1 % so that it reaches 5% by 2001/2. About time too. Experience tells us that improvement can only come by setting targets in this way.

Questions then followed at 3.20 pm to Your President of the Council, Mrs Ann Taylor. Here Honourable Members missed no opportunity to raise proceedings on the Foxhunting Bill or the Wild Mammals Hunting with Hounds Bill, to give it its proper title. This particular Bill, Your Majesty, is due to be debated again this coming Friday when we anticipate that Conservative Members will 'talk it out', thus ensuring its demise. (This is a considerable relief to those of us who do not want to see it reach the Lords and mess up Your Government's entire legislative programme, on which it was elected to govern.) However, a great many Honourable Members are extremely exercised about this. Teddy Taylor alleged that Your Government had sold supporters of the Bill 'down the river'. A Liberal Democrat called for the House to sit on Tuesday and Thursday morning in order to deliver the Bill. I am afraid, Your Majesty, it is quite clear that these people do not fully understand how Parliament works. If it did get to the Lords, goodness knows when it would get back to the Commons and, if and when it did, it would bear absolutely no relation to the Bill which had entered the Lords. Ah well, I guess they will learn eventually.

No Statements or Private Notice Questions. Indeed, for once, no points of order either. And so we were straight on to the continuing debate on the National Minimum Wage Bill. This Bill has just come out of Committee, where Labour Members were eager to force Opposition Members to sit through the night whenever possible, just to punish them for opposing the Minimum Wage. It looks as though tonight will be no different and we are planning to be here until breakfast time if necessary. (My particular stint at counting the votes is between 2 - 5 am, news which I have just gently broken to my husband.)

As I close this message, Your Majesty, the debate is centred on whether or not charities and the voluntary sector should be exempt from the National Minimum Wage, indeed whether there should be any exemptions at all. There are seventeen groups of amendments to be debated thereafter. It is almost bound to be a long night and we are laying in provisions in the Whips Office.

Who knows what time we shall get to Mr Clive Efford's Adjournment debate on the fire station at Shooters Hill. Oh dear, and Your Minister who has to reply is my old friend from the Home Office, George Howarth. So I doubt whether we shall see him in the bar tonight!

Janet Anderson MP, with humble duty reports Tuesday 10 March, 1998

Your Majesty,

I do hope Your Majesty will forgive me if today's Message is rather lacklustre as the House has been sitting all night and Your Vice Chamberlain only managed two hours sleep. It was, however, worth it as we managed to get Your Government's National Minimum Wage Bill through all its stages. Bob Marshall Andrews, the new Labour Member for Medway (who is not always on board with Your Government) told me that he was so elated by this that he had been drinking champagne on the Commons terrace at 6 am this morning.

But on to today's business which began with Questions to Your Foreign Secretary, Mr Robin Cook. The first half of question time was pretty much taken up with questions about the Middle East peace process and the meeting of Your Prime Minister at the weekend with Prime Minister Netanyahu. Mr Cook revealed that he would be travelling to Egypt, Jordan, Israel, the Occupied Territories, Syria and Lebanon next week. Would he, asked Mr Nick Palmer, raise the question of a Palestinian airport in Gaza to which he understood the Israeli government was now ready to agree. Indeed he would, said Mr Cook, together with the establishment of a sea port and an industrial estate on the border.

Two Labour Members failed to be present for their questions, and will undoubtedly incur the wrath of Madam Speaker. Paul Goggins was, however, there to raise the house arrest of former President Kaunda of Zambia. Ministers replied that he had now been charged but they were worried about the wording of the charge and would be keeping a close watch on the situation. Helen Jones wanted to know about human rights in Mexico; and, on Iraq, Your Foreign Secretary confirmed that the process of relaxing sanctions could begin only if Saddam Hussein complies with his obligations under the agreement with the UN Secretary General.

Following questions, Mr Cook was again on his feet for a Statement on Kosovo. The House was silent as he revealed that the security operations around Dreniza in the last week appear to have left at least 80 people dead. Despite claims to the contrary, he said it was simply not credible that all those killed were terrorists and that a local press report claimed that, of the 51 corpses released yesterday by the Serb police, less than half are believed to have been men of military age, 12 were children, 13 were women and 4 were elderly men.

Your Foreign Secretary spoke of his visit to Belgrade last week. He said he regretted that President Milosevic sought to present the events in Kosovo as a legitimate police response to terrorism. He said that President Milosevic had been given ten days to withdraw the paramilitary forces from Kosovo and to commit himself to a process of dialogue with the leadership of the Kosovo community and that, if he did, the sanctions adopted against him would be reconsidered. However, if he did not, said Mr Cook, then further measures would be taken, including a freeze on the funds held abroad by his government.

Mr Julian Brazier then brought in a Bill to require local authorities, when considering adoption or fostering, to make use of married couples unless they can show that no such couples are available who meet the needs of the child. I was not clear what the exact purpose of this Bill was until Mr Brazier got to his feet. All was revealed - what he wants to stop is adoption and fostering by gay couples. This is a particular hobby horse of Mr Brazier's but it has no chance of becoming law. It was opposed by new Labour MP, Hilton Dawson, who was apparently some kind of adoption manager before he joined us at Westminster.

And now, Your Majesty, we are on to two Opposition debates: one on Your Government's Record on Taxation, the other on the Effect of Government Policies on Pensioner Incomes. There is then a very long list of various motions, some of which (Oh, I hope not) could be voted on. And then - possibly a four hour debate on the Fossil Fuel Levy Bill.

Estimated time for rising of the House? About 3 am I should think. And no chance for a lie in tomorrow - whips meeting at 9.30 am!

Janet Anderson MP, with humble duty reports Wednesday 11 March, 1998

Your Majesty,

This morning's Adjournment debates covered Capital financing adjustment for local authority debt repayment, the BBC's coverage of Parliament (there is much anger in the House about the proposed changes), Broadclyst new town, Birmingham health services and Animal testing.

When the House reassembled at 2.30 pm, we began with Questions to Your Secretary of State for Northern Ireland, Dr Marjorie (Mo) Mowlam. It's great to see Mo looking so much better now after all the treatment she received for a tumour. She is such a lovely person and held in very high regard by Members on all sides of the House.

Naturally there were a number of questions about the peace process in Northern Ireland and Dr Mowlam confirmed that the inter-party talks at Stormont are making good progress. She went on to say that it remains Your Government's intention to strive for an early agreement by Easter and to put the outcome to a referendum in May.

There were other questions about extending the Dangerous Wild Animals Act 1976 to Northern Ireland, the National Minimum Wage (the Bill to introduce this was formally approved by the House on Tuesday morning after a marathon all night sitting), and security in the Maze prison. Ministers announced that Your Majesty's ChiefInspector of Prisons would be undertaking a formal inspection ofthe Naze and that his report will be published. Others referred to the Police (Northern Ireland) Bill, currently upstairs in Committee, which will establish an independent Police Ombudsman in Northern Ireland.

And so to Questions to Your Prime Minister during which Your Prime Minister became extremely cross when William Hague had the effrontery to imply that Your Government had refused to sign a UN declaration on human rights in China as a kind of sop to Rupert Murdoch. But later the leader of Your Majesty's Official Opposition went on to the offensive on council tax increases, as did many of his backbenchers. If only I had been able to chip in (but sadly, as a whip, I must remain silent) for the council tax in the Rossendale part of my constituency is to decrease by 14% as a direct result of additional funding provided by Your new Government.

Towards the end, Martin Bell, who really is becoming something of a pathetic joke figure in his white suit, suggested that Honourable Members on the Government benches were unable to ask their own questions, but had questions handed to them by Government Whips. Perish the thought, responded Your Prime Minister. He was, he said, the most democratic leader a party had ever had and, of course, Members could ask any question they liked. (He did have the grace to say this with a broad grin across his face!)

There were then several points of order complaining that the Tories were being beastly to Labour councils, followed by Mr Barry Gardiner's 10 Minute Rule Bill to amend the Housing Act 1996 to enable certain county court cases initiated on or before 1st September 1997 to transfer to a leasehold valuation tribunal. I am afraid, Your Majesty, all of this rather went above my head so I am unable to explain exactly what the Bill is intended to do. However, it was obviously extremely important to Mr Gardiner who bore it to the table of the House as carefully as if it had been Your Majesty's Crown Jewels. It did take him a little time to do this, as he forgot the correct procedure and bounded off to the bar of the House before he had announced who would prepare and bring in the Bill. 'Grab him', shouted Madam Speaker. Dennis Skinner duly did and brought him to a halt. But it was very funny.

And now on to the Report Stages of the School Standards and Framework Bill (up to 10 pm) and the Wireless Telegraphy Bill (after 10 pm). I think we may be here some time, possibly until the early hours. However, we can never be sure as the particular whip in charge of the latter Bill never gets his predictions right. He thought the Minimum Wage Bill would be finished on Monday by midnight (it went on until 10 am); and that the Fossil Fuel Levy Bill would continue last night for four hours when it only lasted two!

Your Majesty may also be interested to know that three Private Members Bills cleared all stages today. One on firework safety, another on public interest disclosure (to protect whistleblowers), and Mr Dennis Turner's Bill which will ensure that beer drinkers will get a proper pint in future. I think Dennis is hoping that a full pint may become known as a 'Turner' so that he can take his place in history.

And, at whatever time, Mr Jonathan Shaw has an Adjournment debate on empty homes and taxation. What can it be about?

Janet Anderson MP, with humble duty reports Thursday 12 March, 1998

Your Majesty,

Your Majesty's Official Opposition even managed today to continue the debate about rural communities and country life during Questions to Your Chancellor of the Exchequer. I dare say this is largely the result of the anticipation of tomorrow's debate on the Wild Mammals (Hunting with Dogs) Bill which is causing some distress to Your Home Secretary. Michael Foster, whose Bill it is, has played a blinder by tabling an amendment to Clause 1 of his own Bill which would make hunting a wild mammal with a dog a criminal offence, and delete the remainder of the Bill. He did this last night which forced the pro-hunters to keep the House sitting until 3.20 am so that they could table their own manuscript amendments. It will be an interesting day tomorrow but it is possible, even allowing for bogus points of order, presentation of petitions and the use of 'I spy strangers', that the Bill could complete its report stage, come back on 27 March for its third reading and then gallop off to the Lords.

However, back to Treasury Questions. There were questions about helping disabled women back into work, the level of domestic savings, the interaction of monetary and economic policy and even Value Added Tax on incontinence pads used in the National Health Service. Dennis Skinner came up with a flamboyant intervention criticising those who said the answer to the strength of the pound problem was to devalue and Gisela Stuart welcomed the reduction of V AT on domestic fuel to 5%. Nigel Evans, the Conservative MP for Ribble Valley, wanted to know why Your Government would not support his Bill to take into account the windchill factor when awarding severe weather payments. He pointed out that his Bill was identical to one introduced by Labour's Audrey Wise before the election. Yet another example, he said, of Your Government saying one thing before an election and doing another afterwards. Funny, I think I've heard that somewhere before. Gordon Prentice wanted Your Government to object to the proposal to abolish duty free within the EU in 1999 since 30 million people patronised duty free shopping every year. Ministers replied that the proposal required unanimity among member states to go through, and that appeared unlikely to happen as things stood now.

Your Majesty's Lord President of the Council, Mrs Ann Taylor, then delivered her usual weekly business statement. A light week for us all as it is the Budget Statement on Tuesday and the subsequent debate will be on a one line whip. The Chief Whip has even said that the whips can have some time off on a rota basis. Hurrah! After this week we shall need it.

And so on to further proceedings on the European Parliamentary Elections Bill, which provides for these elections to be conducted on a proportional representation basis in future. Hopefully we shall complete this business tonight. And fingers crossed that the pro-hunting lobby do not take it upon themselves to carry on the business through the night in an attempt to lose tomorrow's business on the foxhunting bill. If they do, Your Majesty, I fear that most of us will spend the entire weekend in bed.

Janet Anderson MP, with humble duty reports Monday 16 March, 1998

Your Majesty,

As the Culture, Media and Sport Whip, I was particularly concerned to see that all Labour Members with Questions turned up today. On the last occasion of Questions to Your Secretary of State for Culture, Media and Sport, no fewer than nine Labour MPs failed to turn up. Madam Speaker was not amused.

However, today was fine and everyone was present and correct. Several Members asked about arrangements for the World Cup and what was being done to combat hooliganism. Your Minister for Sport, Mr Banks, referred to the recent conference in Blackburn organised by Your Home Secretary at which the police authorities of all the participating countries were represented. English fans must behave, said Mr Banks, but Madam Speaker could not resist a smile when he went on to remind the House that 'the French police don't muck about'.

Francis Maude, Opposition Spokesperson, raised a rather pathetic question, I thought. (I wonder if he's OK. Ann Taylor pointed out to me this afternoon how grey his hair has become since the election.) Was the deal whereby Camelot were now to sell tickets for the Millennium Experience through lottery terminals a 'cash for licence renewal deal, he wanted to know. You would think he could do better than that. Harry Cohen asked about tourism and leisure industries promotions targeted at gay people. To groans, Virginia Bottomley, demanded that if he meant homosexuals, why didn't he use the word homosexuals. Ben Bradshaw (one gay Labour MP who has come out) followed this up with a question about the need to promote tourism in seaside towns - he represents Exeter. This is something Your Government is concerned about. That is why we have set up a backbench 'seaside town' committee of all those Labour Members representing seaside resorts. Richard Spring, from the Opposition front bench, was especially rude to Robin Corbett. Robin could not resist asking him if he had had 'a good lunch?'.

John Randall, who is actually the Conservative MP for Uxbridge, but looks for all the world like a Liberal Democrat with his beard and specs, wanted to know about allocation of World Cup tickets in 2006, when we would, he predicted, have a Conservative government again. 'Dream on' shouted the Labour benches and Your Minister for Sport, Tony Banks, retorted that he'd heard of fantasy football, now we were into the realms of fantasy politics. He would, he said, like to see the Honourable Gentleman's team.

And so on to Questions to Your Minister without Portfolio, Peter Mandelson. The Tories really do not take this seriously. A number of the usual suspects came up with trivial and schoolboyish questions. Trying to be clever, as Tony Banks remarked. Problem is, he went on, they need a brain for that. Wasn't the Dome and the Millennium Experience all a bit of a joke, and wasn't it the Minister himself who was the problem, they droned on. Interestingly, The Honourable Nicholas Soames, who is usually up for this kind of stuff, just sat tight and smiled benignly at Mr Mandelson.

Two Private Notice Questions followed. The first from Gerald Kaufman to ask Your Secretary of State for Culture, Media and Sport if he will make a statement about the responsibilities of the BBC under its charter in relation to its decision to promote the sale of Camelot scratch cards on BBCI next week. Gerald hates the BBC. The BBC had not, replied Your Secretary of State, broken the terms of its Charter and the debate was over fairly swiftly. However, Gerald did say that he intended to raise this matter on the adjournment. He certainly won't give up, that's for sure.

The second Private Notice Question was from Mr Ken Maginnis, the Ulster Unionist MP for Fermanagh and South Tyrone, whose question concerned the murder at the weekend of Mr David Keys, a prisoner on remand in the Maze prison.

Mr Adam Ingram, Your Northern Ireland Minister, replied. A murder inquiry had been launched he said and Your Majesty's Inspector of Prisons was to commence an inspection of the prison on Monday.

And now we are on to the Second Reading debate of the Teaching and Higher Education Bill which commenced its life in the Lords. I fear we could be late as there is provision to move the 10 0' clock rule. Then we are on to the Nuclear Explosions (Prohibitions and Inspections) Bill. I am ashamed to say, Your Majesty, that I have no idea what this is about but it is covered by the Foreign Office.

Various other Orders follow. I do not think it will be as bad as last Monday, when the House did not rise until 10 am the following day. I only hope, Your Majesty, that I am right.

Janet Anderson MP, with humble duty reports Tuesday 17 March, 1998

Your Majesty,

The House was unusually full today for Scottish Questions, and even fuller for Questions to Your Parliamentary Secretary to the Lord Chancellor's Department. This had nothing to do, of course, with a desire to hear the latest on the design and construction of the Scottish Parliament building at Holyrood, or even the future of legal aid and Your Lord Chancellor's wallpaper. Honourable Members were eagerly awaiting the Budget Statement from Your Majesty's Chancellor of the Exchequer, Gordon Brown.

By the time Your Chancellor rose to his feet, not only was the Chamber full, but also the galleries upstairs. Teresa Gorman just made it. 'Shove up,' she begged her colleagues.

There is, Your Majesty, so much in this Budget, I am not sure where to start. The Chief Whip has told us there will potentially be 70 motions which could be voted on next Monday evening (I certainly hope Your Majesty's Official Opposition will not subject us to that).

It was, said Your Chancellor, a Budget to encourage enterprise, reward work and help the family. He claimed the mantle of 'the guardian of the people's money' and stated Your Government's aim to build a national economic purpose around new ambitions for Britain. We were to have the lowest inflation rate for 33 years, increased growth, significantly lower public borrowing (down from a projected £19b to £5b next year) and a budget in balance by the year 2000. And all this under a Labour Government, or at least a new Labour Government. The Opposition benches looked glum.

To assist investment and help industry, companies will no longer have to pay advance corporation tax from next April and corporation tax would be reduced to the lowest rate in history at 30p from next April. Small and medium sized companies would also have their rate reduced to 20p and the Inland Revenue would in future be able to give help to small companies in setting up their payrolls when they took on staff.

A £50m venture capital fund would be opened to help universities expand research and development and make sure that British inventions stayed in and brought success to Britain and a new structure would be established for capital gains tax which would reward long term investment rather than short term speculation. Individual Savings Accounts would be available at supermarkets and post offices and there would be complete freedom to move cash in and out, while accumulated gains from TESSAs and PEPs would be protected.

Your Chancellor then moved on to Your Government's determination to make work pay. The cap on aspirations must be lifted, he said. Under the New Deal all the young unemployed would be offered work or training by April, those unemployed for two years or more would be eligible for a £75 a week employer's subsidy and 70,000 would receive an individual service with expert advice and help. There would too be new employment opportunities for women, particularly the partners of unemployed men.

There would be £50m available from the windfall fund to help homeless young people and changes to the National Insurance system to encourage employers to take on more young people. From April 1999, the Contributions Agency will be amalgamated with the Inland Revenue. While, Your Chancellor said, Welfare to Work had been stage one of Your Government's main project, this Budget was stage two. It was about making work pay. He followed this with the heavily trailed announcement of the Working Families Tax Credit to end the nonsense of many low paid in work receiving benefits and paying tax. No one earning less than 50% of average earnings will pay income tax. We had to make sure, he said, that work will always pay more than benefits.

Continuing the theme of women and families, Your Chancellor, announced that the working families tax credit would give additional help with childcare and cover up to 70% of the cost of high quality childcare, whether it be childminders, day nurseries or out of school clubs. Families were the bedrock of a stable and changing society, he said. There would too be unpaid parental leave available in line with the Social Chapter, and this had the support of the CBI. Poorer families with children under 11 would receive extra child benefit. It was, said Your Chancellor, about giving to those families according to their need and not their structure (reference to the decision last year in future to pay poor single parent families the same as poor two parent families a decision which is not to be reversed). Carers were to be helped too. Women with the care of children and husbands who are incapacitated would in future get the same benefits as did men whose wives are incapacitated.

Moving on to an environmental theme, V AT on certain energy saving materials is to be reduced from seventeen and a half per cent to five per cent, landfill tax is to be increased, an additional £500m put into public transport and another £50m a year specifically to fund public transport in rural communities. Recognising that the car was a necessity for some, the licence fee would be frozen and, for those with the smallest and cleanest cars, cut by £50.

To laughter, Your Chancellor said there would be no change to mortgage interest relief and stamp duty would only be increased by 2% for properties over £250,000.

Free admission to museums and galleries would be maintained, £1.5b would be saved by closing loopholes (including offshore trusts), beer up by 1 p, wine by 4p and no change on spirits. Petrol and tobacco up but another £250m for education and £500m for the health service. This was, said Your Chancellor, prudence for a purpose, to meet the people's priorities.

So there we have it. Investment, enterprise, long term over short term, making work pay, helping women and families and putting education and health at the top of the list. No wonder Labour MPs were jubilant. 'More' they shouted, waving their order papers in the air. And all Mr

Hague could find to say was to accuse Your Chancellor of messing around with a bucket and spade in the summer and was this all he could come up with. And Paddy Ashdown repeated the old chestnut about calls on mobile phones from the Red Lion Pub (something Your Chancellor's press man is apt to do.)

Frankly, I think this is one of the most exciting and innovative Budgets we have seen for years. But then I would say that, wouldn't 1. And, hurrah, no votes now until next Monday. What sheer luxury.

Janet Anderson MP, with humble duty reports Thursday 19 March, 1998

Your Majesty,

Questions today were to Your Majesty's Secretary of State for Agriculture, Fisheries and Food and then to Your Attorney General.

Rather surprisingly subjects covered even included flood defences in the Edgware area which, according to local Labour MP, Andrew Dismore, are quite seriously inadequate. Improvements were being considered, announced Your Minister, Mr Elliott Morley, in conjunction with the Environment Agency and local councils.

As ever, there were lots of questions about BSE, food chains, subsidies to farmers and the lifting of the beef ban. Dr Cunningham reminded the House that, on 16 March, the Agriculture Council agreed by a convincing majority to life the beef export ban for certified herds in Northern Ireland and that, in his opinion, this was a first and important step towards lifting the ban for the UK as a whole. I think everyone is agreed that Dr Cunningham is doing an excellent job and if anyone can get the ban lifted, then he can.

Simon Hughes, the Liberal Democrat Member for Bermondsey, asked if Your Government would give support to urban farms. Ministers replied that urban farms had a role based more on education than production and the Department gives no specific support io farms simply because they are situated in urban areas.

We then moved on to Questions to Your Attorney General, Your Majesty, which were a pretty dull lot and concentrated on international bribery, the Crown Prosecution Service and the use of juries in fraud trials. Your Home Secretary launched a consultation exercise on the latter last month, but it turns out that no-one has yet responded.

Your Secretary of State for Education, David Blunkett, then delivered a Statement on the extra funding for education announced in the Budget on Tuesday. He revealed that £35 million of this would be allocated to schools (there are still 600 of them and most of them primary) which still have outside toilets. This scandal would, he said, be ended by next year. Further funding would also allow schools to replace or improve inefficient heating systems and £40 million from the Budget would go towards new buildings which would help Your Government to deliver its core pledge on class sizes. Mr Blunkett also announced an extension to the Education Action Zones programme which is proving very popular and has produced some imaginative partnerships between schools, LEAs and business at a local level.

On to Business Questions when Your Lord President of the Council announced the Easter recess - one week and one day, and said that she hoped we might have a break at Whitsun but she couldn't promise it. Honourable Members will be dead at this rate.

Janet Anderson MP, with humble duty reports Monday 23 March, 1998

Your Majesty,

Later today we shall be completing our deliberations on the Budget with votes at 10 pm. According to the Treasury Whip there are potentially 88 votes at the end of the debate, though he pointed out that Your Majesty's Official Opposition had only identified 74 points on which they could force a division. So that's OK then! Let us hope the Opposition are not planning to sit up all night.

First, however, Your Secretary of State for Social Security and Women, Harriet Harman, was at the dispatch box to face questions. She was joined by the Minister for Women, Joan Ruddock (affectionately known as the Minister without Salary) who had the opportunity to answer questions on domestic violence and women's health. Your Government is to publish a National Strategy on tackling all forms of violence against women in the Autumn, something to which we are all greatly looking forward. It will cover the question of women's safety at work, on public transport, in their communities and within their personal relationships. The crime of domestic violence was mentioned again by new Labour MP, Helen Southworth, when Your Minister for Women was able to re-emphasise the importance Your Government attaches to this.

On women's health, Joan also referred to the recent parliamentary meeting on ovarian cancer organised by Ann Keen, the Member for Brentford and Isleworth, who is a former nurse. Your Secretary of State for Health, Mr Dobson, has, of course, already set out Your Government's intention to improve the consistency of treatment for cancer in the White Paper 'The New NHS'.

Your Home Secretary then made a Statement on Police Complaints and Discipline. This was in response to a Report from the Home Affairs Select Committee which made a compelling case for change in the procedures governing complaints and police discipline.

Mr Straw praised the honesty and integrity of the vast majority of police officers in this country but said that he was determined to give the police service the powers they need to deal effectively with the corrosive, very small minority of bad officers. He went on to say he was confident that the measures he announced today will strengthen the people's trust and confidence in their police service.

Your Home Secretary said that new procedures would be introduced without delay to tackle poor performance by individual officers. He said too that the standard of proof in disciplinary cases would be changed from the criminal to the civil standard, which has operated fairly in Scotland. In future, it will be possible for officers to face both disciplinary and criminal action on the same facts, bringing the police into line with the position of most others in the public and private sectors. He rejected two of the Committee's recommendations and confirmed that the status quo would be retained on legal representation for all officers and that he was not prepared to allow the hearings to be in public.

Mr Straw also dealt with the 'serious defect' in the present system which allows a police officer to retire on ill health grounds before disciplinary proceedings can be completed. This was something which caused great concern after the Hillsborough disaster to the families of victims. Mr Straw said that, in future, matters could be decided in the absence of officers, with appropriate safeguards. He said too that police authorities would have to refer all cases to him personally where a police officer was convicted of a criminal offence and he would decide whether or not that officer should forfeit his pension. It is, he said, abhorrent that public money should be paid out to those very few officers who abuse their position of trust.

Mr Chris Mullin, Chair of the Home Affairs Select Committee, welcomed Your Home Secretary's Statement and said it was, in his experience, the swiftest and most comprehensive response ever to a report from a Select Committee. Yes, replied Mr Straw, this was a very good example of Parliament and Government working together. Let us hope those journalists who have been bleating about Government ignoring Parliament will take note.

And so, Your Majesty, on to the continuing debate on the Budget, which appears still to be commanding public support almost one week later. A reasonably early night perhaps, for tomorrow we are likely to sit until past midnight. I am sure this hope is shared by Dr Phyllis Starkey for it is she who has the Adjournment Debate on Experimentation in local government. Goodness knows what that is about. Perhaps about installing brains into local councillors, joked the Deputy Chief Whip.

Janet Anderson MP, with humble duty reports Tuesday 24 March, 1998

Your Majesty,

Today's proceedings began with Questions to Your Secretary of State for Health, Mr Frank Dobson, ably assisted by junior Ministers, Alan Milburn, Tessa Jowell and Paul Boateng who really are among the best in the junior ranks.

Robin Corbett wanted to know what targets Your Government proposed to set for reducing deaths from cancer among people aged under 67 years. This gave

Your Public Health Minister, Tessa Jowell, the opportunity to air her usual rant about the need to discourage smoking. (I do believe Tessa would probably ban it if she thought she could get away with it.) We should not forget, she said, that the 15 year old smoker today would, in 30 years' time, become the cancer victim of tomorrow.

Your Secretary of State berated Your Majesty's Official Opposition for peddling untruths about waiting lists. However, he emphasised Your Government's determination to get waiting lists down, and said that the money allocated for that would not, under any circumstances, be diverted to anything else. Other questions concerned better cooperation between health authorities and social services, the cost to the NHS last year of medical negligence claims (£235 million) and celebrations of the 50th Anniversary of the Health Service (all Labour MPs have been asked to organise something in their own constituencies).

Questions were followed by a Private Notice Question requested by Liberal Democrat MP, Alan Beith, to ask Your Secretary of State for the Home Department for a statement on the threat from, and the precautions Your Government is taking against possible attempts to introduce Anthrax to the United Kingdom. This was as a result of a story in today's Sun suggesting that there was a danger of Anthrax being introduced into duty free products. Your Home Secretary suitably reassured the House. He said that this particular threat was first made known to the Home Office on 6 March and that, while it was essential not to be alarmist, Your Government was satisfied that all the appropriate anti-terrorist measures were in place. Mr Straw also said at one point that he had 'taken part in a terrorist exercise'. I am not sure what he meant by that!

Mr James Wallace then introduced a 10 Minute Rule Bill to amend the Crown Estate Act 1961 to require the Crown Estate Commissioners to exercise their functions with due regard to the non-commercial interests of local communities and to regulate the granting of sea-bed leases by the Crown Estate Commissioners.

And so on to further deliberations on the Report Stage of the School Standards and Framework Bill. Opposition Members even managed to draw the recent countryside march into this debate. There will be a number of votes and I think we shall be here past midnight. The votes are, of course, whipped, apart from one. There will be a free vote, possibly in the early hours, on an amendment from Miss Kali Mountford to outlaw corporal punishment in private schools. I think, Your Majesty, most

Honourable Members are probably opposed to beating children in any school!

One Member who is already on the record as being a supporter of corporal punishment is Conservative MP for the Ribble Valley, Nigel Evans. Coincidentally, he also has the Adjournment Debate this evening on Farming in the Ribble Valley.

Janet Anderson MP, with humble duty reports Wednesday 25 March, 1998

Your Majesty,

The first two of this morning's Adjournment Debate were initiated by the Chairs of the Health Committee and the Environment, Transport and Regional Affairs Committee, Mr David Hinchliffe and Mrs Gwyneth Dunwoody. The former was on the subject of children's health and the latter on the proposed strategic rail authority and railway regulation.

These were followed by debates on Sufferers from Adhesive Arachnoiditis, The Rookery Footpath in Barrow on Soar and The Water Industry. I do hope Your Majesty will accept my apologies if I do not go into detail on these deliberations. I have to confess I was still in bed because the House did not rise until 6.30 am this morning and I was not able to get to my bed until 7 am just as my husband was leaving for work) Sadly, it looks as though there may be a repeat of this tonight.

However, despite the fact that there were many sore heads and sleepy faces around the place, the House reassembled again at 2.30 pm for Questions to Your Secretary of State for International Development. Members wanted to know about aid to Sierra Leone, Your Government's commitment to the international poverty eradication strategy, the encouragement of literacy in developing countries and what Your Government is doing to help reduce the amount of coercive abortion which takes place in China.

At 3 pm Your Prime Minister faced the usual round of questioning. The first, from lawyer, Gareth Thomas (Clwyd West), continued the French theme, following Your Prime Minister's seemingly very successful trip to Paris. Could Your Prime Minister, asked Mr Thomas, now deliver a coup de grace, bring forward reform of the House of Lords, and thus do something about the ancien regime. Your Prime Minister replied that he was delighted to be back on English ground today and could we 'stick with that'. Mr Blair also invited Your Leader of the Opposition to divulge to the House what was his position on abolition of the voting rights of hereditary peers. Mr Hague sat tight despite frantic gestures from Government backbenchers urging him to get to his feet.

Tony McNulty, one of the new Labour Members, who is always good value at Question Time, welcomed the fact that Conservatives were now campaigning for a Yes vote in the London referendum and particularly that possible candidate for the London Mayor, Jeffrey Archer, had said he would give up writing books if he were elected. Almost worth it, said Tony.

Sir Peter Tapsell tried to accuse Your Prime Minister, rather clumsily, of spending more time in the French Parliament than in the British Parliament (or at least I think that's what he meant). It didn't really work though. As Your Prime Minister pointed out, he is available under the new arrangements for Prime Minister's Question Time for exactly the same length of time as were his predecessors. And lately, he has also been seen in the division lobbies on a few occasions which has given great heart to the troops. While they do not expect for a minute that Your Prime Minister should be here every day, they do like to spot him in the lobbies or the tea room every now and again.

Gwyn Prosser, Member for Dover and Deal (Labour gain from the Tories last May) spoke glowingly of the Port of Dover which Your previous government had wanted to sell to the French. 'Did I hear someone ask for David Shaw?' asked Your Prime Minister with a grin. David Shaw was the previous Conservative incumbent in Dover and Deal and was generally regarded in the House as a loud mouthed hooligan. 'The fact that My Honourable Friend won the seat,' said Your Prime Minister, 'probably united both sides of the House.'

Your Deputy Prime Minister then delivered a robust Statement about Your Government's proposals for a Greater London Authority and the election of a London Mayor and there is also to be a new Metropolitan Police Authority, accountable to Londoners. 12 years after the demise of the Greater London Council, it is certainly exciting to know that Your

Government intends to breathe life back into the capital city. Last Friday's Statement on the future of the London Underground will certainly help too.

And so, Your Majesty, on again to the Government of Wales Bill (at least up to midnight) and no-one seems to have a clue when the votes will be or on what and goodness knows how long the speeches will be. I am terribly fond of my Welsh colleagues, Your Majesty, but I do wish some of them would be a little less verbose.

At whatever hour, this will be followed by Mr Gerald Kaufman, Chair of the Select Committee on Culture, Media and Sport, who has the Adjournment Debate on the subject of the BBC Charter and Camelot scratch cards. Gerald never misses an opportunity to have a go at the BBC. It should be good fun. And hopefully we shall be home before breakfast, so there will be no champagne in the smoking room at 6 am tomorrow!

Janet Anderson MP, with humble duty reports Thursday 26 March 1998

Your Majesty,

First Order for Questions today was to Your Secretary of State for Education and Employment, David Blunkett, who certainly seemed to have recovered from his all night session on Tuesday.

I am afraid, Your Majesty, I was not able to be terribly attentive during Question Time as I was dashing around trying to get the entire Glasgow University Labour Club (of which my eldest son is vice chair) into the Strangers Gallery. However, having managed to obtain 30 tickets (by all sorts of devious means) I was then able to concentrate on the proceedings.

There were questions about the application of the Private Finance Initiative to the provision of new schools. Your Minister, Dr Kim Howells, announced that there were no fewer than 16 projects announced or under consideration. It really is good news that we have got this initiative up and running because there was always some scepticism about the likely availability of private finance. Other questions covered the out of school childcare initiative which will create 20,000 new places, the need for better pastoral arrangements in primary schools with a high turnover of pupils, transport to denominational schools and the consultation document on millennium volunteers.

But, of course, what everyone was waiting for was the Statement from Your Minister for Welfare Reform, Mr Frank Field. The House was full and it was, at 2,800 words, one of the longest and most comprehensive statements, apart from the Budget, I have known for some time. Your Prime Minister and Your Chancellor of the Exchequer were on the front bench which showed the importance Your Government attaches to this important reform.

Mr Field pledged that, as the new welfare contract is established, we will have a new welfare state fitting a modem nation in the new millennium.

His Green Paper 'New Ambitions for our Country: A New Contract for Welfare', he said, set out the principles of reform based on the twin pillars of work and security; work for those who can; security for those who cannot. The proposals are certainly ambitious and wide ranging and I will not go into all the detail, Your Majesty, in this message. However, Mr Field did rightly say that the need for change is overwhelming and that the system as it stands, promotes fraud and deception, not honesty and hard work.

He went on to say that Your Government wants to spend more in some areas - on health and education, and on help for severely disabled people with the greatest needs. But we want to spend less in others: to get the bills for social and economic failure down by cutting unemployment, tackling low pay and raising skills, rooting out fraud and abuse and encouraging greater self-provision where it is appropriate.

There were to be changes to the rules governing benefit to the disabled to encourage them into rather than discourage them from work. He said that while the basic state pension, uprated at least in line with prices, would remain, there was obviously a need to encourage people also to make private provision to supplement the state pension. There would, he said, be a Green Paper on pensions later this year.

People would no longer lose benefit when they lost their jobs as a result of having made insurance provision to cover items such as credit card bills and car loans. Childcare would be expanded still further, and, again, a Green Paper will be published after Easter, since Your Government sees the provision of high quality services to be very much part of the welfare contract with the people. A Disability Rights Commission is to be established, Disability Living Allowance and Attendance Allowance (contrary to press speculation) will remain universal, national benefits but, at the same time more needed to be done to ensure that help was targeted at those most in need. Incapacity Benefit which costs almost £8 billion a year (more than we spend on the whole of the police in England and Wales, will, for future claimants, be reformed. There would now be an emphasis on what people could do, rather than what they couldn't do. And so it continued - 16 pages in all - and warmly welcomed, even (albeit rather grudgingly by Your Majesty's Official Opposition).

And later, Your Majesty, we are on to the Welsh Bill (again - Oh, I do hope this is the last day). But the real issue exercising the minds of my colleagues in the North West region, is the decision of the Labour Party no longer to hold their conference in Blackpool. This has been seen as a terrible snub to the North. I do hope we might be able to reach a compromise solution which would provide some reassurance that this great party of ours has not become Southern based and too yuppified for words. I know I shall certainly have my ear bent about it on Rawtenstall market on Saturday morning.

Janet Anderson MP, with humble duty reports Monday 30 March, 1998

Your Majesty,

A rather tedious day today, Your Majesty. I suspect everyone is now rather tired and looking forward to their Easter break, albeit still 10 days away.

First Order for Questions was Your Secretary of State for the Home Department, Mr Straw, who I am sure is currently very preoccupied about arrangements for the World Cup, especially following the tragic death of a football fan at the weekend. Shadow Home Secretary, Dr Brian Mawhinney (who is reportedly planning to leave the front bench) continued on this theme and asked Your Home Secretary about the FIFA sponsored knife, which has been in the news lately. Was this, asked Dr Mawhinney, known at the time of the Blackburn Conference organised by Your Home Secretary on the subject of policing the World Cup. Mr Straw replied that it was not. He went on to say that strong representations had been made to the French authorities to withdraw the knife from sale, but that, sadly, those representations had been ignored.

One question concerned honours and peerages - Dennis Skinner announced that he did not want one. Simon Hughes, Liberal Democrat from North Southwark and Bermondsey, asked if Your Home Secretary would reform the inquest system. He replied that the inquest system was an inappropriate say of inquiring into major disasters (such as Hillsborough and the Marchioness) and that legislation would be brought forward as soon as there was an opportunity. There were lots of questions about asylum seekers where Your Government announced that it was considering a range of measures for speeding up the asylum process. Angela Smith from Basildon wanted vulnerable witnesses protected in court and Your Home Secretary said he was looking at ways of doing this.

I am afraid it was all really rather dull. The only light hearted moment was when Conservative David Amess revealed that he had been invited to a briefing meeting for Home Office Questions by Labour MPs so that he could collect a supplementary question. As Ministers pointed out, had he done so he might have come up with a rather better supplementary than he did.

With no Statements, Private Notice Questions or 10 Minute Rule Bills we moved swiftly on to further proceedings on the Scotland Bill, despite attempts by Conservative Members to disrupt the business, as usual. This time, all the usual suspects were labouring the point about Your Prime Minister's relations with Mr Rupert Murdoch. Surprisingly, Madam Speaker dealt with it all in a very good humoured way and said she was not prepared to accept hypothetical points of order.

We anticipate, Your Majesty, that the Scotland Bill will continue up to 10 pm with two possible votes, followed by a number of Orders which are potentially votable. However, I suspect Steve Webb will not have to wait too long for his Adjournment

Debate on Rail Services between London and the West Country. Minister responding is, of course, Glenda.

Janet Anderson MP, with humble duty reports Tuesday 31 March, 1998

Your Majesty,

Questions today were to Your Secretary of State for Environment, Transport and the Regions, and Deputy Prime Minister, John Prescott. This is always a pretty hectic question time because there are so many Ministers and so many subjects covered by Mr Prescott's super ministry, as it as been dubbed.

Hugh Bayley from York wanted Your Government to take action to reduce the amount of sand and gravel dredged from river beds in environmentally sensitive areas. It turned out that this was apparently a matter for the mineral planning authority. I doubt whether this will dissaude Mr Bayley, however, from pursuing the matter. He is one of our more intense Members and also Parliamentary Private Secretary to Your Secretary of State for Health. This does not mean, sadly, that he restricts himself to health matters. Quite the reverse. He once received a roasting from the Chief Whip after refusing to shut up in a late night debate we wanted to close down so that people could go home.

Other questions were on local authority funding and the review of the landfill tax which, said Your Minister, Michael Meacher, was working, but needed to be higher to ensure a significant increase in waste recycling, recovery and minimisation, hence the increase announced in the Budget. Someone wanted to know about the accountability of the proposed Regional Development Agencies which will, it turns out, be required to consult the designated regional chamber and account for their activities to the chamber.

We were then on to transport. Michael Connarty wanted more freight on the railways, while Conservative MP, Howard Flight was exercised about the transport needs of rural areas (the Chancellor of course announced an additional £50m a year for public transport in rural areas in the Budget). Howard represents Arundel and South Downs, so you cannot get much more rural than that. There were, as usual, all sorts of odd questions about obscure roads in Honourable Members' constituencies. Poor old Glenda has to deal with them all. She once said to me that if she was given a speech which did not once mention the word 'bypass' it made her day.

Honourable Members were concerned to learn that Glenda had no plans to discuss the West Coast Main Line with the Franchising Director. As someone who travels on the line regularly, I know only too well that further investment is long overdue. They also need to do something about the food on the trains. We had all thought it would improve once Richard Branson took over, but no such luck.

Questions were followed by a Statement from Your Secretary of State for Health, Mr Frank Dobson. Everyone agrees that Frank is doing an excellent job and, thankfully, his preoccupation with high matters of state has done nothing to dent his reputation as master of the most vulgar jokes in the House!

The Statement was to announce the eleven areas in England which will become Health Action Zones, where special arrangements will be made to benefit local people by both modernising the local health services and taking concerted action to tackle the root causes of ill health. (And, no doubt, to make it easier for Tessa to persuade people to give up smoking!)

Some of the proposals for the individual zones are very exciting. In Luton, they are going to particularly address the health needs of Asian women. In Manchester, Salford and Trafford, they are going to adopt a holistic approach to mental health. North Cumbria will work with local transport services to improve access to health services in rural areas. Plymouth will be developing new approaches to improving dental health, particularly in children. And many others besides. And, we are told, this is only the first wave. Mr Dobson urged the continuing development of local partnerships so that we could build on this first stage. This really is taking health seriously at last.

Conservative David Atkinson then introduced a 10 Minute Rule Bill on Millennium Conformity and the need to make sure computer systems could cope with the move into the next century. This is rather worrying, and thank Goodness, Your Majesty, that Your Prime Minister is taking it so seriously. Madam Speaker told me she had been strongly advised to make sure she was not on a plane at midnight on 31 December 1999.

And so to Scotland - again. Committee of the Whole House and lots of amendments about what the Scottish Parliament will and will not do. There is almost bound to be a division on whether or not the Parliament should have power over abortion legislation. No doubt the anti abortionists will argue vehemently that it should, presumably on the grounds that they might find it easier to get the law amended in Scotland. They will, however, be defeated - even though it is a free vote.

And that will be that - apart from Des Turner's Adjournment Debate on Sewage treatment and disposal. I think I shall give that a miss and have a relatively early night for a change.

Janet Anderson MP, with humble duty reports Wednesday 1 April 1998

Your Majesty,

April Fools' Day and no-one in the Whips office has yet attempted to hoodwink anyone. Cannot quite believe it. Moreover, the weekly Whips' meeting at 12 Downing Street this morning was extremely good humoured. We didn't even complain about Doris' coffee (on which you could dance, according to my colleague, Bridget Prentice, the Member for Lewisham East).

Meanwhile, in the Chamber, there took place this morning an assortment of Adjournment Debates. One from Harry Cohen was on the subject of Tibet. Dear old Harry rather defeated the point of his debate, however. For Your Foreign Minister, Derek Fatchett, had to be in the Chamber to respond making it necessary for him to cancel a meeting with the Chinese Prime Minister, at which they were to have discussed - Tibet!

The most entertaining of these debates had to be Mr Martin Bell's on the subject of the Policy of the Arts Council towards touring light operetta: the case of the D'Oyly Carte Opera Company. Clearly there are serious fans of Gilbert and Sullivan in the House (though I have to say that I personally rather regard them as the musical equivalent of Enid Blyton). Sir Patrick Cormack for one. So exercised was he that he managed to raise the subject again later in the day during questions to Your Chancellor of the Duchy of Lancaster. They always, he alleged, sang off the same hymn sheet. That was, retorted Minister Peter Kilfoyle, precisely the function of the Press Secretary to Your Prime Minister, Alistair Campbell, who has this morning been up before the Administration Committee.

Strangely enough, the subject of Mr Campbell was not raised at Prime Minister's Question Time from the Opposition Benches. I suspect that was because veteran Labour MP and senior backbencher, Gerald Kaufman, got in first. Wasn't it disgraceful, he said, that the Tories dared to criticise Alistair Campbell. They were, after all, the party who had employed Sir Bernard Ingham, who had misused a letter from the law officers, accused a member of the then cabinet of being 'semi-detached' and had been described by John Biffen as 'the sewer rather than the sewage'. Well, there was no answer to that really. (No wonder there was such a large turnout for the Justice for Jammu and Kashmir dinner last night in Gerald's honour.)

To groans (as ever), Liberal Democrat Leader, Paddy Ashdown, rose to his feet. (He really is not taken terribly seriously - possibly because he gives the appearance of trying too hard). Oh dear, it was so predictable. When did Your Prime Minister meet Rupert Murdoch, he wanted to know and when was he going to do something about predatory pricing. Your Prime Minister responded that the Competition Bill before the House dealt with predatory pricing, that he met all the major newspaper proprieters regularly and that they were dedicated to the success of their businesses as he was dedicated to the success of his. Bravo.

David Crausby from Bolton asked Your Prime Minister to welcome the apparent conversion of Your Leader of the Opposition to the National Minimum Wage. The activities of the Opposition were not, boomed Madam Speaker, a matter for Your Prime Minister.

Once again, Dennis Skinner managed to bring the House down, Your Majesty. As he rose to ask a supplementary, everyone noticed that he had a pager (these are issued to Labour MPs by the Whips office) in his hand. Apparently reading from the pager, 'Could I congratulate,' Dennis began, whereupon he groaned and threw the pager into Terry Lewis' lap. I don't suppose we shall ever succeed in getting Dennis on message.

And so on to the Regional Development Agencies Bill, Report Stage and Third Reading. We expect the Third reading vote at midnight. And then there is something entitled Criminal Procedure (Intermediate Diets) (Scotland) Bill (Motion). This apparently has something to do with the need for retrospective Scottish legislation to prevent burglars, drug traffickers and other serving sentences in Scottish prisons from being released. As the Chief Whip said this morning, Heaven forbid, they may end up in England. Or, as one of my colleagues, quipped, as Labour councillors in Glasgow.

Janet Anderson MP, with humble duty reports Thursday 2 April, 1998

Your Majesty,

I must say the House of Commons already has an air of getting ready for the Easter break about it. Honourable Members are clearly ready for their holiday, albeit rather short, which commences next Thursday. So only a week to go, and let us hope no more all night sittings.

First Questions today were to Your President of the Board of Trade, Margaret Beckett and her Ministers, including the Scot who represents Makerfield (and still describes himself as the Socialist MP for Makerfield - I wonder if Peter Mandelson knows) Ian McCartney. You are always guaranteed a lively question time with Ian, and today was no exception. However, he has an extremely broad Scots accent. There was an amusing interlude last Friday when my fellow whip, Jim Dowd, had to respond to a debate in Ian McCartney's absence. He was congratulated by Conservative Nigel Evans who said that at least they could understand what Mr Dowd said, in contrast to Mr McCartney. Jim, who is very good at quick witted responses, replied that, in his experience, the Honourable Member for Makerfield, was always able to make himself understood, whether verbally or otherwise. Ian also has a reputation for being rather fierce if provoked!

However, Your Majesty, back to Questions. Ministers revealed that Your Government had invested £160 m in the encouragement of research and development, that they did understand the difficulties faced by manufacturers as a result of the strong pound, that there was a new Internet-based service for matching overseas customers with British suppliers and that Your Government had also launched a safety awareness campaign to specifically warn of the hazard of burns and scalds in the home, underlining that pre-school children were most at risk and that the kitchen was the place where many such accidents happen - most of them with chip pans I shouldn't wonder.

Your Secretary of State for Northern Ireland, Dr Marjorie Mowlam, then made a statement on the Narey Inquiry Report into the Maze Prison which was published today. Dr Mowlam commissioned this report following the escape of prisoner, Liam A verill, and the shooting of the L VF prisoner, Billy Wright. Dr Mowlam also referred to the subsequent killing of David Keys, into which a separate inquiry is being conducted by Sir David Ramsbottom.

The Maze contains, of course, Your Majesty, the largest concentration of convicted terrorists in the Western world and holds over 500 paramilitary prisoners. As Dr Mowlam said, the only prudent option is to hold them all in one place and, although the concentration of prisoners has many security advantages, there is a price to be paid.

She went on to list a number of steps Your Government was taking to improve security at the Maze and pointed out that Martin Narey had made 59 specific recommendations and Dr Mowlam said she would return to Parliament in 3 months' time with a progress report on their implementation. Goodness knows what the solution is, but Mo is certainly the best person for the job.

Your Lord President of the Council, Ann Taylor, then delivered the usual Business Statement for next week when we shall discuss the Lottery Bill and the Crime and Disorder Bill among other things. This was followed by an Opposition debate on the International Arms Trade on which there will be a vote at 7 pm. Your Foreign Minister, Tony Lloyd, is scheduled to speak at the beginning and end of this debate. However, Opposition Members may object and, if they do, the debate will be wound up by my fellow Whip, Greg Pope. Which is why he is currently trawling the House of Commons Library in an attempt to ascertain just what is the Wassenaar Arrangement.

We should be finished by 10 pm Your Majesty and Mr Derek Wyatt (who used to work for BSkyB and took a serious drop in salary when he got elected) has the Adjournment Debate on the second crossing of the

River Swale. Most Honourable Members will, I suspect, be safely on their way home to their constituencies by then.

Janet Anderson MP, with humble duty reports Monday 6 April, 1998

Your Majesty,

Your Secretary of State for Defence was first Order for Questions today. It was a fairly quiet session as many Honourable Members will still be making their way back from their constituencies (the first vote is not until 7 pm and it is not Government but Opposition business today).

Ministers revealed that the total cost of British forces in Germany is about £ 1.3 billion a year; that epidemiological studies into the health of UK Gulf veterans are continuing and that a number of events are planned to mark the 80th anniversary of the foundation of the Royal Air Force and the 50th anniversary of the Berlin airlift.

Questions to Your Lord President of the Council then followed and concentrated on the Report of the Modernisation Committee which recommends a number of changes to behaviour and procedures in the Chamber. Nicholas Soames, while saying he welcomed most of the Report, remarked that it might be a good idea for new members to spend some time in the Chamber before making suggestions for change. Mrs Taylor said she thought that was insulting to new members. 1 am sure he did not intend it to be. He told me last week that he probably had more friends on our side of the House than on his own!)

No statements, no Private Notice Questions, no 10 Minute Rule Bills. What a boring day indeed.

The first Opposition debate was on Trade Union Recognition. Clearly this is an attempt by the Opposition front bench to try and embarrass Your Government on this issue on which we shall unquestionably have to find some compromise. Personally I cannot for the life of me see why it should be unacceptable to expect 50% of the total workforce in a company to support recognition as the CBI would like.

Mr John Monks of the TUC would not, of course, agree.

There will be a vote on the Opposition Motion at 7 pm and then we move on to another Opposition debate on Manufacturing Industry. No doubt the Opposition will be greatly exercised about the strength of the £, alleged splits in the Cabinet and whether or not interest rates should rise. I doubt, however, Your Majesty, that many will take much account of what they say.

And so we should be home relatively early this evening, once Mrs Margaret Moran has had the opportunity to raise the subject of Electronic Government on the Adjournment.

My apologies, Your Majesty, for such a brief message but it would be economical with the truth to say there was much worth reporting.

Janet Anderson MP, with humble duty reports Tuesday 7 April, 1998

Your Majesty,

Questions to Your Foreign Secretary (who is not terribly popular with his team as he has organised a three hour team meeting on the first day of the recess) began in lively fashion with a question from my former roommate and MP for Delyn, David Hanson. David wanted to know about progress on a peace settlement in the Middle East.

There are, of course, Your Majesty, mixed views on this in the House. There are those who think Your Foreign Secretary's recent visit was a triumph and others who think it was a disaster. What worried me was the length of the reply drafted for Your Foreign Secretary by his civil servants. A whole page. Madam Speaker would not like that. However, in the event, she decided to live with it.

Gerald Kaufman made a moving tribute to Your Foreign Secretary's stance, and urged him to keep the pressure on Netanyahu to observe the Oslo Accord. He also welcomed the fact that Your Prime Minister was soon to visit Gaza. Questions quickly moved from the Middle East, an area about which Your Foreign Secretary said he was deeply concerned, to Cyprus and accession to the European Community. It is Your Majesty' s Government's firm view that Cyprus has a valid application for membership of the European Union and that the people of Cyprus are entitled to have that application judged on its merits. According to Steve McCabe from Birmingham Hall Green, this represented the fulfilment of yet another Manifesto commitment by Your Government. Cypriots in his constituency, he said, would be delighted. Reservations were expressed, however, about the refusal of Mr Rauf Denktash to take up President Clerides' offer of a mixed delegation on accession. It was a source of great sadness, said Your Foreign Secretary, that this offer had not met with a more positive response.

Following questions, Sir Patrick Cormack, raised on a point of order the decision of the BBC to press ahead with changes to the broadcasting of

Parliament and asked Madam Speaker to make available copies of her correspondence with the BBC. Reporting of Parliament should, said Madam Speaker, be available to as many people as possible. It was clear that Madam Speaker feels very strongly about this and she confirmed that she had put the correspondence in the House of Commons Library.

The Labour Member for Lincoln, Gillian Merron, then moved her Football Sponsorship Levy 10 Minute Rule Bill. This would establish a Football Levy Board with powers to impose levies on football organisations and to allocate sums for the benefit of association football. The aim of the Bill is to help the smaller clubs which lose out to the Premier League.

The Second Reading debate today was on the subject of the National Lottery Bill which has just come to the Commons from the Lords. This provides for the establishment of a panel to assist the Director General of the National Lottery in selecting who should run the National Lottery. It also creates a new good cause, of health, education and the environment. It also establishes a New Opportunities Fund to implement these initiatives and the National Endowment for Science, Technology and the Arts.

Your Secretary of State, Chris Smith, made an excellent speech describing Your Government's proposals for transforming the Lottery into a 'People's Lottery', and the debate continues as I write. In fact, the Member on his feet at the moment is none other than Your former Prime Minister, John Major. Like his colleagues, he appears to be hellbent on attacking Your Government for using lottery money to fund initiatives which they claim are not 'additional'. I think we can knock this argument down pretty swiftly. We are going to use the money for additional healthy living centres, additional after school clubs and additional IT training for teachers so you cannot get more additional than that. But we will, I am sure, have some fun in the Standing Committee on which I am considering putting Bernie Grant (on the basis it's better to have him on the inside than on the outside).

Janet Anderson MP, with humble duty reports Wednesday 8 April, 1998

Your Majesty,

Last day before the Easter hols so suffice it to say that Honourable Members are demob happy. This was evident at Prime Minister's Questions, of which more later.

Earlier today, as we Whips were having our usual weekly gathering at 12 Downing Street (discussing who we wanted elected to the National Executive Committee of the Labour Party, who had misbehaved recently and therefore must be kept here late at all costs to cause them maximum inconvenience, and simultaneously wishing Your Prime Minister well in Northern Ireland) backbenchers were raising every conceivable subject under the sun in the Chamber under 'Matters to be considered before the forthcoming adjournment' which always takes place before a recess.

Alice Mahon was concerned about breast cancer screening, Gwyneth Dunwoody about the BBC's reporting of Parliament, Alan Hurst berated the local Conservative administration in Essex for cutting back on school transport and Dari Taylor wanted a bypass in her constituency, or at least around it. Bob Blizzard came out with a bizarre story about a pit in Mountbatten Road in his constituency which has apparently been caused by the siting of a water main around it, and is daily growing in size as the weather causes more erosion. Andrew Rowe wanted more help for fruit pickers in Kent; he said you just couldn't get them these days (I imagine that is because being on benefit pays better than fruit picking in Kent) and John Cryer wanted more to be done to protect children travelling to school. He pointed out that in 1971 70% of primary school children walked to school. Now the figure had dropped to 10%. Surely some of this is due to wider car ownership!

Northern Ireland Questions predictably dwelled on the peace process and everyone wished Your Prime Minister and Your Secretary of State well in their deliberations in Ulster. It was a relatively low key affair, however, as only two Ministers were present. As Northern Ireland whip,

Jim Dowd, pointed out at the Whips meeting, the problem today was not having enough Members to ask questions, but ensuring sufficient Ministers to answer them.

At 3 pm, Madam Speaker announced Questions to Your Prime Minister, only today it was Your Deputy Prime Minister and Secretary of State for Environment, Transport and the Regions (when does he sleep?) who was at the dispatch box. This was the first time he had stepped in for Your Prime Minister. How would he do? In the event, he was brilliant. He even managed to use the word socialist, whereupon Andrew Mackinlay shouted from a sedentary position that this was truly 'old' question time.

Mr Prescott began in a very statesmanlike way, not least since the first subject was Northern Ireland and even Gillian Shephard, who was replacing the Leader of Your Opposition, Your Majesty, managed to be reasonably conciliatory. However, once we got onto farmers, Mr Prescott really came to life. How dare Conservative Members criticise us, he shouted, they were after all the party who had given us BSE and deregulated the milk industry. It got better. Would he confirm, asked Tam Dalyell, that the source of a particular piece of intelligence was MOSAD. Bluntly, he would not, since it would, he said, not be in the national interest.

However, John, who used to be a commichef in a hotel, really came into his own when Conservatives referred to the Minimum Wage. When he had been a commichef, he said, and that meant a trainee chef; it had no political significance (though he thought the hotel manager had sometimes doubted this) he had been subject to the Wages Council Act, which your previous administration had abolished. And when John Bercow, a rather odious little Tory MP from Buckingham, tried to provoke Your Deputy Prime Minister, he certainly got a reaction. This was the man, he boomed, who had been Chairman of the National Federation of Conservative Students when Norman Tebbit closed it down because it was too 'right wing'. Well, the thought of anyone being to the right of Mr Tebbit always brings the House down. Today was no exception.

On and on he went. 'More' cheered Labour backbenchers. Michael Fabricant, the Conservative MP from Mid Staffs who looks for all the world as though he wears a wig but won't admit it, could be described as 'hair today and gone tomorrow', said Mr Prescott (he has a small majority). He berated the Tories for not backing the consultation on the European workplace Directive and invited them to tell the House whether they were going to campaign in the forthcoming local elections on the slogan 'vote Tory and we'll take your holiday rights away'. And, finally, when Gary Streeter (who sometimes tries to be too clever for his own good) asked Your Deputy Prime Minister to what did he attribute the fact that Britain was now more dynamic, self-confident and outward looking than for some time, back came the response. It was, said Mr Prescott, entirely due to the real effect of Your new Labour government. Bravo. What a performance.

Difficult to follow that, but Frank Dobson, Your Secretary of State for Health, did so with a statement on the Blood Transfusion Service, which seems to be in a bit of a mess, but I am sure we'll sort it out. Fraser Kemp, who up to recently has most been concerned with getting Coronation Street's Dierdre freed from Risley Remand Centre, introduced a 10 Minute Rule Bill to return the Lindisfarne Gospels to the North East.

This was opposed by some Honourable Members who thought they should stay in the British Museum. As a Geordie by birth, I have to say I agree with Fraser.

We now, Your Majesty, proceed to the Second Reading on the Crime and Disorder Bill. (What a dreadful title. It sounds for all the world as though we intend to create crime and disorder.) I suspect there will be no vote on this as it has fairly broad support across the House. I do hope I am right as a number of we whips are off to a very nice restaurant for an end of term, bonding dinner, to return on Monday 20 April suitably refreshed, I hope, for the next stint.

Janet Anderson MP, with humble duty reports Monday 20 April, 1998

Your Majesty,

First Order for Questions today was Your Secretary of State for Culture, Media and Sport. We had anticipated questions from Your Majesty's Official Opposition about Rupert Murdoch, BSkyB and Mr Tim Allan and we were not disappointed. However, thankfully there were some rather more serious Conservative Members present who chose to concentrate on the subject as opposed to schoolboy antics.

As ever, there were questions about concessionary television licences for pensioners. This is an extremely tricky one as some pensioners get them and others have to pay the full fee. Sadly, it would cost millions to extend them to all pensioners and Ministers confirmed that the issue would be addressed when the licence fee came up for review in two years' time. However, Your Ministers could not resist pointing out that Honourable Members opposite, including Your former Secretary of State, Mrs Virginia Bottomley, had voted against a Private Members Bill introduced by Mr David Winnick on this very subject in the last session. Mrs Bottomley had the grace to look rather sheepish at that point.

Other questions concerned Lottery funding for piers. Mr Ronnie Fearn wanted more for his pier in Southport which is apparently visited by 144,000 people every year and Mr Ivor Caplin reminded the House that the West Pier in Brighton is the only Grade 1 listed pier in the country. Mr Nigel Waterson wanted more help for community theatre groups like the one in his Eastbourne constituency which goes under the odd name of the Rude Mechanical Theatre Group and Mr Ross Cranston pointed out that free access to museums was all very well but why did they have to meet the cost of producing education packs.

Your Secretary of State, Chris Smith, chose his response to Ross Cranston's question to pay a warm tribute to the late Dennis Howell, who was once famously dubbed the Minister for Drought. He would, said Chris, be remembered with very great affection by all who had known him.

Austin Mitchell (whose wife Linda McDougall was moved to write in The Times this weekend that if Anthea Turner had stolen her husband she would have been doing Linda a favour!) was anxious to highlight the contribution to the economy of the creative industries. 'Yes,' shouted Dennis Skinner, 'we've made a killing out of The Full Monty'.

And so we moved on to Questions to Your Majesty's Minister without Portfolio, Mr Peter Mandelson, who answers for The Millennium Experience, or rather The Dome. Rhodri Morgan, rather strangely, took the opportunity to say that people wanted the Right to Roam as well as the Right to Dome. Andrew Mackinlay said we had got the date of the move into the Millennium wrong and it should be the last day of 2000 and not 1999, which moved Michael Fabriqant, in an appalling attempt at a French accent, to speak of 'le date de fermature'.

Following questions, Your Secretary of State for Northern Ireland, Mo Mowlam, rose to make a Statement on the successful conclusion of the multi-party talks in Belfast on Good Friday - to resounding cheers from all sides. Labour backbencher, Candy Atherton, whispered to me that David Trimble looked rather lonely on the opposite benches. 'Shall we go and sit next to him to give him some support,' she asked.

Mo rightly referred to the agreement as 'unique' and really spoke for everyone when she said that 'the achievement of a peaceful and just society would be the true memorial to the victims of violence'.

A Business Statement followed, as Wednesday's Business will now have to be changed to accommodate the Northern Ireland business. We shall be taking the Bill in all its stages on the Floor, so a late night I rather suspect.

As for tonight, if Conservative Eric Forth and his chums want to make life difficult, then tonight's their night. Two statements have taken up a lot of time - more than an hour on the first one alone. We then have Lords Amendments to the Bank of England Bill up to 7 pm, Opposed Private Business to do with the Lloyds TSB Bill (apparently there has to be legislation to allow them to merge) up to 10 pm. I suspect we shall then go back to the Bank of England, followed by a rather complicated and obscure Data Protection Bill. Thankfully only two backbenchers have put in to speak on this and Your Majesty's Home Secretary has been told forcibly that for every minute over 20 his speech takes, we shall make sure he remains here for an hour. Let's hope the threat works.

Janet Anderson MP, with humble duty reports Tuesday 21 April, 1998

Your Majesty,

Second day back from the Easter holidays has been relatively uneventful, I am afraid. Perhaps it is because we are all recovering from too much 'first day back' celebrating yesterday evening.

First for questions today was Your Secretary of State for Scotland, Mr Donald Dewar, who is, of course, set to be the First Minister of Scotland in the Scottish Parliament. There were questions about health inequalities in disadvantaged communities in Glasgow, the number of criminal convictions in Scotland, the compliance of computer systems used by the emergency services for the millennium and social exclusion in rural areas.

As ever, Tam Dalyell (who doesn't look too well these days and brings his own cushion into the Chamber to sit on) had an obscure question about the Iranian defector, Mr Abolghasem Mesbahi, and the Lockerbie bombing. I don't think Tam will ever give up on this one. Gerald Howarth from Aldershot wanted to know about progress towards the design for the Scottish Parliament. Ministers replied that from 70 firms submitting bids, 12 have been chosen to take part in competitive interviews in May and, thereafter, 3 or 4 firms will be asked to prepare indicative design proposals for the Holyrood site which will go on public display, and that the design team will be appointed in July.

There were then questions to the Parliamentary Secretary at the Lord Chancellor's Department, Geoff Hoon (who has apparently framed a small piece of Your Lord Chancellor's new wallpaper and stuck it on his wall). He revealed that the Court Service is planning initiatives to save £4.25 million in 1998/99; £9.95 million in 1999/2000; and £12.05 million in 2000101 and that these savings will come from computerisation of administrative tasks in both the Crown and county courts, improved energy efficiency and the better use of resources.

A Member of Parliament called Laurence Robertson (of whom I have never previously heard, nor indeed seen) then introduced a Bill to deregulate racecourses followed by the Second Reading debate on the Finance (No 2) Bill. This was, said Your Chief Secretary to the Treasury, a mark of Your Government's continuing determination to modernise the economy, to provide for a sustainable rate of long term growth, and to ensure everyone has a share in rising prosperity. It is, Your Majesty, a rather dull and dry debate, as one might expect.

There will, I suspect, be two votes at 10 pm and then we are on to a number of orders on which there may be further votes. A midnight finish? I fear so. However, this will give me plenty of time to sort out the Standing Committee on the National Lottery Bill which meets for the first time this Thursday. A certain Minister is trying to hold up the proceedings because he wants to go to Bologna to attend the opening of an exhibition. I shall take great pleasure in informing him that such misguided priorities are forbidden and he will not be on a plane to Bologna, or anywhere else until I have got this Bill through. I sometimes wonder whether these Ministers understand that we do, from time to time, report on their progress or otherwise to Your Prime Minister. I suspect they don't.

Janet Anderson MP, with humble duty reports Thursday 23 April, 1998

Your Majesty,

I am afraid the House is rather like the Marie Celeste today. We are on a one line whip for a debate on the Adjournment on the subject of the Royal Air Force and I fear most Honourable Members are already safely back in their constituencies as I write this.

However, first this afternoon at 2.30 pm Your Chancellor of the Exchequer rose to take questions at the Dispatch Box. Given the few Members in the Chamber it was a singularly uneventful occasion. All the usual stuff about the strength of sterling came up. Your Chancellor made it clear that Your Government had no intention of going back to the days of boom and bust which would not be in anyone's interests, and certainly not in the interests of manufacturing industry.

There were questions, inevitably, about EMU and when we might join up.

Sally Keeble wanted to know what had been the impact of the Budget on families with average earnings of £16,000. They will, it turns out, see a real increase in their disposable income of about £10 a week.

Your Lord President of the Council then announced the business for the next two weeks. The first three days of next week will be taken up with the Finance Bill and Thursday will see a debate on Economic and Monetary Union.

So, I am afraid, Your Majesty, today was all rather boring. I should own up and admit it is largely because there is a grand Labour Party fundraising ball at the Hilton tonight hosted by Your Home Secretary and Your Prime Minister. I suspect that many of my colleagues are busy getting into their finery for that, which is where I am off to now.

I imagine things will be back to their usual hectic selves next week.

Janet Anderson MP, with humble duty reports Monday 27 April, 1998

Your Majesty,

Questions today were to Your Majesty's Secretary of State for Social Security, Harriet Harman.

Honourable Members were particularly exercised about the future of pensions. Would Your Government means test the basic pension, they wanted to know. Your Government would stick to its manifesto commitments, responded Minister John Denham. He also referred to the fact that his fellow Minister, Frank Field, would be addressing the National Association of Pension Funds Annual Conference on the future of pensions on 14 May. A major announcement perhaps?

Ministers also revealed that an astonishing 100,000 giro-cheques were lying around unclaimed in post offices and that £400 million had been made available for last winter and next for Winter Fuel payments to help pensioners with their fuel bills.

Other questions concerned welfare reform. The White Paper, A New Contract for Welfare, was published on 26 March and views upon it are being sought by the 31 July 1998. There were also questions about the future of child maintenance and the Child Support Agency which Your Government is determined to reform - though I suspect, as with welfare, this is such a minefield that it is taking a while to make decisions about what should be done. New Conservative MP, Julie Kirkbride (a former Telegraph journalist and recently married to Shadow Northern Ireland Secretary, Andrew Mackay) bemoaned the fact that too many pensioners had to call upon their savings to survive and Alan Williams wanted to know what Your Government was doing to promote good parenting. Strangely Harriet did not seem to know there was a Cabinet Sub-committee on the family, chaired by Your Home Secretary, which was looking at this very subject. Oh dear, maybe those press reports about the reshuffle are accurate after all.

There was then a Private Notice Question about nuclear waste and the resignation of Anthony Pointer, the Chief Constable of the UK Atomic Energy Authority police, followed by Your President of the Council who made a Statement on Your Government's White Paper 'Tackling Drugs to Build a Better Britain'. Mrs Taylor said that there were some signals that levels of drugs misuse were relatively stable across England and Wales as a whole, but that the problems remained acute and a fresh long-term approach was now needed.

Mrs Taylor emphasised the need for a partnership approach and the need to combine firm enforcement with prevention. She also said that tackling social exclusion was an important part of dealing with the problem, and announced that primary school age children would indeed receive education about the effects of drugs misuse. The White Paper sets out a 10 year strategy for Your Government. As Your Prime Minister pointed out in the introduction, the fight is not just for Government. It is for teachers, parents, community groups, those working in the field and everyone who cares about the future of our society.

And now, Your Majesty, on to further stages on the Finance (No 2) Bill with three votes expected before 10 pm. The Adjournment Debate this evening has been secured by Mr George Galloway MP, one of our more colourful colleagues (who once admitted that while he was on a War on Want trip abroad, he had known several women 'carnally'). Sadly, this came as something of a shock to his now estranged wife. George's debate is about Venezuela. So no surprise there. Heaven forbid that George should ever seek to raise anything about his own constituency of Glasgow Kelvin. After all, Your Majesty, foreign countries are so much more interesting.

Janet Anderson MP, with humble duty reports Tuesday 28 April, 1998

Your Majesty,

Yet another day on the Finance Bill today, Your Majesty, when we shall be discussing duty on beer, hydrocarbon oil, tobacco and gambling. I suspect that is probably as far as we shall get this evening, as Treasury Whip, Bob Ainsworth (a former panel beater in the car industry who is one of our most effective whips) has done a deal with Your Majesty's Official Opposition to ensure we finish at 10 pm every evening. If only all our whips were so efficient.

However, we began at 2.30 pm, Your Majesty, with questions to Your Secretary of State for Health, Mr Frank Dobson. Your Majesty may recall me mentioning that Frank has probably the best line in risque jokes in the Commons. However, I fear I could not possibly repeat to Your Majesty the one he told me in the tea room yesterday! Frank is generally regarded as having done a good job at Health and he was, as ever, on top form for questions.

Simon Hughes, Liberal Democrat spokesperson on health, chose to question Frank about the 'rough ride' he had received at the Royal College of Nursing conference recently. Not a good idea, as it turned out. Typical, said Frank, of the whinging, moaning contribution one had come to expect from the Honourable Member.

Your Secretary of State also announced today that £288 million of the extra resources for the National Health Service in 1998-99 was being allocated to health authorities today in order to deliver the waiting list targets which are also being announced today. Julian Lewis bemoaned the fact that women in mixed, acute psychiatric wards were being raped and David Heath wanted to know how many applications had been approved in the South West under the Investing in Dentistry initiative. There really is a serious lack of NHS dentists. I was told last week by my local Health Authority Chief Executive that it is virtually impossible to get dental treatment on the National Health Service in my constituency.

Questions were followed by Mr Elfyn Llwyd's 10 Minute Rule Bill to amend the Town and Country Planning Act, to what end I know not, I am afraid. And then on to further deliberations on the Finance No 2 Bill.

For my part, Your Majesty, I am back into the Standing Committee on the National Lottery Bill. This is the legislation which will make the Lottery non profit making by 2001 and divert more lottery funding to health and education. Rather surprisingly, Liberal Democrat, Ronnie Fearn (who once famously played a pantomine dame), chose to vote against the clauses which would do just that. I suspect, as we speak, a press release, alerting voters in the forthcoming elections to the fact that Liberal Democrats are opposed to healthy living centres, after school clubs and IT training for teachers, is being prepared in the Labour Party bunker at Mill Bank Tower. I cannot imagine where they got the idea from!

Janet Anderson MP, with humble duty reports Wednesday 29 April 1998

Your Majesty,

This morning's Adjournment debates covered such diverse topics as Land reform in Scotland, Former British prisoners of war and civilian internees in the Far East, Alcohol misuse as a public health issue, Sanctions against Libya and Lockerbie and Palestinian refugees and the Middle East peace process.

The House then reassembled at 2.30 pm for Questions to Your Secretary of State for International Development, Clare Short. Clare revealed that six countries have so far qualified for debt relief worth around $5.7 billion under the Heavily Indebted Poor Countries Initiative and Your Government would continue to press for its full implementation. Lindsay Hoyle, the New Labour Member for Chorley, wanted to know if her Department was involved in the Russian Resettlement Project for retraining unemployed former Soviet Army officers in Russia. What a bizarre question. It turned out that the Department had no involvement at all, so goodness knows where Lindsay got that one from.

Your Prime Minister rose to the Dispatch Box at 3 pm for his weekly Question Time. Ann McGuire, who won Stirling at the General Election from Your Former Secretary of State for Scotland, was the first up. She chose to highlight what Your Government has done in its first year. Was it any wonder, she said, that no-one was saying 'Bring back the Tories'. William Hague, Leader of Your Majesty's Official Opposition, chose to attack on hospital waiting lists, but I'm not sure he succeeded in landing any direct hits - even though this is a difficult issue for us. Waiting lists have indeed gone up. Your Prime Minister, however, pledged that they would indeed go down over the lifetime of this Parliament.

Tony Coleman somehow managed to get in a plea for voters to vote Labour on May 7th, not easy under Madam Speaker's eagle eye at Question Time.

Dennis Skinner attacked the Tories for seeking a weak £. Taking us down memory lane, Dennis regaled us with stories of what had previously happened to Governments which devalued. 'Weak £s don't get you into Downing Street,' he thundered. It was, said Your Prime Minister, one of the most imaginative bids he had come across for the Presidency of the European Central Bank.

The Welsh MP, Rhodri Morgan, rounded it all off by asserting that we were devolving power to Scotland, Wales and London in order to counter the charges that Your Government was run by a bunch of control freaks. Your Prime Minister noted that the Opposition were now in favour of these policies, including the election of a London mayor. Perhaps, by the time of the next election, he speculated, they will be in favour of a minimum wage and trade union recognition too.

The rather boisterous House then calmed down for a serious Private Notice Question about the situation in Sudan. There were obviously very strong feelings about this on all sides of the House. Your Government was doing what it could to help, replied Your Secretary of State for International Development. However, the real answer, she went on, was peace and she hoped that the international community would put pressure on for progress towards that end to be made in the talks in Nairobi on Sunday.

The deliberations on the Finance Bill continued thereafter and will go on up to 10 pm. Rather strangely, we learn that the Liberal Democrats are going to oppose the income tax clause. Do they not understand that, if this clause were defeated, Your Government would not be able to collect income tax. As was pointed out in the whips meeting this afternoon, this could potentially mean no money for Ministers' salaries. So we shall, Your Majesty, make doubly sure that the Liberal Democrats are soundly defeated.

Janet Anderson MP, with humble duty reports Thursday 30 April, 1998

Your Majesty,

Dr Jack Cunningham, Your Secretary of State for Agriculture, Fisheries and Food was first Order for Questions today, though this did not deter him from having his usual good lunch in the Members' Dining Room beforehand. Your Majesty may recall that Jack was the Secretary of State whom William Hague accused of being in the Smoking Room when he should have been in the Chamber for a Statement on beef on the bone. In the event, he left it to his junior, Jeff Rooker, who is himself not terribly popular having banned beef on the bone, Vitamin B6 (thus denying women all over the country relief from pre-menstrual tension, and who is now considering banning green top milk).

However, they were all present today for Questions. Dennis Turner, Chair of the Catering Committee, managed to invite Honourable Members to dine in the Commons tonight in order to sample the golden chips and mushy peas. (Dennis has also incurred the wrath of Honourable Members as his committee has decided to ban smoking in the dining rooms). A new Member I did not recognise, asked why Airtours were still serving Argentinian beef in their in-flight meals and Ministers undertook to look into the complaint. This prompted me immediately to telephone Airtours, who are the largest employer in my constituency, to alert them.

In fact, the whole of Question Time was pretty much dominated by questions about beef and related issues and, if it wasn't beef, it was fish. One of the more interesting questions concerned the reform of the Common Agricultural Policy. It is apparently estimated that lower support prices will save UK consumers around £1 billion per year, equivalent to a 3% reduction in retail food bills. Let's just hope it is passed on to the consumer.

Questions were followed by a Private Notice Question on events in Kosovo, in the former Yugoslavia. This was taken by Your Foreign

Secretary, Robin Cook. It was good to see him back in the Chamber again following his recent nuptials.

Mrs Ann Taylor, Your Lord President of the Council, then announced the business for the following week, or at least from Tuesday, since we (thankfully) have Monday off. Business that week will include the Second Reading of the Competition Bill. No doubt we can expect some unhelpful remarks from some 'colleagues' about

Mr Rupert Murdoch and whether or not Your Prime Minister did or did not telephone the Italian Prime Minister. On Wednesday, more Scottish business will follow and, on Thursday, we have the Police (Northern Ireland) Bill. However, Your Majesty, since Thursday 7 May is local elections day in many parts of the country, including London, I suspect we whips shall be more generous than usual and allow as many Honourable Members as possible to be off to their constituencies.

And so, Your Majesty, we are on to the main business of today, a Government motion on Economic and Monetary Union, which will end at 7 pm. Mr Charles Wardle then has the Adjournment debate on the gripping subject of Battle Fire Station.

Janet Anderson MP, with humble duty reports Tuesday 5 May, 1998

Your Majesty,

Honourable Members drifted back today, Your Majesty, after their long weekend, not looking very rested, I have to say. Presumably, like me, they have been spending their weekend doing the rounds of constituency advice surgeries, school fetes etc. My worst one this weekend was presenting the prizes at a local dog show, which was a complete shambles.

However, there was at least a reasonable attendance in the Chamber for questions to Your Deputy Prime Minister, Mr John Prescott, who has been much in the news in recent days for describing one of Your Prime Minister's policy advisers as a 'teenybopper'. Opposition spokesperson, David Curry, could not resist referring to this in his question when he asked Your Minister for Transport, Glenda Jackson, whether she agreed with the teenyboppers. Quick as a flash, our Glenda responded that she thought the use of the word teenybopper was unfortunate "given the comparative age of Your Leader of the Opposition' but that she could not imagine him anyway 'bopping anywhere'.

Several questions cropped up about the forthcoming poll on Thursday for the local elections, and also in London to see whether Londoners would like an elected Mayor. Former taxi driver, Clive Efford (now the Labour MP for Eltham) welcomed the proposed London assembly and said it was time we got rid of all the quangos in London. Taxi drivers were mentioned again when Linda Perham, Member for Ilford North, which undoubtedly contains many cabbies, wanted to know when Your Government would take action to regulate minicabs in London. Linda referred particularly to the number of sex attacks on women in London in minicabs. There is a Private Member's Bill to deal with this currently before the House which is sadly being blocked (for what reason we know not) by one single Conservative MP.

Your Prime Minister then rose to make a Statement about European Monetary Union and the decision to appoint Wim Duisenberg, the current President of the European Monetary Institute, as the first President of the European Central Bank.

Your Majesty's Official Opposition were clearly determined to make the most of this and William Hague put in a pretty competent performance. However, his backbenchers were so badly behaved that Madam Speaker described their behaviour as 'disgraceful'. And, sadly, for Mr Hague, Your Prime Minister managed to wipe the floor with him. Would Mr Hague have blocked the appointment of Mr Duisenberg, he wanted to know. Poor William Hague chose to nod his head at this point. Aha, said Your Prime Minister, thank heavens Mr Hague was not in charge of the negotiations for to have blocked the appointment would have been a disaster for Britain. Your Prime Minister also chose to remind Mr Hague that he had warned of a £ going through the roof and markets in turmoil and this had not happened. However hard Opposition Members tried to pretend the events in Brussels had been damaging, the more convincing was Your Prime Minister in his firm belief that they had not. He really does get better and better at slapping the Opposition around in the Chamber.

He's also not bad when it comes to some of the errant Members on our own side. Tony Benn tried to pretend that the euro meant the end of civilisation as we know it, but he really is a voice in the wilderness these days.

Mr Richard Allan then introduced a 10 Minute Rule Bill to provide for the compulsory registration of dogs and later we shall debate the Magistrates Courts (Procedure) Bill on which we are not expecting any votes so I dare say an early night is in prospect. Hoorah!

Janet Anderson, with humble duty reports Wednesday 6 May, 1998

Your Majesty,

As I was on bench duty this morning, I had the opportunity to listen to the whole of one of the Adjournment debates. It was on the subject of the forthcoming abolition of duty free shopping, which really is inevitable, however much Honourable Members with ports or airports in their constituencies may object. They were mainly concerned about the loss of jobs, but they really ought to accept that you can buy perfume cheaper in Blackburn Town Centre than you can in duty free shops.

Other debates were concerned with infertility treatment, affordable housing in London, the Territorial Army and water fluoridation. The House then adjourned until 2.30 pm.

First up for Questions was Your Chancellor of the Duchy of Lancaster, David Clark, who, if the newspapers are to be believed, is due to be reshuffled to make way for Mr Peter Mandelson. Certainly the journalist from the Sun who entertained me to lunch today in the 'Inn of Happiness' (a Chinese restaurant) thinks so. However, he was still in place today and ready to answer questions on whether Charter Mark holders could have their awards withdrawn, the exchange of expertise between

United Kingdom and Commonwealth civil servants and the sort of background checks that are made on people who are appointed to public bodies.

It was then, Your Majesty, the turn of Your Prime Minister who was in good form. (I thought he was in excellent form yesterday too, despite what the political writers have written today.) Few Honourable Members lost the opportunity to congratulate their local councils giving Your Prime Minister the opportunity to urge everyone to vote Labour in the local elections tomorrow. Derek Twigg from Halton was really funny. Would the Prime Minister, he asked, congratulate his local council on having the second lowest council tax in the North West. However, he went on, there were no local elections in his area tomorrow - but there was a by-election in one ward and the Conservatives had not even been able to find a candidate. What a wonderful opening. There were, said Your Prime Minister, actually 240 seats around the country where the Conservatives had failed to put up a candidate.

Jean Corston wished Your Prime Minister happy birthday though she doubted whether he would have much time to spend with his family. Jean went on to welcome Your Government's initiatives on working hours, low pay and childcare. It all, she said, contrasted starkly with the Party opposite, for whom 'spending more time with the family' meant getting the sack.

It was noticeable, Your Majesty, that there was a better than usual turnout of junior Ministers to support Your Prime Minister today. The reshuffle must be imminent.

Your Foreign Secretary then responded to a Private Notice Question about arms sales to Sierra Leone allegedly in breach of the UN arms embargo. This is not good news and No 10 were greatly exercised about it yesterday. Your Foreign Secretary confirmed that no Ministers had been consulted, or taken any decisions or even discussed the matter. It was all down to civil servants. So that's alright then.

Dr Nick Palmer (very bright and member of MENSA, but has the kind of detached look often worn by people of great intellect) introduced a 10 Minute Rule Bill to provide for the cost of keeping an animal pending a court case to be met. Goodness knows what has prompted that one. It seems to have something to do with farmers facing bankruptcy.

And then, Your Majesty, we are back onto Scottish business - again. There is a lot of ill feeling that we have spent so much time on Scottish and Welsh business and our Scots and Welsh colleagues are pretty reluctant to stay down tomorrow so that we can all campaign in the local elections. They jolly well should, since they have no local elections themselves. It has been noted!

But, thankfully, we do not expect a vote until 10 pm so some of Your Majesty's Government Whips are off to the excellent eaterie in Kennington, the Lobster Pot, for oysters. And they give us 10% discount, which cannot be bad.

Janet Anderson MP, with humble duty reports Thursday 7 May, 1998

Your Majesty,

With most of our colleagues away campaigning in the local elections, the House today had a rather empty feel about it. However, we must be ever vigilant for fear of Tories calling votes unexpectedly so we have made sure we have kept enough of the troops back just in case.

Your Secretary of State for Education and Employment was first for questions today safely guarded by his dog, the ever faithful Lucy, who always appears to be asleep but rarely is. Hilton Dawson, the new Member for Lancaster and Wyre, asked about the need for better access to further and higher education for those leaving care. Ministers said they took this very seriously because 70% of those leaving care had no academic qualifications at all, and 50% remained unemployment. They also pointed out that those leaving care were much more likely to go on to become members of the prison population later in life and that this was one of the issues to be tackled by the Social Exclusion Unit.

Mr Jim Murphy, former president of the National Union of Students, and new Member for Eastwood, suggested that when the first annual report of the New Deal was produced, it should include details of what had or had not been achieved by Your last Government under the 'Old Deal'. Wonderful idea, said Mr Blunkett, thank you very much. Eric Clarke, a burly Scot, former miner and National Union of Mineworkers official, chose to come in on the back of a question on music in schools to say he hoped that attention would be paid to the need to preserve our brass and silver bands in our industrial and mining areas.

Your President of the Council, Ann Taylor, then delivered the weekly Business Statement, informing us that next week we would be discussing the Second Reading of the Competition Bill, remaining stages of the Scotland Bill (surely not again), Lords amendments to the Social Security Bill and the remaining stages of the Tax Credits (Initial Expenditure) Bill.

There is also to be a debate on the modernisation of the House of Commons and a non sitting day on Friday. Hurrah!

Mr Michael Howard, the Shadow Foreign Secretary, was quick on his feet at the end of the statement. On a point of order, he seemed to be implying that Your Foreign Minister, Tony Lloyd, should resign for knowingly misleading the Select Committee over arms sales to Sierra Leone. That, said Madam Speaker, was a matter between Mr Lloyd and the Select Committee, and not a matter for her. Poor old Tony, there is a general feeling that he has rather been dumped on. He must be feeling dreadful.

And, Your Majesty, there are bits and pieces to do with the Working Families Tax Credit, announced by Your Chancellor in the Budget, followed by business on the Police (Northern Ireland) Bill. However, we are pretty sure it will not be a late night, as we happen to know that the Ulster Unionists are booked on the 9.45 pm flight to Belfast. It's just as well to know these things in the Whips office.

Janet Anderson MP, with humble duty reports Monday 11 May, 1998

Your Majesty,

Sadly, as I write this, Members of Parliament are rather thin on the ground in the House today. This is presumably because there is no vote until 10 pm tonight, and I guess some will still be in their constituencies holding post mortems on last Thursday's election results. I always warned my party that, once we had a Labour government, they would run the risk of losing council seats locally. They didn't believe me at the time, but they do now!

However, there were sufficient Honourable Members to guarantee a reasonably decent attendance during Questions to Your Home Secretary, Mr Straw. Many of the questions were concerned with Your Government's White Paper 'No More Excuses' and the Crime and Disorder Bill which is currently before Parliament. The first includes proposals for tackling crime amongst young people, and substantially to reduce the time between arrest and sentencing of young people. This 'fast track' approach to juvenile offenders was, of course, one of the five pledges on which we fought the last general election.

The Crime and Disorder Bill will impose a statutory duty on local authorities to provide for crime prevention and establishes Community Safety Orders to deal with the problem of criminally anti-social neighbours. It will also, thanks to an amendment tabled this morning, give police the powers to pick up children who are playing truant and return them to school. And about time too.

Other questions concerned the number of prisoners with drug and mental health problems. At the last count, this was 28,000 but as this figure was reached as a result of a survey some considerable time ago, Your Government intends to commission a new survey of the prevelance of mental disorder in the prison population.

Ben Chapman, the former civil servant who won the Wirral South by-election for Labour just before the general election, wanted to know what was being done to tackle organised crime and Dale Campbell Savours, the Member for Workington, wanted Identity Cards introduced which he was sure would be helpful in combating crime.

The House then moved on to the Second Reading debate on the Competition Bill, which started its life in the House of Lords. I wonder whether we shall see any rebels on this? Many Labour Members are, of course, exercised about the way in which Mr Rupert Murdoch is selling The Times cheap - predatory pricing they call it. An amendment by Lord McNally was carried in the Lords to prevent Mr Murdoch doing that. However, Your Prime Minister has made it plain that we shall not be supporting the amendment in the Commons because it is fundamentally flawed and anyway there is no need for it. Personally, I don't really care, Your Majesty, if Mr Murdoch gives his newspapers away.

We shall then be asked to pass the draft Broadcasting (Percentage of Digital Capacity for Radio Multiplex Licence) Order 1998, whatever that is and Ms Claire Ward, one of our youngest Members, will conclude the proceedings with her Adjournment Debate on Secondary school transfer in Hertfordshire.

Rather a dull day, I fear, Your Majesty. The best performance was by Your President of the Board of Trade, Mrs Margaret Beckett, who in a previous role in the Government Whips' office in the 1970s did, I understand, perform the duties of Vice Chamberlain for a while.

Janet Anderson MP, with humble duty reports Tuesday 12 May, 1998

Your Majesty,

The Government benches were packed for this afternoon's Question Time. You will not, therefore, be surprised to learn, Your Majesty, that it was Your Foreign Secretary who was in the firing line today - something he has probably become rather accustomed to in recent days!

There were lots of cracks from the Opposition about' close reading of the text' and being 'well informed' (or not), but they failed to score any direct hits. I am afraid Your Foreign Secretary is head and shoulders above most of them when it comes to intellect and quick wit.

Many questions concentrated on ethical foreign policy, the need to restore a credible and democratically-elected civilian government in Nigeria, refugees on the Thai Burma border, Your Government's aim to get the UN negotiations on Cyprus resumed and, as ever, a number of questions about the Middle East. Nicholas Winterton certainly did not mince his words when he bobbed up on this one. Was not the problem, he said, that there was not one single Arab Leader who trusted Netanyahu. He's quite right, of course.

For some reason, Madam Speaker decided to allow a Private Notice Question following questions 'To ask the Secretary of State for Foreign and Commonwealth Affairs if he will make a statement on the supply of arms to Sierra Leone in the light of the Prime Minister's statements about the outcome of events there'. So poor old Robin was in for a long stint at the dispatch box. He handled himself brilliantly. Here was a man whose whole body language announced that he was in control.

But Opposition Members were determined to have a go. So much so that Madam Speaker got extremely cross and almost named John Bercow (he is one of the regular troublemakers). 'The Foreign Secretary will be allowed to answer in silence,' she boomed. Labour backbenchers were generally helpful, apart from Diane Abbott who, as was noted in the Whips report, 'sank to the occasion' and accused Minister, Tony Lloyd, of misleading the Foreign Affairs Committee (of which, sadly, Ms Abbott is a member). David Winnick said it was a bit rich of the Tories to criticise us when Your former Government had been selling arms to the Argentinian junta up to the day on which the Falklands were invaded. Even Dennis Skinner waded in with a helpful intervention, praising Your Foreign Secretary for being a 'master of his brief who had managed to read the Scott Report in a mere three hours. Perhaps we are succeeding in turning this one round, Your Majesty, by placing the emphasis on the restoration of an elected government in Sierra Leone. But there is no doubt that it is our darkest hour so far, which is why we made sure that Minister Tony Lloyd was surrounded on the terrace by his mates last night. It helps to have friends, and Tony has a lot of them.

Mr David Prior, son of Jim Prior (and advocate of smoking cannabis) then introduced a Bill to establish procedures to place restrictions on the closure of rural and community hospitals - and so we find ourselves back on Scottish business - again!

The sooner we get this Scottish Parliament up and running the better. Let us hope there are not too many votes, not least because British Airways are holding a reception at the London Aquarium at County Hall. Their receptions are always good and the champagne flows freely. What a pity we shall have to tell them we've all switched to British Midland because the food and service are much better.

But we should be back in time for Mr Christopher Fraser's Adjournment Debate on Prostate cancer screening.

Janet Anderson MP, with humble duty reports Wednesday 13 May, 1998

Your Majesty,

This morning's Adjournment debates covered the Misuse of drugs, United Kingdom Plutonium disposition policy, Combating election fraud in Northern Ireland, Prosecution and sentencing policy in fatal road traffic accidents involving pedestrians or cyclists and the Impact of the long life assets Capital Allowance provision on British Aviation. I am afraid, Your Majesty, I cannot give you precise details of each debate since I was attending the usual weekly meeting of Whips at 12 Downing Street. However, they certainly appear, as ever, to have included a wide range of issues and, however, obscure, Your Majesty may be sure they will certainly be important to the individual Member.

Questions to Your Secretary of State for Northern Ireland today were dominated by the Bloomfield report on the victims of violence and the announcement that Adam Ingram was to be given Ministerial responsibility for this. Everyone said they wished for a successful outcome in the referendum on 22 May and the achievement of a peaceful society and there was a general condemnation of those Honourable Members who were being less than enthusiastic about this. There was also a general welcome for Your Chancellor's recent announcement for increased funding to help the unemployed in Northern Ireland for although the number has decreased by 4,000 over the past year, there are still 59,000 people unemployed in the province.

The Northern Ireland theme continued into Questions to Your Prime Minister as

Mr Norman Godman' s first question was on that very subject. Your Prime Minister welcomed the Bloomfield report and its 20 recommendations and went on to thank all the other political parties for their support. Your Government had too, he announced, allocated £5 million to help the victims of violence. Your Prime Minister also revealed, in answer to David Crausby from Bolton, that there were now 100,000 modern apprenticeships, which was 50% up on one year ago.

William Hague, for Your Majesty's Opposition, had (unwisely as it turned out) decided to question Your Prime Minister on Your Secretary of State for Foreign Affairs, Sierra Leone, and associated matters. But Your Prime Minister was ready for him and came out fighting. What a contrast, he asserted, between this Government and the last. Your Government now was being attacked by the Opposition for helping to restore a democratically elected regime to a country previously ruled by a military junta, whereas they had been found guilty of gun running to Iraq. William Hague persisted. 'The Honourable Gentleman might impress a 6th form debating society,' retorted Your Prime Minister, 'but he doesn't impress me.' Well that brought the House down. 'More' shouted all the Government backbenchers.

Bev Hughes asked about exclusions from schools. There are 13,000 pupils apparently currently excluded and we are going to do something about it. Quite right - it really is too easy an option for headteachers to take. Phil Woolas from Oldham wanted to be congratulated on setting up the All Party Clothing and Textile Group (with a strong membership and free subscription), and he duly was.

Dr George Turner then introduced a Bill to make new provision with respect to home to school transport for pupils in maintained schools, and so we were on to the main business: Lords amendments to the Social Security Bill, all 186 of them.

I fear, Your Majesty, there is a late night (or early morning) in prospect. At least the weather is mild enough for us to sit out on the terrace - always a pleasant experience on summer evenings.

Janet Anderson MP, with humble duty reports Thursday 14 May, 1998

Your Majesty,

Questions today were to Your President of the Board of Trade, Mrs Margaret Beckett, who always puts in a competent and well polished performance at the Dispatch Box. It is Margaret's Department which is dealing with two rather tricky issues at the moment - the Competition Bill and the question of trade union recognition. She has so far managed both extremely well and we await the White Paper on the latter any day now. It is rumoured that Your Majesty's Government will be producing proposals likely to be acceptable to both the CBI and the TUC.

However, questions were mainly concerned with other matters today.

Gordon Prentice was concerned about supermarkets selling bread below cost price and the effect this is having on independent bakers. Others continued the debate about the strength of sterling and the implications for exports. Mrs Beckett reinforced the determination of Your Government not to return to the boom and bust policies of the past. Ian McCartney (who is rumoured to be in line for promotion) confirmed that Your Government remained committed to maintaining the universal postal delivery service and also told the House that the Low Pay Commission would be making its recommendations to Government on the National Minimum Wage by the end of May.

Your Foreign Secretary, who has certainly had a busy week, then made a Statement on the recent nuclear tests in India. There was no doubt about the strength of feeling about this from Honourable Members on all sides. Mr Cook said Your Government had already expressed dismay to the Indian Government and that yesterday the Acting High Commissioner for India was summoned to the Foreign Office so that we could express our concern at the test programme. There were also worries about any consequential action by Pakistan. As Gerald Kaufman pointed out, the world could be facing what could turn out to be the most dangerous nuclear missile race. Mr Cook called upon the whole

House to join Your Government in sending a united message on behalf of Britain that we oppose and condemn these nuclear tests.

Your Majesty's Lord President of the Council, Mrs Ann Taylor, followed Mr Cook with the usual Business Statement informing us that the annual scrutiny debate on the Common Agricultural Policy would take place next week. Your Majesty's Official Opposition have also chosen to debate the subject of Sierra Leone on Monday next, so poor Robin will be at the Dispatch Box again.

Opposition Members were also anxious to know the truth about the rumours that the House my not rise until mid August. What they don't know - yet - is that we may have to sit on at least one weekend too in order to get all the Northern Ireland legislation through. We shall save that particular piece of news for a little later.

Proceedings continued on the Tax Credits (Initial Expenditure) Bill and we are confident we have struck a deal to allow Honourable Members to vacate the premises by 7 pm, which should go down well with everyone.

Janet Anderson MP, with humble duty reports Monday 18 May, 1998

Your Majesty,

Today has been such a hot day it probably accounts for the good attendance in the Commons Chamber - it is the only part of the Commons to enjoy air conditioning. So, even though the first vote is not before 7 pm, there were plenty of Honourable Members present for Questions to Your Secretary of State for Defence, the amiable Scot, George Robertson.

Laura Moffatt, a former nurse, wanted to know about the state of defence medical services, which have apparently been criticised in a recent report from the Defence Select Committee. Several other Honourable Members spoke up in similar vein on this question. Your Secretary of State made it plain that Your Government would not tolerate anything other than a first rate medical service. When asked by former Defence Minister, the Hon Nicholas Soames, if Your Secretary of State would speak urgently to Your Secretary of State for Health to ensure that skilled medical staff from health trusts around the country could be made available as necessary, Mr Robertson replied that he certainly would.

Other questions concerned recruitment to the army. Ministers revealed that, in the year to 31 March, the Army recruited 13,926 soldiers, the highest number since 1991. Could this be part of our Welfare to Work project I wonder or possibly national service by another name! Certainly seems a good idea to me. One particularly interesting question was about the availability of satellite television facilities on board Royal Navy ships. It turns out that only carriers can receive it when at sea. Dr Reid (one of Your Majesty's brightest and best junior Ministers in my view) announced that 'in view of the potentially beneficial effects on morale,' he had directed that Your Government should explore the possibility of making satellite television available on all Royal Navy ships at sea. That should certainly cheer up the troops. I imagine it was no coincidence that the question was asked by Mr Jim Murphy, the young Member for

Eastwood, a former President of the National Union of Students, one of the keenest footballers in the House, and a very smooth operator indeed.

The business continued with an Opposition debate on Sierra Leone (what a surprise), led by Mr Michael Howard, Your Majesty's Shadow Foreign Secretary. The Opposition case was seemingly that any inquiry into what had happened over Sierra Leone should be public and overseen by a senior High Court judge. I cannot imagine what is wrong with Sir Thomas Legg QC. Apparently because he has worked in the civil service this makes him unsuitable. However, as Your Foreign Secretary pointed out, surely it made him best placed for the job. (Good job Your Majesty's Official Opposition do not know that Sir Thomas is married to the former secretary to Tony Benn!) Your Foreign Secretary also announced that Sir Thomas would be assisted by an assessor, none other than Sir Robin Ibs, formerly of ICI and Lloyds TSB, whom Your Majesty's former Prime Minister, Margaret Thatcher, had appointed to advise her on efficiency. That one brought the House down.

Robin really was on excellent form and supported by no fewer than five Cabinet colleagues on the front bench. To great laughter, he apologised for misleading the House when he had accused Your former Home Secretary, Michael Howard, of having lost 13 cases in the courts. He had, he said, overlooked four others, so the total was 17. It really is a bit rich, Your Majesty, for Michael Howard to accuse Your current Ministers of evading their responsibility. This, after all, was the man who invented a distinction between 'policy' and 'operations' and was once famously grilled by Jeremy Paxman who ended the interview in exasperation with the question 'let's just get one thing straight, Home Secretary, if every prisoner in Parkhurst crawled across the walls tonight, you would not be responsible'. It is an interview which, quite rightly, has received a number of awards and I don't think any of us will ever forget it.

Your Foreign Secretary certainly warmed to this type of theme when he reminded Your Shadow Foreign Secretary that, when (as Home

Secretary) he had been informed that 537 prisoners had been released early, he said he thought he 'should have been consulted'.

So really, Your Majesty, it wasn't a particularly important or gripping exchange, just the usual knockabout stuff. Your Foreign Secretary was clearly in command - you could tell by his body language. But I do not think that the issue of Sierra Leone is going to be foremost in the minds of my constituents as they make their way home from the factories this evening.

The next debate is another Opposition debate on the Territorial Army, for which we have one speaker, and then Sir Michael Spicer has the Adjournment Debate on The future of nursery education. I think there is one simple answer to that and that is that at least nursery education does have a future - now.

Janet Anderson MP, with humble duty reports Tuesday 19 May, 1998

Your Majesty,

Yet again, Your Majesty, today's proceedings have a particularly Scottish flavour but, so far as the Scotland Bill is concerned, this is the very last day. Hurrah! At the end of today, and after considering no fewer than 270 amendments, we shall at last have reached the Third Reading of this marathon bill. The vote (if there is one) will be at around 10.45 pm, after which I suspect several large malts will be consumed in the Smoking Room in celebration.

First off today, however, was Questions to Your Majesty's Secretary of State for Scotland, Donald Dewar. Almost every time we have Scottish questions, Your Minister, Sam Galbraith, is forced to reveal that he once worked as a brain surgeon on the Isle of Skye. Today was no exception. This was in response to a question about hospital waiting lists in the Highland Health Board area. There are apparently 3616 on the waiting list, but over 80% of patients are seen within 3 months. The latter statistic is the one we should be highlighting. It was, in my view, unwise to select waiting lists as a measure. As my local health chiefs said to me on Friday, they will never go down.

Other questions concerned land reform in Scotland, a subject upon which Your Secretary of State has apparently received 300 written replies during the consultation period; as ever, one from Tam Dalyell on the Lockerbie bombing; and another on the future funding of child care provisions previously provided under the Urban Programme. On the latter, Ministers confirmed that during 1998-99 Your Government will be making almost £4 million extra available to local authorities in Scotland to develop and encourage childcare in their areas.

Scottish questions were followed by Questions to the Parliamentary Secretary in Your Majesty's Lord Chancellor's Department. These were, not surprisingly, dominated by Your Government's proposals to reform the legal aid system. There are an awful lot of worried lawyers who stand to lose out, and not before time given the millions they have had under the old system. The Parliamentary Secretary, Geoff Hoon (who is being tipped for promotion in the reshuffle whenever it comes) reminded the House that Your Government intends to create a Community Legal Service and to do so it is essential to re-focus legal aid on social welfare issues.

Mr Alasdair Morgan then introduced a 10 Minute Rule Bill, again with a Scottish dimension. His Bill would require Scottish local authorities to make reciprocal arrangements for the operation of bus and rail concessionary travel schemes for visually impaired and blind people within their areas. Undoubtly a popular measure, but this Bill, Your Majesty, stands no chance of becoming law, which is probably just as well as the cost implications would be enormous.

The only respite from Scotland today was another excursion into Foreign Affairs. Thankfully, however, Your Foreign Secretary was spared today and the Statement on the current situation in Indonesia was made by junior Minister, Derek Fatchett. He confirmed that Your Government's top priority is to ensure the safety of British citizens in Indonesia, that regular World Service broadcasts were giving advice to them, as well as the emergency telephone lines which had been set up in Jakarta to provide 24 hour information.

Mr Fatchett referred particularly to the tragic death of a British citizen in Jakarta on 14 May and extended Your Government's deepest sympathy to his family. The motive was apparently robbery and the death was not related to the mob violence. Derek went on to say that the situation in Indonesia was changing very rapidly and Your Ministers had made their concerns very clear to the Indonesian authorities. He also confirmed that Your Prime Minister took the opportunity of the G8 Summit to discuss the situation. Let us just hope, Your Majesty, for a peaceful transition in Indonesia.

And so we were back to Scotland and the Scotland Bill but I will not waste Your Majesty's time with the remainder of the amendments.

Suffice it to say that, so far as English Members are concerned, the sooner we get the Scottish Parliament and the Welsh Assembly established the better.

Janet Anderson MP, with humble duty reports Wednesday 20 May, 1998

Your Majesty,

Honourable Members took the opportunity of this morning's Whitsun adjournment to raise all manner of constituency and other issues. I am sorry that I cannot let Your Majesty have exact details of these at the time of writing. I was, as usual on a Wednesday morning, occupied in the weekly Whips strategy meeting. We were able to meet this morning in the Cabinet room at No 10 which was an interesting experience. Apparently this was because Your Prime Minister was recording a Party Political Broadcast and, while he was not permitted to do this from No 10, he could do so from No 12 Downing Street. So we swopped offices. As we took our seats, Your Chief Whip asked if we would like to know in whose seats we were sitting. Given the rumours about a reshuffle, we replied that we would prefer not to know!

The House then reassembled at 2.30 pm for Questions to Your Secretary of State for Wales. There was a general welcome, at least on Government benches, for the decision to twin seats for the Welsh Assembly in order to ensure fair representation between women and men. Other questions concerned Your Government's decision to enter into a Public/Private partnership with British Aerospace for the development of the new Airbus which will directly secure over 2,000 jobs in the UK, a significant number of which will be based in North Wales; and a rather heated exchange about the damage being caused to industry in Wales by some of the more unwise comments of the Leader of Your Majesty's Official Opposition about relations with Europe.

At 3 pm Honourable Members were ready for the weekly bout of Questions to Your Prime Minister. The House was so packed that Ian Pearson had to give up his seat for Debra Shipley, who is expecting a baby in two weeks' time. Poor Debra is going to need all our support for this is her first child and her partner is dying from cancer. It's at times like those that you realise the number of friends you have in this place. Everyone rallies round.

However, back to Prime Minister's Questions, Your Majesty. Your Prime Minister began by congratulating Madam Speaker on her celebrations today of her 25th year as a Member of Parliament but was soon into fighting mode, fielding a number of questions about the single currency and, inevitably, the conduct of Your Foreign Secretary. Your Majesty's Official Opposition, and indeed Mr Paddy Ashdown, chose to make much of tomorrow's figures on hospital waiting lists. Apparently the numbers are set to rise but I do believe Your Government is making progress on reducing waiting **times** so let us wait and see what the Opposition have to say about that. There was uproar when Mr William Hague accused Your Prime Minister of 'always blaming someone else'. That was a bit rich, I thought.

A similar tack was tried on reducing class sizes. Some class sizes have indeed risen, but, said Your Prime Minister, that was the fault of the Opposition when they were in Government. (So he did blame someone else!) Anyway, he pointed out, there were already 100,000 children now enjoying small class sizes as a result of Your Government's early action. Moreover, he said, this had only been possible as a result of the legislation to phase out the Assisted Places Scheme, which Conservative Members had voted against.

So, Your Majesty, we had all the usual banter. Nicholas Winterton, as ever, made a pretty good fist of standing up for his constituency of Macclesfield, when he managed to praise just about everything connected with Macclesfield, including Macclesfield Town who had just been promoted to the Second Division. Your Prime Minister replied that he had no plans to visit Macclesfield but, in any event, he now felt he knew a lot about it.

There followed a Statement from Your Prime Minister on the G8 Summit which took place in Birmingham at the weekend. He referred particularly to the support he had met, both in Birmingham and Geneva, for the Northern Ireland Agreement. He went on to emphasise the importance of Britain playing a strong, international role in support of sound economic and political policies throughout the world, as a champion of free trade and in the fight against international crime. He said he believed that the Summits had contributed to these goals and that the results were good for Britain.

Mr Gwyn Prosser, the Member for Dover, then introduced a 10 Minute Rule Bill to make provision for special status for ports of entry to the United Kingdom so far as the law affecting local government and policing is concerned. I am not entirely clear, Your Majesty, what his Bill seeks to do, but no doubt it is of huge importance in Dover and it will get him lots of good local publicity.

The House is now discussing the first day's business on the Human Rights Bill, which incorporates the European Convention on Human Rights into British law. As I write, there is some dispute about whether or not a particular vote on a protocol affecting capital punishment will be a free vote or not. Apparently, Your Home Secretary considers that we have to retain the ability to impose capital punishment on deserters in times of war, and that it should not, therefore, be a free vote. I think there may be some difficulty about this and Your Chief Whip is being consulted.

We should finish that lot by 11 pm and then Mr Michael Fabricant has the Adjournment on English heritage and the restoration of church bells. Presumably, there are some church bells in his constituency which have not enjoyed the heritage Millennium funding. However, Your Majesty, I do not think many Honourable Members will stay behind to find out. If they have any sense, they will, by then, be making their way home to bed. Or at least we Whips certainly hope so!

- -

Janet Anderson MP, with humble duty reports Thursday 21 May, 1998

Your Majesty,

Everyone is winding down today, Your Majesty, in anticipation of the Whitsun break, though I dare say many Honourable Members, like me, will be holding constituency advice surgeries.

However, there was a reasonable turnout for Questions to Your Chancellor of the Exchequer, Gordon Brown. Government backbenchers did an excellent job of highlighting what Your Government is doing for families. Your Chancellor confirmed that the childcare disregard would be improved this year and the childcare tax credit introduced next year at the same time as the working families tax credit. He said that these measures, together with an increase in Child Benefit next year and the establishment of a National Minimum Wage, would make the average family £20 a week better off.

Ministers also revealed that the balance of payments is forecast to record a deficit in the next two years, equivalent to less than 1 % of GDP, which by historical standards is small. It also transpires that in 1997/98 government borrowing averaged just £50 per household, compared with an average of £ 1,500 per household over the years 1992/93 to 1996/97. Your Chancellor also lost no opportunity to remind the House that Your Majesty's Government was determined to avoid a return to the boom and bust policies of the past and that the aim continues to be for a stable and competitive pound over the medium term. There were several references to the speech by Mr William Hague, Leader of Your Majesty's Opposition, in France earlier this week against a single currency and the even deeper division which had emerged in the Conservative party on this issue as a result.

Your Majesty's President of the Board of Trade, Margaret Beckett, then made a Statement on Your Government's long awaited White Paper, Fairness at Work. This was generally welcomed by the House, though Conservative Members were less than enthusiastic. Mrs Beckett made it plain that there was to be no return to wildcat strikes or strikes without ballots. She also said that Your Government would consult widely and take advice before specific legislation was brought forward. The reduction in the time limit for unfair dismissal from two years to one year will be particularly important in my constituency. As predicted, a compromise between the TUC and the CBI seems to have been achieved with the threshold figure of 40% of the total workforce in any company voting for trade union recognition in order for it to take place. I would have thought the TUC should certainly welcome the suggestion that where 50% of the workforce favour trade union recognition, that recognition would be automatic.

Conservative MP, Douglas Hogg (who will forever be linked in the minds of Honourable Members with BSE) attacked the proposals with great vigour.

Mrs Beckett retorted that it was a bit rich coming from someone who was a member of one of the remaining closed shops - the legal profession. This produced much laughter from all sides.

The usual Business Statement from Your Lord President of the Council, Mrs Ann Taylor, followed, announcing the business for the first week back after the Whitsun break. Thankfully, Honourable Members were restrained in using this opportunity to raise their usual constituency concerns, since we are anxious to get on with the annual scrutiny debate on the Common Agricultural Policy and send colleagues away happy before 8 pm if we can. A very welcome early night, Your Majesty, and, judging by the haggard look of some of my friends, much needed.

Janet Anderson MP, with humble duty reports Tuesday 2 June, 1998

Your Majesty,

Sadly I missed the first part of Questions to Your Secretary of State for Health as I was busily trying to sneak 17 students from Blackburn College into the Strangers' Gallery. Mission accomplished, I was just in time to catch Ann Widdecombe, the formidable and newly appointed Shadow Health Secretary, do her best to savage Mr Frank Dobson. She did not quite score a direct hit, but I suspect she will eventually. She came pretty close with her questions about social services funding during the winter period when more elderly people need to be admitted to hospital. However, good old Frank batted it back in his usual 'is that the best the Honourable Lady can do and what a shower the Tories are' manner.

There was an interesting question about what Your Government is doing to reduce the death rate from cancer among people aged under 65. Apparently our target is to reduce the rate by a further fifth by the year 2010. Ministers also revealed that, in the last year, representation of ethnic minorities and women on Health Trust boards had improved and that Your Government had produced a leaflet 'Life begins at forty' on men's health. This particular leaflet has been distributed through working men's clubs. I suspect it has not received much attention in the Rosemount Working Men's Club in Stacksteads, of which I happen to be an honorary, though not a full member. (Only men are allowed to be full members!)

Thankfully, there were no statements today. I was forced last night to make this point forcibly to Your Majesty's Opposition, who were threatening to keep us here late. We had, I reminded them, had three statements yesterday in order to protect their Opposition Debate today. Suitably admonished, they capitulated and we got the main business yesterday rather earlier than we might otherwise have done.

Back to today's business, however, and Questions were followed by Jane Griffiths who introduced a 10 Minute Rule Bill on Cities (Process and Criteria for Designation). I suspect that Jane, who represents a Reading constituency, is arguing the case for revised criteria which would be met by Reading.

The main business today is an Opposition motion on Britain's Electoral System endorsing the view that Britain's current electoral system should be retained. This is rather surprising, given the battering Conservative Members received at the last election under that very system, but I suppose they have their reasons. Perhaps one is that Your Home Secretary has to deal with the debate for Your Government, and I rather suspect he would prefer to retain the present system too.

So, I am afraid it has not been a terribly exciting day, Your Majesty. This evening, a small group of us are off to dinner with the Saudi Ambassador, which I suppose will be a dry occasion. Let us hope it helps to foster good diplomatic relations between us and at least we can pop back to the Strangers Bar afterwards for a nightcap. Just in time to catch Desmond Swayne's Adjournment Debate on the detention of Mr George Atkinson in Dubai. As George's sister lives in my constituency, I guess I had better look in on that too.

Janet Anderson MP, with humble duty reports
Wednesday 3 June, 1998

Your Majesty,

It was, unfortunately, my turn to move the Adjournment this morning and set through the first hour and a half of a rather tedious debate on the value of and procedure concerning referenda. In fact, a great deal of the debate concentrated on whether the plural of referendum was referenda or referendums. Alan Clark even asked Madam Speaker to make a ruling. It was, she replied, simply a matter of taste. Other Members raised constituency issues, mainly to do with health matters, apart from Tess Kingham who wanted to question Ministers about Your Majesty's Government's policy towards Western Sahara.

The House then duly adjourned until 2.30 pm when Your Secretary of State for International Development, Clare Short, rose to take questions. There were all the usual questions about the debt of poor countries. Apparently we have speeded up the implementation of the Heavily Indebted Poor Countries Initiative and the G8 Summit in Birmingham resolved to do more to help heavily indebted post-conflict countries. Your Government has also, according to Ms Short, provided £3 million in aid to Sierra Leone since the restoration of President Kabbah's democratically elected government. There was also reference to the Roll Back Malaria Initiative. It was not entirely clear what this is but it seems to have something to do with pharmaceutical companies.

Your Prime Minister was looking very cool and confident at Prime Minister's Questions today. He even congratulated Labour MP, Andrew MacKinlay (not known for his sycophantic support for Your Government) on his 'independence of mind' and said he would do his best to make sure he retained it. John Hutton, Labour MP for Barrow and Parliamentary Private Secretary to Your President of the Board of Trade, managed, by contrast, to ask an extremely sycophantic question without appearing to do so. He asked Your Prime Minister to confirm that Labour Governments were good news for the National Health Service and, to loud cheers, revealed that Your Government had now given the go ahead for 30 new hospitals to be built across the country, 30 more than had been built under Your previous Government, as Your Prime Minister was quick to point out.

Roger Stott, Labour MP for Wig an, who specialises in Northern Ireland affairs, congratulated Your Prime Minister on his handling of the referendum etc. and said he personally had spent some time knocking on doors in Derry to secure a 'yes' vote. This makes a change from Roger's usual boast, often late at night in the bar, when he cannot resist regaling us with tales of when he was 'dodging bullets in the Falls Road'. But his heart is in the right place.

Apart from that, there really wasn't anything desperately interesting except for an exchange between Your Prime Minister and the leader of Your Majesty's Official Opposition on which party had the most corrupt local councillors. Mr Hague attacked us on Scottish Councils. Yes, but we have acted, replied Your Prime Minister. What about Westminster, he went on, the Conservatives had failed to take action there. That, retorted Mr Hague, was in 1988 when Your Prime Minister had been wearing a CND badge. Rather puerile, I thought, and a remark which justifiably provoked a shout from across the Chamber that in 1988 Mr Hague had been 'in nappies'. Ouch!

Your Deputy Prime Minister then made a Statement about the Channel Tunnel Link. He made much of the difficulties we had inherited on this from Your previous Government. He said that Your Government did want the project to proceed, but not at any price. He had, he thought, managed to secure a Public Private partnership which would work. There would, however, be many more months of negotiation on the detail and he had already negotiated a mechanism to prevent any of the parties involved enjoying excessive windfall gains at the taxpayers' expense.

Mr Chris Leslie then introduced a 10 Minute Rule Bill to provide for drinks containers, whether bottles or cans, to be returned to the retailer on a deposit and redemption scheme; and we were then into the further Committee stages of the Human Rights Bill. It could, I fear, be late Your Majesty. However, since I have been allowed away to give the after dinner speech at the Annual Dinner of the National Federation of Tour Operators, it will not affect me tonight.

Janet Anderson MP, with humble duty reports Thursday 4 June 1998

Your Majesty,

Your Secretary of State for Agriculture, Fisheries and Food, Dr Jack Cunningham ('Jackboots' as he is affectionally known in some sections of the press), was first up for Questions today. Food safety and farming incomes were among the major topics. There was even a question about beekeepers and junior Minister, Jeff Rooker, revealed that there are no fewer than 10 billion bees in the country and they produce 4,000 tonnes of honey a year. At least he is not seeking to ban them. Jeff is, of course, the Minister who banned beef on the bone and Vitamin B6 (to the great distress of all those women who took it to relieve pre-menstrual tension) and who is now seeking to ban green top milk, though some of us are fighting a serious rearguard action against that one.

The House was also told that the Cattle Tracing System was on course to be launched on 28 September and that there were systems in place to keep the number of forms which farmers need to complete to the minimum. I am sure my local farmers would express surprise at this. I spent some time with them at the weekend learning about suckler cow quotas and associated matters. They tell me that the number of forms they have to complete is more than ever before.

For once there were no Private Notice Questions or Statements, so we were straight onto the Business Statement from Your Lord President of the Council, Mrs Ann Taylor. She announced that included in the business for the next fortnight would be further proceedings on the Higher Education Bill, which has returned from the Lords. This promises to herald our second rebellion with a number of Labour Members (albeit mainly the 'usual suspects') having tabled an amendment seeking a return to the maintenance grant system. I really do not understand how these self-claimed upholders of left wing socialism can possibly justify a return to a system which allowed children from middle class families to be funded through higher education by working class families' taxation, but there we are.

The subjects raised by individual Members during Business Questions covered the usual wide range. While there was opposition from some Conservative Members to the possibility of the House sitting on a Saturday (which we may have to do, Your Majesty, in order to get through all the Northern Ireland business), other Members said they would be willing to do so in order to ratify the Ottawa Convention on Landmines. Others said how refreshing it had been this morning not to have to listen to the usual stream of politicians on the Today programme and to have soothing music instead. This was, of course, one of the programmes which hit the dust as a result of the strike at the BBC. And now we are threatened with a strike by the underground drivers. It's quite like old times, though I suspect they will be surprised by the response they receive from Your new Government. Striking is really terribly old Labour.

The main business today, however, is the Registration of Political Parties Bill, which is designed to prevent candidates misleading voters. No candidate will, for example, in future be able to stand as a 'Literal Democrat' or a 'Conversative', which have both been tried in the past.

We do not anticipate any votes on this for it is likely to be supported by all the political parties. It would, indeed, be in their interest to do so. And so, Your Majesty, an early night is anticipated. Hurrah!

Janet Anderson MP, with humble duty reports
Monday 8 June, 1998

Your Majesty,

Your Secretary of State for Social Security, Harriet Harman, was first up for questions today. Poor Harriet, it is almost impossible to see her in action now without recalling the hatchet job done on her by the Observer newspaper last week. One really does wonder whether she is going to recover.

However, today she put up a passable performance, ably assisted by junior Minister for Women (and without salary!) Joan Ruddock. It was Joan who had the first question asked by the Member for Stockton South, Dari Taylor, who was one of the first of our candidates to be selected from an all women shortlist. Not surprisingly, the question was about the impact of the women's website in increasing access to government information for women. I must say I didn't know there was a Minister for Women's website, but apparently there is and over 100,000 'hits' have been made on it since last October.

As for Harriet, she had to deal with questions about family friendly employment which she said was good for families and good for business. What the exact definition of family friendly employment is something of a mystery, but I am sure Harriet has it clear in her own head. There were other questions about the extension of second tier pensions to groups not presently covered. Proposals on that will be included in the pensions Green Paper later this year, together with other proposals for stakeholder pensions and citizenship pensions, the latter being for carers not able to make provision for themselves.

There was then a Private Notice Question about Your Government's decision to discontinue reprocessing of nuclear material at Dounreay. Your Minister, John Battle, deftly batted away all the difficult questions. Thank goodness John did not become a priest, which was his original choice of vocation. Anyway we came through it OK. Of course, this has nothing whatsoever to do with the rise in popularity of the Scottish

National Party!

It was no accident, Your Majesty, that two further Statements followed. The main business today is the Teaching and Higher Education Bill, on which we are expecting something of a rebellion from a small number of 'colleagues' - if there are votes on the relevant amendments, of course. There are ways of trying to prevent this and Your Majesty may be sure that we are actively pursuing them. We are also encouraging as many colleagues as possible to speak, in order to prolong proceedings on the statements, as some of Your Ministers are not able to turn up to vote until later in the evening. The two bones of contention in this Bill are whether students should pay tuition fees at all or whether we should return to the maintenance grant system, which is what the rebels want. How on earth they can justify the retention of a system under which effectively working class families paid taxes to education middle class children is beyond me. But there we are. The other is the apparent anomaly whereby Scottish and EU students at Scottish universities only pay three years' tuition fees for a four year course, but English and Welsh students pay four years. The plain fact is that no-one below a certain income will pay any tuition fees at all, but some people seem to have conveniently forgotten that.

The second statement was from Your Chancellor of the Duchy of Lancaster, Dr David Clark (will he be reshuffled I wonder) about the Millennium Date Change. It does seem that business is making progress on dealing with this and that companies are correcting their business critical IT systems, whatever that means. Though, worryingly, Dr Clark said that a few showed end dates for this which were uncomfortably close to the end of 1999. Apparently a 'Year 2000 Team' has been set up in the Cabinet Office to keep an eye on developments and Dr Clark said that he would continue to report to the House on a quarterly basis.

The third Statement was on Eritrea and the task fell to Tony Lloyd, lately of Sierra Leone fame. Your Majesty will be interested to know that Your Royal Air Force has now evacuated 40 Brits and 60 Australians, Canadians and South Africans from Asmara, the capital of Eritrea. Tony said that the temporary cessation of hostilities had by and large held and that Your Government would continue to press both parties to agree a formal ceasefire.

And so, Your Majesty, on to the Education Bill, which will run at least up to 11 pm. This will be followed by Julie Kirkbride (the rather nice Conservative MP who is married to Opposition Northern Ireland spokesman, Andrew Mackay) who has an adjournment debate on Planning permission in respect of playing fields. It will be interesting to see what points she raises, given that it was Your Majesty's former Conservative Government which did more than any other to sell off school playing fields.

Finally, our grateful thanks to Your Majesty's Private Secretaries, who entertained us to an excellent lunch today. It was both enjoyable and informative and my colleagues in the Whips Office were delighted to have the opportunity.

Janet Anderson MP, with humble duty reports
Tuesday 9 June, 1998

Your Majesty,

I suspect the rather subdued atmosphere around the Commons today is due to some over indulgence yesterday evening during what was a fairly long stint - the House rising just before midnight. Your Secretary of State for Social Security, Harriet Harman, was even spotted in the Smoking Room buying rounds of drinks (or at least one round anyway). I can assure Your Majesty this is not a regular occurrence.

So Questions to Your Deputy Prime Minister or Secretary of State for Environment, Transport and the Regions was a relatively quiet affair. Ann Campbell, as ever, wanted more to be done to encourage cycling. Ann is pro cycling and anti smoking and is not terribly popular with some of the Whips following her successful campaign to ban smoking in the division lobbies.

There were all the usual questions about various road schemes in the individual consitutencies of Honourable Members. Liberal Democrat, Simon Hughes, wanted the cap removed on local authority spending. Your Government is currently reviewing the whole system of local government finance but I doubt whether we shall do what the Liberals want. It seems to me that there does have to be a limit on what local authorities spend. Goodness knows what some of them would get up to otherwise.

Tony McNulty wanted safeguards to ensure disabled access on the privatised rail network. Conservative, Eric Pickles, could not resist climbing on to that particular bandwagon, demanding that Your Government condemn the proposed industrial action by the RMT union which would, he said, make life very difficult for the disabled who depended on public transport.

Following Questions, Shadow Foreign Secretary, Michael Howard, leapt up to raise a point of order on when Your Foreign Ministers had known about the investigation into Sandline. Apparently, the Permanent Secretary at the Foreign Office gave evidence to the Select Committee this morning and said that junior Minister, Baroness Symons, had been briefed on the investigation prior to her claiming in the House that she had not. Madam Speaker made it very plain that this was not a point of order for her, and that Honourable Members would have to await the report of the Select Committee.

Andrew Rowe then moved a 10 Minute Rule Bill to set up a Youth Parliament. This seemed to involve a large number of young offenders being allowed to roam around Parliament during the summer recess. And so back to the Teaching and Higher Education Bill which should be uneventful, unlike last night when 33 Labour MPs voted with Your Majesty's Official Opposition. Tony Benn was one of them. He had had the benefit of a free education, he said. Funny, I was under the distinct impression that the former Viscount Stansgate had been educated at a rather posh public school!

This will be followed, Your Majesty, by some European Communities business where we expect Conservative Members to make a lot of fuss about quota hopping. And then Barry Gardiner has the Adjournment debate on Gas industry regulation.

Janet Anderson MP, with humble duty reports Wednesday 10 June, 1998

Your Majesty,

This morning's Adjournment debates covered the usual range of subjects chosen by individual backbenchers. These included Preventative health care and home insulation, planning guidance on the use of sports grounds and the provision of magistrates' courts in Suffolk. This latter topic is exercising the minds of many Honourable Members as Your Government tries to streamline the court service to save money. Other debates were Claire Curtis-Thomas (who has just returned from maternity leave) on Mr Ray Herring and the Merseyside Policy, and Jim Fitzpatrick (who uncharacteristically voted against Your Government on student finance this week because the Fire Brigades Union, of which he is a former member, asked him to) on leasehold reform.

The House then adjourned until 2.30 pm when Your Chancellor of the Duchy of Lancaster, Dr David Clark, was up for questions. There was much debate about the length of time some of Your Majesty's Ministers were taking to reply to letters. There were some, claimed Eric Forth, who didn't even sign them. (This is a complaint I have heard before from Nicholas Soames who tells me that Your Financial Secretary to the Treasury is the worst culprit.) Others complained that letters from civil servants to members of the public were often slow in coming too, and that when they did they were sometimes irrelevant to the original enquiry and, heaven forbid, not in line with Government policy.

Prime Minister's Questions saw a packed Chamber today and, all in all, it tas pretty good humoured. William Hague tried to suggest that Your Government was about to tax rubbish to which Your Prime Minister retorted that the greatest amount\ of recycled rubbish came from the Opposition benches. (Are we going to tax rubbish? I assume he was referring to the landfill tax but it was not clear.)

Roger Casale said he looked forward to welcoming Your Prime Minister to his Wimbledon constituency for the All England tennis finals and said he hoped Your Prime Minister would have time to look in on the primary school where government funding had enabled every child to be 'wired up to a computer'. Oh dear, is this a Home Office initiative to replace tagging I wonder? Lawrie Quinn congratulated Your Agriculture Secretary on his work to help to get the beef ban lifted and said this would be warmly received by farmers in his Scarborough and Whitby constituency.

And Conservative, John Wilkinson, scored an own goal by criticising the decision to abolish duty free, which was actually taken by his lot in 1991 and would now require every EU country to agree to overturn it. There was also much laughter when Marion Roe suggested that Your Prime Minister should take lessons from Your previous government on health policy. I don't think so somehow.

Candy Atherton then introduced a 10 Minute Rule Bill to restore damage to sites of special scientific interest. This was followed by the usual string of bogus points of order. One was from Francis Maude, the new shadow Chancellor, who really should have known better. He sought to criticise Your Paymaster General, but it turned out that he had not paid Your Paymaster General the courtesy of informing him. That is a cardinal sin in Madam Speaker's eyes and a suitable apology was eventually extracted from a redfaced Mr Maude.

And so we are now, Your Majesty, being treated to the rantings of Dr Ian Paisley and his colleagues on the subject of the Northern Ireland (Sentences) Bill. You could be forgiven for thinking some of these people have no interest in a peace settlement actually I think that is probably right. Thank God for David Trimble & co.

I imagine there will be a vote, forced by Paisley and his friends, but otherwise the Bill has all party support so, with any luck, we may not be too late. However, I dare say the bars and dining rooms will be full of Honourable Members celebrating (or not celebrating) the outcome of the Scotland v Brazil match. My eldest son has even donated his' Jimmy hat' to the Whips office for the occasion. It is, Your Majesty, a quite tasteless tartan hat, with tufts of orange hair peeking out the sides - and it plays 'Scotland the Brave'.

-

Janet Anderson, with humble duty reports Thursday 11 June, 1998

Your Majesty,

I am afraid today's business is singularly uninspiring so I do hope Your Majesty will forgive the comparative brevity of today's message.

The House began with Questions to Your Secretary of State for Education and Employment. The first question was from Helen Southworth (Warrington South) and enquired about access to the New Deal for people from ethnic minorities. Ministers replied that local partnerships would deliver the New Deal in accordance with the Department's racial equality strategy. Andrew Smith, who is Your Minister in charge of the New Deal, is apparently doing a great job according to one of his senior civil servants I was speaking to the other day, so let us hope the New Deal continues to deliver. There were other questions about the New Deal too. Laura Moffatt, who is a former nurse and increasingly active in the Chamber, spoke about a particular constituent of hers, Maureen Wells, who has been a carer since she was married, but who now wanted to take her place in full employment and was benefiting from the New Deal.

Barry Sheerman wanted to know what Your Government was doing to increase the number of pupils gaining A level passes and said more should be done to help those universities who wish to increase the numbers of students from mainstream comprehensives. And I think we were all reassured to learn from junior Minister, Estelle Morris, that Your Government has no plans to boost teacher recruitment by lowering the entry requirements to the profession. Thank goodness for that. Given the under-expectation so many of our teachers have for our children, we should perhaps consider raising the entry requirements instead.

Questions were followed by a Statement from Your Chancellor of the Exchequer, of which we were given warning on our electronic pagers. The Statement was about Economic and Fiscal Strategy. This was indeed the only lively occasion of the day and the first outing for new Shadow Chancellor, Francis Maude. Opposition Members were surprisingly vocal. There was a lot of hooting and laughing throughout Your Chancellor's speech whenever he mentioned public/private partnership. I cannot, Your Majesty, quite understand why, unless Conservative Members have still not grasped that the Labour Party has changed and there is no going back.

Your Chancellor spoke of Your Government's intention to reduce the debt level and increase investment as a proportion of Gross Domestic Product. Effectively, he was announcing an entirely new regime to apply to public spending control and a fundamental reform of the rules that govern our public finances. He also said that, later this month, he would set out the results of a wholesale revision of our spending priorities and the purposes of government support in each department.

The comprehensive spending review on which Your Majesty's Government has been engaged for some considerable time will then be complete with a new definition of the role of government so that it is enabling and empowering, not centralising and controlling.

Your President of the Council then made the usual Business statement. Next week will be largely taken up with business on the Northern Ireland (Sentences) Bill, though Your Majesty's Official Opposition have also chosen one of their days to debate National Health Service Waiting Lists and the Crisis in Scottish Local Government. The motion to limit the spending of Derbyshire County Council will also now be taken on the floor of the House, as is usual with these matters, though Your Government's Business Managers had tried very hard to restrict it to a Committee upstairs.

Later this evening, Your Majesty, there will be a debate on the Cardiff European Council. It looks as though it will run to 10 pm with plenty of speakers, though most of us will be gone long before then I suspect as we are only on a one line whip - the first for a very long time indeed.

Janet Anderson MP, with humble duty reports
Monday 15 June, 1998

Your Majesty,

I am afraid, Your Majesty, that the only thing on the minds of most Honourable Members today is the England v Tunisia match - despite the quite disgraceful behaviour of our fans in Marseille. Indeed, some Members have pooled resources to buy a wide screen television which has been set up in a downstairs Committee Room. I gather that even Your Prime Minister managed to look in for some of the Scotland v Brazil game.

However, there was, nevertheless, a reasonable turnout for Home Office Questions but even Your Home Secretary could not resist a smile as a cheer resounded around the Palace of Westminster when England scored their second goal. But back to the serious matter of Home Office Questions, and it was quite a sombre occasion today.

There were a number of questions about the treatment of sex offenders and whether and when they should be released back into the community. I thought it was a bit rich of Shadow Home Secretary, Norman Fowler, to say he was in favour of a national register of sex offenders. When we pressed for this before the election, the Conservative government would have none of it.

Other questions concerned the treatment of rape victims in court. As Your Majesty will know, Your Home Secretary has announced a number of changes. It will not be permitted for a victim's past sexual history to be taken into account, nor will it any longer be possible for the defendant to cross examine the victim himself. Again this was something we supported before the election, but Your then Government would do nothing about it. It was prompted by the widespread public concern following the harrowing case of Julia Mason, who was cross examined in court by the man who had raped her and, even worse, he was wearing the same clothes he had worn at the time of the attack.

And really, Your Majesty, that was just about that. No light hearted moments, no jokes, just everyone wishing, I suspect, that they were watching the football.

We are now debating the Committee Stage of the Northern Ireland (Sentences) Bill which will take up much of our time this week. If weekend press reports are accurate, Your Majesty's Official Opposition have decided not to support it. Rather foolish if you ask me, since it will simply serve to highlight the fact that we would never have got this far down the road to peace under a Conservative government.

It looks as though we shall probably finish early too, so Barbara Roche, Your Minister for Small Firms, will not have to wait too long to respond to the Adjournment Debate about the Distribution of European Union Structural Funds in the United Kingdom.

Janet Anderson MP, with humble duty reports Tuesday 16 June, 1998

Your Majesty,

Your Secretary of State for Foreign Affairs should have been at the dispatch box today for Questions. However, as he was attending the European Council in Cardiff his place was taken by his able junior Ministers, Derek Fatchett, Doug Henderson and Tony Lloyd. By 3 pm we had only reached question five. This was because the answer to question three on Kosovo virtually amounted to a statement.

Your Minister, Tony Lloyd (who must be greatly relieved now that Baroness Symons has replaced him in the firing line on Sandline and Sierra Leone) revealed that he had last week handed a letter from Your Prime Minister to President Milosevic expressing Your Government's grave concern at the continuing violence in Kosovo. The Contact Group Foreign Ministers apparently agreed last Friday that the economic pressure on Belgrade must be maintained and that flights by Yugoslave carriers to their respective countries would be banned.

Other matters raised included Kashmir, which, Ministers said, obviously lay at the heart of the difficulties between India and Pakistan. It emerged that the EU Heads of Mission Troika visit to East Timor, scheduled for early June, had been postponed because of Indonesian security concerns. Regional leaders in the Great Lakes region of Africa had also apparently been urged during a EU Troika visit to the area to avoid any recourse to the use of violence. Cheryl Gillan, the new shadow junior Minister, made her debut at the dispatch box (she was previously small businesses) on this question.

Mr John Bercow then introduced a 10 Minute Rule Bill to prevent anyone who does not pay income tax or is resident outside the country from benefiting from legal aid. Seems rather sensible, but what a shame it had to be introduced to such a tiresome little man. Bercow constantly bores us with his attempts to be more clever than anyone else, reeling off statistics and so on. So irritating did this become in a recent debate on sport that Labour wag, Stephen Pound from Ealing, was moved to comment 'Personally, I'd rather have a sex life'.

As with yesterday, Your Majesty, today was a rather simple day. No Statements or Private Notice Questions, but straight on to the Opposition debate on hospital waiting lists. Your Majesty's Official Opposition are obviously hoping to score some direct hits on this one. However, Your Majesty's Secretary of State for Health, Frank Dobson, was, as ever, in fine form. He announced that Your Government would be creating an extra 3,000 hospital places as part of the strategy to reduce waiting lists in the National Health Service. This will lead to the biggest increase in hospital beds for 30 years. The debate also coincides with a report which says that the NHS is one of the most efficient health care services in the world. Apparently the cost of health care for a family of four in the NHS is about £2,090 per year compared with £8,060 in the private sector.

This debate will be followed after the 7 pm vote by another Opposition one on Scottish local government, where, as Your Majesty will undoubtedly know, some of our Labour colleagues North of the border are suffering some local difficulties, all entirely of their own making. This is unlikely to be a pleasant debate for us, but at least we can say that Your Government is taking action to deal with the problems, unlike Your previous Government which consistently failed to take action against corruption in Westminster.

The Adjournment, once again, is about a road - The A27 from Sompting to Shoreham. Glenda seems to have been spared the pain of doing this one, for her place is to be taken by Nick Raynsford.

Janet Anderson MP, with humble duty reports Wednesday 17 June, 1998

Your Majesty,

The first two of this morning's Adjournment debates were unusual in that they were debates on matters which had been considered by Select Committees of the House. The first was on the Disability Living Allowance and the second on the subject of Peace Support Operations in Bosnia Herzegovina. Debating Select Committee reports was a rare occurrence under Your Majesty' s previous Government, so this was indeed a welcome departure from what had become usual practice.

Other debates concerned the millennium bug and its impact on public services, Your Majesty's Government's response to the publication of the International Union for the Conservation of Nature and Natural Resources Red List of rare plants (whatever that is) and enforcement procedure under the Food Safety Act 1990.

The afternoon began with Questions to Your Secretary of State for Northern Ireland, Mo Mowlam. The best supplementary question was probably from young
Gareth Thomas, the Labour Member for Harrow who is one of the new Members who is doing really well. He accused Your Majesty's Opposition of playing party politics with the peace process by effectively abandoning the bi-partisan approach.

An extremely relaxed Prime Minister then appeared in the Chamber for his usual weekly bout of Questions. Not surprisingly, there were references to the World Cup. Jim Murphy asked Your Prime Minister to congratulate the Scottish fans on their exemplary behaviour and to condemn the minority of English hooligans who had brought shame on their country and their team. Everyone agreed of course. The Leader of Your Majesty's Opposition warmed to this theme and asked Your Prime Minister if he would support Conservative amendments to the Crime and Disorder Bill effectively to apply Anti Social Orders to soccer hooligans. Your Prime Minister could not resist pointing out that Conservative Members had, up to now, been pretty lukewarm about Anti Social Orders, but that he would consider any sensible suggestions for dealing with these people.

Yvette Cooper spoke about a new scheme in York to try and improve on the number of convictions for rape. Apparently there are convictions in only 9% of cases. Your Prime Minister referred to Your Home Secretary's proposals for action in this area which would prevent defendants from cross examining their victims in court, stop any court taking into account a woman's previous sexual history, and also give the judge the power to clear the public gallery where it was desirable to do so. These suggestions, Your Majesty, have received the widest possible support from women's groups across the country. Indeed, I am sure they will be raised at the Annual Meeting of the Townswomen's Guild in Birmingham tomorrow, where, as a Vice President, I should be, but sadly whips duties will prevent me from doing so.

A Statement from Your Prime Minister followed on the outcome of the European Council meeting in Cardiff which Your Prime Minister had chaired.

The meeting had apparently been mainly concerned with economic reform and employment; enlargement and the necessary accompanying policy reforms; the future development of the EU; and foreign policy issues, notably Kosovo. The environment, crime and drugs were also discussed and agreement was reached on the need to implement the Amsterdam Treaty provisions on integrating environmental protection into EU policies.

Your Prime Minister also said how delighted he had been to welcome Nelson Mandela to Cardiff.

Dr Alan Whitehead then introduced a 10 Minute Rule Bill on the disposal and re-use of white goods. This apparently is an attempt to make sure Zanussi fridges are not left lying around in lay-bys by placing a value on goods when they have reached the end of their natural life. So, as Your Majesty will see, there is no matter too trivial for Your Parliament to consider.

The remainder of the evening win be taken up with further debate on the Human Rights Bill and the Northern Ireland (Sentences) Bill. We were facing six and a half hours on the former and three hours on the latter. Thankfully Opposition Whips have been persuaded to agree to three hours on each. Hurrah. So home before midnight if we are lucky.

Janet Anderson MP, with humble duty reports Thursday 18 June, 1998

Your Majesty,

The main issue today, Your Majesty, is of course the announcement by Your Government of the minimum wage which, we believe, will benefit 2 million people. This was warmly welcomed by Labour backbenchers and indeed almost everyone apart from Your Majesty's Official Opposition. It fell to Labour's Derek Foster, who was our Chief Whip in Opposition, to remind the House that it was Churchill himself who, in 1909, pronounced that there ought to be a minimum wage. Didn't that, said Derek, show what an uphill task lay ahead if the Conservative Party were to modernise itself.

Dennis Skinner asked if tips would be taken into account and claimed that, if they were to be, Ministers would find themselves in trouble. Mrs Beckett said she could not recall receiving tips herself, but confirmed that tips, gratuities and bonuses would only be taken into account if they were paid through the payroll.

The Statement on the National Minimum Wage, to be set at £3.60 per hour, with exemptions for 16-17 year olds and those on apprenticeships, and a lower rate of £3.20 to apply to 18-21 year olds, phased in over two years, was made by Your President of the Board of Trade, Mrs Margaret Beckett. It was a busy day for Margaret, as she earlier had to take Questions. She told the House that the review of energy sources for power generation is expected to reach conclusions this month. She also said Your Government recognises the difficulties that are created for exporters and manufacturers by the strength of sterling, that the Bank of England had taken these into account in deciding on the level of interest rates, and that she was working in partnership with business to develop measures to promote the competitiveness of British firms and would publish a White Paper in the Autumn.

The usual Business Statement followed, when Your President of the Council, Ann Taylor, announced the business for the next two weeks. This will involve yet more business on Northern Ireland and a number of debates initiated by the Opposition parties. Sadly, the pressure of legislation has been such that the Opposition's entitlement to days of their own has been building up and we now need to deliver. Currently, we are trying to persuade them to give up one of the days to facilitate Northern Ireland business. However, given that they appear to have abandoned the bipartisan approach, this does not now seem likely.

Your Majesty's Secretary of State for Health, Frank Dobson, then made a Statement about Bristol Royal Infirmary, the hospital where a number of children died or suffered brain damage following heart surgery. Mr Dobson announced that he had decided to set up a public inquiry into children's heart surgery at the hospital to be chaired by Professor Ian Kennedy, professor of health law, ethics and policy at University College, London.

This was followed by further business on the Northern Ireland (Sentences) Bill and we shall later be discussing the Church of England (General Synod) (Measures) - at least, Your Majesty, some Honourable Members will be. I suspect not too many.

Janet Anderson MP, with humble duty reports
Monday 22 June, 1998

Your Majesty,

I suspect the highlight of today will be the Private Notice Question asking Your Secretary of State for Northern Ireland if she will make a statement on the burning of the Lovell and Christmas factory in Ballmoney on Saturday and the effect this disaster will have on local employment and impact on the local pig industry. Apart that is from a potential vote later this evening during proceedings on the Crime and Disorder Bill to lower the age of consent for homosexuals to 16.

However, the day began, Your Majesty, with Questions to Your Secretary of State for Defence, Mr George Robertson. There was a lively exchange about the destruction of United Kingdom land-mine stocks. Ministers confirmed that Your Government is committed to ratifying the Ottawa Convention and that, in the last year alone, we have destroyed some 450,000 anti-personnel landmines, some 50% of the total.

Andrew MacKinlay (who has been enjoying some publicity recently following his question to Your Prime Minister about alleged sycophancy from Labour Members!) caused some amusement when he managed to insert a reference to the 'New Labour Manifesto' into his question about aircraft carriers. Honourable Members could not resist a chuckle when Andrew said it was a manifesto to which he was signed up and proud to be associated with. Not, I suspect, if there is an opportunity for more publicity were he to do otherwise.

Ministers also revealed Your Government hopes to make an announcement before the summer recess on progress towards the establishment of a defence diversification agency and that a ruthless examination is being undertaken of our procurement processes to ensure faster, cheaper and better delivery of our future requirements.

There was a short question and answer session with Your President of the Council, Mrs Ann Taylor, when Conservative Member, Simon Burns (who sadly separated from his wife recently) asked if parliamentary recesses could be timed to coincide with school holidays. And the Hon Nicholas Soames could not resist the urge to complain that he had tabled a written question on tourism and it had taken Ministers four days to come up with a non answer.

Your Majesty will be aware of Conservative allegations that Your Prime Minister had 'doctored' Hansard during an exchange on Northern Ireland. Madam Speaker ruled today that Hansard had indeed contained an accurate account of what Your Prime Minister had said. So let us hope that is the end of that.

We are now, Your Majesty, on to further proceedings on the Crime and Disorder Bill. Amendments have been tabled to give the police greater powers over soccer hooligans, which I am sure will have the unanimous vote of the House. This will be followed by the vote on the age of consent, if it happens. I am sure that too will be approved by a majority but we expect the Strangers Gallery to be packed nevertheless.

There is so much interest from the public that the Admission Order Office tell me they are taking no bookings for the gallery; it will be first come, first served. Let us hope, Your Majesty, there will be no trouble.

Later this evening there are no fewer than 16 Orders, all potentially votable, and an Adjournment Debate on The fishing and cockle industry in Essex.

Janet Anderson MP, with humble duty reports Wednesday 24 June 1998

Your Majesty,

I was able to sit in the chamber for the first of this morning's Adjournment debates as I was the whip on duty on the bench. It was on the subject of Crime in London and very interesting it was too. There were quite a lot of references to domestic violence and the need to tackle it, and praise for the agencies active in this area, but demands for Your Majesty's Government to do more. Quite right too. Only the other day I met a woman who had, in her first marriage, been persistently dragged up and down the stairs by her hair by her husband. It really is a serious problem, which often also involves children, and we all await Your Government's National Strategy, to be announced in the autumn, with eager anticipation.

Other debates this morning were on the subject of Vitamin B6, where Your Government was severely criticised yesterday by the Select Committee for restricting the access of people to high doses of this supplement. I guess the problem is that these decisions are still too often taken by men, and they are hardly likely, Your Majesty, to suffer from pre-menstrual tension! There was also a debate on immigration cases involving domestic violence. This is a problem where a woman is admitted to this country for marriage and then suffers domestic violence. If the marriage breaks up within the first year, then she risks deportation, so there has long been a call for an end to the 'one year rule' as it can trap women into violent marriages.

The House then adjourned until 2.30 pm when Madam Speaker resumed the chair. Sadly Wednesdays are a long day, Your Majesty, and Madam Speaker was telling me only this morning how tired she was and had even found her customary one hour walk at 8 am difficult. I told her we were all feeling the same as the pace since the election had been quite simply relentless.

So we began the afternoon with Questions to Your Secretary of State for Wales, which were relatively dull. What is, of course Your Majesty, always noticeable with Welsh Questions (as with Scottish Questions) that all the Conservative Members who participate have constituencies outside Wales (and Scotland).

And then on to Questions to Your Prime Minister who, I must say, was looking extremely relaxed and well today. Both of his normal sparring partners, William Hague and Paddy Ashdown, were missing. Their places were taken today by Peter Lilley and Alan Beith.

The main issues to emerge were the single currency and the announcement yesterday of 25 Education Action Zones, one of which, I am very pleased to say Your Majesty, is in the Borough of Blackburn with Darwen, which includes part of my constituency. These zones will be run by partnership with local companies (Blackburn Rovers are involved with ours); they consist of a cluster of primary and secondary schools and the zones will receive an extra £1million a year. Both Linda Gilroy (Plymouth) and Geraint Davies (Croydon) thanked Your Prime Minister for granting them zones in their areas. The really good thing it that the salaries and conditions of teachers within these zones can be varied, so we can pay the good ones more and the bad ones less! Peter Lilly, who stood in for William Hague, was not terribly impressive. At one point, he seemed to be having problems reading his notes. He could, suggested Your Prime Minister, put them **on** the dispatch box. On the single currency, Your Prime Minister pointed out that the Conservatives were pledged never to join; the Liberal Democrats pledged to join no matter what the economic circumstances; and it was only Your Majesty's Government which took the sensible view that we would join if it were in the national economic interest to do so and, if it were not, we would not.

There were, of course, references to the front page of today's Sun newspaper which has come out firmly against the euro. As backbencher, George Turner, reminded the House, the decision would be taken by the British people through the ballot box and not by the Sun. Good old George. He's not normally known for being over helpful to Your Majesty's Government, but today he was. Denis

Canavan, however, was as unhelpful as usual. He wanted a free vote on the question of tuition fees for English, Welsh and Northern Irish students who attend Scottish universities. Denis is particularly peeved at the moment because he has been kept off the list of candidates for the Scottish Parliament. This is hardly surprising since the only time he is in this place is when he makes the effort to vote against Your Government. Denis was cheered by the Tories, which was, said Your Prime Minister, 'an interesting alliance'. And so on to further stages on the Human Rights Bill. The votes will come we know not when. However, I suspect there will be no votes at all, because there is hardly a Tory in the place, and I have seen the Hon Nicholas Soames leg it out of Members' Entrance. He certainly did not have the appearance of someone who intended to return this evening. So, hopefully Your Majesty, a relatively early night for all of us.

Janet Anderson MP, with humble duty reports, Thursday 25 June 1998

Your Majesty,

Questions today to Your Majesty's Chancellor of the Exchequer were dominated by references to the Comprehensive Spending Review which is due to be complete in about a fortnight's time. Bill Rammell (one of the Labour backbenchers who will be unhappy about the delisting of test cricket) asked if some of the available funding released by the review could be directed towards social housing. He said that, while there had been a 33% increase in social housing in one year, thanks to the release of local authority capital receipts, more needed to be provided simply to compensate for the 62% decline between 1992-97.

George Turner, who represents a rural Norfolk constituency, wanted more to be done for rural areas, particularly in respect of public transport and, inevitably, there were calls for even greater spending on health and education. I have to say, Your Majesty, that in my constituency everyone is perfectly happy with the increased funding they have already received for health and education. The £1,000 every school received for books was particularly welcomed.

Treasury Questions was followed by a statement from Your President of the Board of Trade, Mrs Margaret Beckett, about Your Government's Review of Energy Sources for Power Generation. The review was set up following the crisis in the coal industry last Autumn, amid claims that the electricity market was rigged against coal. The Review has apparently confirmed that there are indeed serious distortions in the electricity market and that, as a result, prices have been higher than they should have been. Mrs Beckett confirmed that the aim of Your Majesty's Government was to put all fuels on a level playing field, and not to give priority to any one.

As a result, Your Government is to promote competition by reform of the wholesale electricity trading arrangements and by pressing forward with competition in electricity supply. Together with other measures, Your President of the Board of Trades said she was confident Your Government could remove the current distortions which work against coal. She said that her proposals were open for consultation until Monday 20 July and, until then, she intended to defer decisions on power station consents.

The Statement was followed by the usual Business Statement, during which Honourable Members are able to bob up and down and ask anything they like, but it is usually to do with their constituencies. We now know that next week's business is all three line whips, on the Finance Bill, the Human rights Bill and the Data Protection Bill – late nights again I suspect.

But, for now, we are debating a Liberal Democrat motion about the way in which private business is handled. This is an attempt to get through two Private Member's Bills, one to license minicabs and the other to do with energy efficiency. The majority of Labour Members are already on their way home, as we shall only keep back the minimum number we need. Apart from the London Members, that is, who are all attending a Fundraising Dinner at the Royal Lancashire Hotel.

Janet Anderson MP, with humble duty reports Monday 29 June, 1998

Your Majesty,

Questions to Your Majesty's Secretary of State for Culture, Media and Sport, are always highly entertaining, thanks to the presence on the front bench of Your Minister for Sport, Mr Tony Banks. Today was no exception. When challenged about the allocation of tickets for the World Cup, he declared that he was not 'Tone the tout'. When Helen Jones from Warrington North complained that her constituency had received no money from the Millennium Fund, he responded by saying that 'was a bit of a bummer'. However, he was at his best and most agitated when young Claire Ward said she was disappointed that the French authorities were to allow the sale of drink at the match tomorrow (against Argentina I believe - yes, Your Majesty, I fear that World Cup fever is beginning to affect even me!). It was outrageous, boomed Your Minister for Sport, that French town should be expected to change their normal way of life because English soccer hooligans couldn't hold their drink. Quite right too.

Today was the first outing at the Dispatch box for Peter Ainsworth, Opposition Culture Secretary. Peter was previously Opposition Deputy Chief, a position I happen to know he was loathe to give up - not least because it paid a salary and being in the Shadow Cabinet does not. Peter was certainly aggressive but I'm not sure he scored any direct hits. His jokes were pretty poor - talk of bandwagons with two wheels missing and so on. He was also personally nasty to Your Secretary of State, calling for his resignation (how original) and suggesting that would give him time to write a 'proper' book. This was a reference to Chris Smith's recent collection of speeches 'Creative Britain' which was not an unmitigated success, it has to be said.

Opposition Members tried to make the most of the recent Select Committee Report which had criticised the Department saying not enough emphasis was placed on tourism. But I think we got away with it. We talked a lot about what we were doing for seaside towns and so on - despite the fact we recently announced that this year would be the last year the Labour Party Conference would meet in Blackpool. Actually it probably won't be as long as they do something about that dreadful conference venue, the Winter Gardens. Someone who would feel quite at home in the Winter Gardens would be the Liberal Democrat for Southport, Ronnie Fearn (who once played a pantomine dame). He wanted to know when Your Government was going to spend more money on piers. Ronnie is well known for his concern for piers; in fact he talks about little else.

And so, Your Majesty, no statements, private notice questions or even points of order. After questions to Your Minister without Portfolio, who is responsible for the Dome, which went quite well (principally because Madam Speaker did not call Diane Abbott), we had a brief spell of questioning the Member responsible for the Church Commissioners. We were then on to the beginning of the first Opposition debate of the day, on the subject of The Economy. So far, Your Majesty, this has been a lively debate about which party had put up taxes more. You would think we would have all tired of this argument by now. But no, they say we have put up taxes when we said we wouldn't. Not true, actually, what we said was that we would not increase the rate of income tax. Your Chief Secretary suggested that the Liberal Democrats were the very model of fiscal responsibility when compared with the Conservatives. They only wanted 1p on income tax, he said, whereas Conservative proposals would put at least 3p on income tax.

Who was it who said there are lies, damn lies and statistics. And I suspect the average man in the street cares not one jot and thinks everyone is being economical with the truth.

The second debate, Your Majesty, will be about class sizes. Another chance for Your Official Opposition to have a swipe at Your Government. We are confident that David Blunkett and Steven Byers will be more than a match for them.

-

Janet Anderson MP, with humble duty reports Tuesday 30 June, 1998

Your Majesty,

I am sure Your Majesty will not be surprised to learn that the most important task of the Government Whips today is to try and ensure that there are no votes during the course of the England v Argentina match this evening. We think we have agreement with Your Official Opposition to deliver that. However, if the match should run into extra time, an emergency meeting will have to be held.

Earlier in the day, however, the House was more concerned with Questions to Your Secretary of State for Health, Mr Frank Dobson. This is always guaranteed to be a lively occasion, especially since the appointment of Ann Widdecombe as his Opposition Shadow. Today's Question Time turned into a high spirited exchange on waiting lists and whether or not they had come down, and what was the length of the waiting lists for the waiting lists! Frank was clearly delighted to be able to announce that waiting lists had indeed come down. To be able to do so in answer to a question from Dennis Skinner made it doubly rewarding.

When challenged by Ann Widdecombe, Frank retorted that this was merely a first step towards reducing the lists still further. Much like, he said, the first step taken by all those prisoners who managed to escape during Ms Widdecombe's tenure as Prisons Minister. That cheered our side up a lot.

Other questions revealed that more NHS dentists are to be provided in Shropshire and that Public Health Minister, Tessa Jowell, is to produce a White Paper on tobacco control later this year. I can assure Your Majesty that this will not go down a storm in the Strangers Bar of the House of Commons - or anywhere else for that matter. There has already been an outcry because smoking is banned now in all the dining rooms.

Shadow Foreign Secretary, Michael Howard, then tried to raise a point of order about this morning's meeting of the Foreign Affairs Select Committee, which had received a letter from Your Foreign Secretary on the subject of Sandline. This was not a point of order, proclaimed Madam Speaker. However, this is clearly not a subject which will go away, Your Majesty. We have all just received a message on our pagers to say that the backbench Foreign Affairs committee has been cancelled this evening. When I asked the Foreign Affairs whip why this was, he replied that frankly they had enough on their hands already!

Mr Christopher Fraser had the 10 Minute Rule Bill slot today with a Bill to prohibit the sending of facsimile messages offering for sale goods of services or seeking answers by questionnaire without prior permission of the recipient. I cannot say this has ever happened to me but it has obviously happened to others.

And so on to the Finance Bill - again - which should keep us going until at least 11 pm. The only other thing which merits a mention today is the publication of the Eyre Report into Covent Garden etc which was not the subject of debate in the House. Just as well, since I gather Sir Richard is calling for millions more in public funding to be poured into the Royal Opera House. I somehow do not think, Your Majesty, this is a view which will find favour with Your Secretary of State for Culture, Media and Sport. In fact, I know it will not. He rather takes the view that if Glyndbourne can be run as efficiently as it is, why should we not expect similar results from Covent Garden. No doubt, this will lead to further 'Luvvies desert New Labour' headlines, but I guess we can live with that.

Mr John Wilkinson has the Adjournment debate on the Future of RAF Northolt which will be dealt with by the extremely able and effective Defence Minister, Dr John Reid.

-

Janet Anderson MP, with humble duty reports Wednesday 1 July, 1998

Your Majesty,

This morning's Adjournment debates included the subject of Guidance for gap year students. I was sorry I missed this, Your Majesty, as I have two teenage children currently considering gap years before university. The other debates covered the 50th Anniversary of the NHS, Pedlars (sorry I missed that one too), Your Government's response to the World Conservation Monitoring Centre for Living Marine Aquatic Resources report 'Reefs at risk (from Tam Dalyell of course) and the future of Oxted and Limpsfield (War Memorial) Hospital.

The NHS came up again in Questions to Your Prime Minister when David Crausby (rather out of character for him) bowled Your Prime Minister a blinder. 1998, he said, was the 50th anniversary of the founding ofthe NHS under a Labour Government, and the 25th anniversary ofthe introduction of Value Added Tax under a Conservative Government. Which of these events, he asked, did Your Prime Minister feel people would prefer to remember. Well, responded Your Prime Minister, he had so far not received a request from Your Majesty's Opposition for a celebration of the introduction of Value Added Tax.

However, before that we had Questions to Your Secretary of State for International Development. Most of the questions were about aid to developing countries and encouraging democracy and so on. Austin Mitchell raised an interesting question about the need to get young people involved in assisting with aid work. A peace corps of young people was what was needed, he said.

There were no questions on landmines, but this was soon rectified later in Questions to Your Prime Minister. To loud cheers, Your Prime Minister announced that Your Government will be bringing forward to Bill next week to ratify the Ottawa Convention. This was prompted by a question from Lindsay Hoyle (the son Lord Hoyle) whose Chorley constituency contains the Royal Ordnance Factor which operates the landmine clearance unit. What Lindsay does not know, however, is that the Bill is not even written yet. The Parliamentary draftsmen are going to have to work extremely hard to get it ready on time. Though you do wonder, Your Majesty, given that we have always been committed to this, why the Bill was not written before now.

There was one rather difficult moment when new Member, Jane Griffiths, from Reading, was admonished by Madam Speaker for not restricting her question to matters which were the responsibility of Your Prime Minister. Poor Jane got bogged down in a convoluted question about the Conservatives' commitment to the national minimum wage. And, by the time Betty had finished with her, she looked absolutely terrified. (Betty can be a bit harsh sometimes.) Anyway, all of Jane's chums rallied round, she got her question out in the end, and Betty had the grace to say 'Well done that lot', referring to Jane's chums.

There was then a Private Notice Question about redundancies at Dawson International, followed by further proceedings on the Finance Bill, which thankfully we shall conclude tonight.

Let us hope, Your Majesty, it will not be too late. We are all suffering the after effects of drowning our sorrows following the England defeat. However, Your Government's Whips office turned up trumps. A vote was expected at 10 pm, but a small group of parliamentary stalwarts agreed to delay the proceedings (by talking about anything which popped into their heads) and they managed to do so until 10.45 pm. Out went the message on the pagers as we all held our breath as the England squad was reduced to 9. The next vote, it said, will be after extra time, or penalties if required. I suspect, Your Majesty, that several Honourable Members will have saved that particular message for posterity.

Janet Anderson MP, with humble duty reports Monday 6 July, 1998

Your Majesty,

There is only one topic on the lips of Labour Members today, Your Majesty. That is the report in yesterday's Observer newspaper about Labour lobbyists allegedly promising access to Government which has been followed up in all the papers today. I suspect the result will be that several people who expected to be earning an awful lot of money will now find their earnings potential seriously reduced. I dare say Your Prime Minister had to be scraped off the ceiling when he heard about it. Thankfully, when Your Majesty's Opposition applied for a Private Notice Question on the subject this morning, Madam Speaker refused the application.

However, back to the Chamber and Harriet Harman, Your Secretary of State for Social Security, certainly had a great deal of exposure today. Harriet was first up for Questions which covered the need to tighten up on housing benefit fraud. Your Government has given local authorities new powers to fight landlord fraud and rules on paying benefit direct to landlords have been tightened. This was, Your Majesty, long overdue. In my constituency alone, the local authorities often have to payout thousands of pounds to landlords whom they know are defrauding the system.

Other subjects included the Child Support Agency (of which more later) and an interesting question to Your Minister for Women, Joan Ruddock on the value of women's juries in influencing policy. Joan revealed that an evaluation of what the juries had recommended on a whole range of issues, including parental leave, regulation of childcare, and part-time working, would be available in the early Autumn.

Harriet then made a Statement about Your Government's proposals in respect of the Child Support Agency. She emphasised that Your Government, above all, wants work for parents and security for their children. Interestingly, Harriet made the point that, in identifying the need for reform of the Child Support Agency, she would not seek to make party political criticism of Your previous Government. As she said, we are all wiser with the benefit of hindsight.

The problem is, Your Majesty, that there are a staggering 1.8 million children living in families on Income Support or Family Credit in respect of whom fathers pay no maintenance at all. This clearly sends out the wrong message to boys who will one day themselves become fathers. The new proposals will involve replacing the byzantine complexity of the current formula for assessing and collecting maintenance with a new formula based on a simple percentage. In future, for one child 15% will be deducted from the father's net income; for two children 20% and for three or more children 25%. This will mean that the Child Support Agency will be able to spend dramatically less time assessing maintenance and spend more time ensuring it is paid. Moreover, it is a system which everyone will understand. Pending the necessary legislation, Your Government will provide more telephone lines and service outside normal working hours; further action to tackle the backlog; and an extra £12 million this year to sharpen up the service. Your Government's approach could not be better illustrated than by the title of the Green Paper published today - 'Children First'.

We are now, Your Majesty, debating Estimates relating to further education, freedom of information, and a number of Orders.

I suspect there are no votes, which is just as well as some of us are off to the Hurlingham Club for the annual Lords v Commons swimming gala. I dare say the Lords will thrash us again, just as they did in the Karting Challenge earlier in the year. We really must find more work for their Lordships to do so they have less time to practise their sporting activities.

-

Janet Anderson MP, with humble duty reports Tuesday 7 July 1998

Your Majesty,

As ever with Questions to Your Majesty's Deputy Prime Minister, the Government bench was packed with Ministers, there being no fewer than eight of them in the Commons. It is, therefore, difficult for all of them to get an equal chance to answer questions.

There was one interesting question on the effects of air pollution. Apparently the Department of Health's Committee on the Medical Effects of Air Pollution estimates that each year between 12,000 and 24,000 deaths are brought forward by short-term exposure to certain air pollutants from all sources, including traffic. That should spur Labour MP, Anne Campbell, on with her campaign to make everyone cycle everywhere and give up smoking.

Other questions covered the Bill presently before Parliament to establish Regional Development Agencies, the best value pilot schemes in local authorities in Leeds, Newham and York and the consultation paper on improving local financial accountability, to which there have been 491 responses.

The questions turned to transport when Glenda Jackson told the House that Your Government has increased the funding to local authorities for measures to promote walking and that the White Paper on integrated transport policy will soon be published. Integrated public transport, she said, will be a key element in generating new transport choices for people.

Mr Howard Flight then introduced a 10 Minute Rule Bill to make provision with respect to the form and appearance of United Kingdom passports. I was not able to be in the Chamber for this, but I imagine it had something to do with retaining our old blue hardback passports in preference to the dark red 'Euro' ones.

And on, Your Majesty, to an Opposition debate on the subject of the Release of Information to Select Committees. This, of course, has to do with whether or not Your Foreign Secretary should release to the Foreign Affairs Select Committee certain telegrams. Your Government's argument was that we should all await the outcome of the Legg Inquiry and that nothing should be done to prejudice the conduct of that inquiry by premature disclosure of parts of the evidence. I think this really is a 'village' matter, Your Majesty, ie. one with which Honourable Members are totally preoccupied but which is of no or little interest to the man or woman in the street.

However, we did all have a little chuckle when we discovered that the Chairman of the Committee, one Donald Anderson, had written to the Prime Minister apologising for what had gone on and saying that he had in fact tried to do a deal with Your Foreign Secretary's PPS, Ken Purchase. Foolishly, Donald copied this letter to all Members of the Select Committee, which includes the off message Diane Abbott. He may as well, Your Majesty, have published it in The Times. Ken Purchase is not at all amused at being fingered in this way, but since Ken is not entirely on message all the time, I guess the Whips have won all round.

The votes on this will be at 10 pm and we then have an hour and a half s debate on Social Security for Lone Parents - oh dear. Why this is on the floor of the House is beyond me. Apparently the Opposition asked for it, but surely we don't always have to give in to them. But perhaps the single parents issue has gone away now, and they are all instead gearing themselves up for the Competition Bill tomorrow night.

Janet Anderson MP, with humble duty reports Wednesday 8 July, 1998

Your Majesty,

This morning's adjournment debates covered the usual range of subjects of relevance to Honourable Members' individual constituencies including EU structural funds for London, The economy of disadvantaged areas in Wales, Women in science and engineering and an interesting one on Village schools and rural communities. Your Majesty's junior (and rising star) Education Minister referred to a number of village schools with excellent records, despite having as few as 30, or even 24 in one case, pupils.

The House then adjourned, Your Majesty, for Questions to Your Chancellor of the Duchy of Lancaster. However, no-one was terribly interested in Freedom of Information today. Everyone was waiting intently for Questions to Your Prime Minister, and the inevitable line of attack from Opposition Members on the Labour Party and Labour lobbyists. Thank goodness we were ready for them.

In the event, the Leader of Your Majesty's Official Opposition, newly returned from his bout of sick leave, was rather disappointing. I suspect he is still not entirely recovered. Of course, he used all six of his 'slots' to repeatedly ask questions about Sunday's Observer article about the former employees of the Labour Party who are now making lots of money in lobbying and associated activities. As we expected, however, Your Majesty's Prime Minister was well able to cope with it, although I suspect he is still extremely angry about it. He had, he said, asked the Cabinet Secretary to look at the rules and regulations to see whether there was a need for them to be strengthened. He could not resist pointing out that they were in fact rules which Your Majesty's present Government inherited from Your previous Government.

It was during Prime Minister's Questions that Your Prime Minister was also able to reveal that the alleged leaking of the Strategic Defence Review, some of which has appeared in today's newspapers, had in fact apparently come from a Shadow Minister on the Opposition Benches. Would Mr Hague sack the culprit, he enquired. The Leader of Your

Official Opposition ducked that one.

And so we were indeed on to the Statement on the Strategic Defence Review from Your Secretary of State for Defence, Mr George Robertson. He firstly announced that there was to be an inquiry into the leaking of the White Paper and said that he would take full responsibility for the situation. Good old honest George.

This Review, Your Majesty, is unique in three key ways. First, it has been foreign policy led, not Treasury driven. Second, it has been unprecedently open and inclusive (which may, of course, be why it leaked). Thirdly, it has the wholehearted support of all of the Service Chiefs.

The Review proposes to acquire four additional roll on roll off container ships and four large C-17 aircraft and will also enhance the Army's supporting arms. I do hope, Your Majesty, that this will mean good news for the Royal Ordnance Factory in my constituency. It is also proposed to increase the size of the Regular Army by 3,300 and to establish a number of joint initiatives within the services, the most important of which is probably the creation of a new pool of Joint Rapid Reaction Forces. This would, said Mr Robertson, enable us to mount more than one Bosnia size operation at a time.

It was good to know that there was also to be progress on disarmament with the number of warheads on Trident to be reduced from 96 to 48.

The Statement was generally well received. I think we all acknowledge that Your Secretary of State has done an excellent job on this one.

Later this evening, we shall be debating the Competition Bill, Your Majesty. There may be a small rebellion on the 'Murdoch' amendment, but I anticipate we shall be able to contain it to the usual suspects. I certainly hope so.

Janet Anderson MP, with humble duty reports Monday 13 July, 1998

Your Majesty,

Questions to Your Majesty's Home Secretary today revealed that he had visited 9 prisons during his tenure so far and that Your Government is looking at options for closer and more integrated working between the Prison Service and probation services. Minister for Prisons, Joyce Quin, also announced that the Prison Service was piloting the reintroduction of disinfecting tablets in some prisons to reduce the levels of hepatitis and HIV.

There were no Statements, Private Notice Questions or even 10 Minute Rule Bills, so we were straight into the first Opposition debate of the day on the subject of Manufacturing and Industrial Relations. At least, Your Maj esty, that was supposed to be the subject of the debate. As Madam Speaker pointed out, 32 minutes into the debate manufacturing had hardly been mentioned. The Opposition frontbench instead chose to concentrate on lobbyists, cronyism and the activities of lobby companies established by former Labour advisers. Eventually Madam Speaker got very cross indeed and berated Shadow Ministers for straying from the motion. It was only then that they got around to the subject in hand, although John Redwood could not resist one or two further references to lobbyists.

I have to say Your Majesty that there is much bewilderment about the way in which this story about lobbying has continued to run. As a journalist said to me, it is probably because the press were getting very fed up with not being able to criticise Your Government. They were, therefore, going to latch onto anything they possibly could and, sadly, Mr Derek Draper et al have given them the chance. Let us hope that Your Prime Minister will be able to take effective action to kill the story once the Cabinet Secretary has reported to him on whether or not the rules and regulations need to be strengthened.

Thankfully, when Your President of the Board of Trade rose to the dispatch box, we got on to some serious stuff about manufacturing and industrial relations. She particularly referred to the part of the Opposition motion which referred to the 'growth in industrial unrest'. On the contrary, she said, this year had been the best year of industrial peace since 1891.

There will be a vote at 7 pm, Your Majesty, and then the House will be debating the second Opposition motion which accuses Your Government of failing to reduce social security costs. Given the mess we inherited which is the social security system, it is a bit rich to make this accusation after Your Government has only been in office for 15 months.

The contentious business, Your Majesty, will come on after 10 pm when the House will again debate the Lords amendments to the Teaching and Higher Education Bill on tuition fees. I fear we could be here until the early hours. This will certainly be the liveliest point of what has hitherto been a relatively dull day.

Janet Anderson MP, with humble duty reports Wednesday 15 July, 1998

Your Majesty,

The first of this morning's Adjournment debates was indeed aptly timed. Mrs Virginia Bottomley had secured a debate on The work and future prospects of the British Council. This did not go entirely to Virginia's plan for she could not have known when she put in for it that Your Chancellor of the Exchequer would be announcing an increase in funding to the Council during his Statement yesterday. The other subjects covered Your Majesty's Government's preparations for the Buenos Aires Conference on Climate Change, Treatment of the UK art market, Train Services for Northampton and Maritime safety in the fishing industry.

As was to be expected, Questions to Your Secretary of State for Northern Ireland were dominated by Drumcree and the tragic deaths of the three brothers over the weekend. Fiona Mactaggart (one of Labour's millionaires allegedly, who owns a castle in Scotland) referred particularly to the women of Northern Ireland and how so many of them had borne the brunt of the troubles. I suspect all Honourable Members at that point were, Your Majesty, thinking of the boys' mother. However, when we got on to the need to ensure women were elected to the Northern Ireland Assembly, Michael Fabricant could not resist claiming this was all politically correct claptrap, and why couldn't women make it on merit and charm like Your Secretary of State for Northern Ireland and Madam Speaker.

This was followed by the best Prime Minister's Question Time we have had since the general election. Your Prime Minister, Your Majesty, was on top form and at his patronising best. He accused the Leader of Your Official Opposition of' dancing around the dispatch box as if he were at a sixth form debating society'. That always angers Mr Hague, who said Your Prime Minister always resorted to that charge when he couldn't answer the question. Not true, as it happens.

Mr Hague had clearly decided to concentrate on the charge that spending on social security had risen whereas Your Government had promised to reduce it. There was a need, retorted Your Prime Minister, to separate out social security spending on pensions, child benefit and people with disabilities, and spending on the costs of social and economic failure such as unemployment benefit and benefit to people who should be in work, but were not. Your Government was in the business of protecting the former by reducing the cost of the latter. What, he asked, would the Opposition cut. Would it be pensions, or child benefit or help to the disabled? This banter continued. What really brought the House down, however, was when Your Prime Minister finally lost patience at the fourth attempt to explain the equation. 'Got it?' he shouted across the dispatch box.

Well, Labour MPs went wild, Your Majesty, waving their Order Papers in the air and cheering loudly. I suspect that, combined with Your Chancellor's Statement yesterday, will ensure they return to their constituencies this weekend happy bunnies indeed.

Your Secretary of State for Education, David Blunkett, then made a statement about the impact of the Comprehensive Spending Review for Education and Employment. He announced that a new scheme called 'Surestart' would provide £540 million for comprehensive support for those pre-school children who face the greatest disadvantage. This will include childcare and play; primary health care, early education and family support. There will, Your Majesty, also be an extra 190,000 nursery places for three year olds in England by the year 2002, doubling to two thirds the number of 3 year olds who currently have access to a free nursery place.

David also promised that, with the money diverted to education yesterday, it would now be possible to achieve the pledge on class sizes earlier than had previously been thought. No five, six or seven year old will be in a class of more than 30 by September 2001. There will be an extra £160 million available to adapt or build 2,000 extra classrooms and an extra 6,000 teachers employed to ensure that youngsters learn the basics. More money for universities too. This is certainly, Your Majesty, education, education and education.

We are now considering Lords amendments to the School Standards and Framework Bill which we anticipate will go on until midnight. However, we shall have to be careful with the votes as all Ministers and partners have been invited by Your Prime Minister to a reception at No 10 between 7 - 8.30 pm. This has rather unkindly been dubbed the P45

Party, Your Majesty, in anticipation of the forthcoming reshuffle. We shall all be watching very carefully to see who gets special attention from Your Prime Minister, on the grounds that they may well be the ones in line for the bullet!

Janet Anderson MP, with humble duty reports Thursday 16 July, 1998

Your Majesty,

I fear there may be a few sore heads around the place today. Your Prime Minister's reception for Ministers and partners last night was excellent, with a seemingly never ending supply of champagne. However, it has not curbed the speculation about the reshuffle which, had it not been for Northern Ireland, I suspect would have taken place by now. Let us hope Your Prime Minister will get it over and done with soon, if only to stop everyone feeling so twitchy.

Otherwise the atmosphere around the House is pretty quiet. In fact, many Honourable Members have already left for their constituencies as we are only on a one line whip for a debate on public expenditure. But first came Questions to Your President of the Board of Trade, Mrs Margaret Beckett. Consumer Affairs Minister, Nigel Griffiths, (who is reputed to be in his office every morning at 6 am) berated Your Majesty's Official Opposition for blocking the Fireworks Bill, a Private Member's Bill to improve firework safety. It was introduced by Labour MP, Linda Gilroy, and its sad demise is now Linda's sole topic of conversation - apart from her need for a better office.

Your President of the Board of Trade told the House that the CBI had forecast growth in both manufacturing output and investment this year and next, and that improving productivity was at the heart of Your Government's drive to improve the competitiveness of UK companies. One of her junior Ministers, Ian McCartney, announced that about 2 million workers will benefit from the proposed minimum wage rates, 1.4 million of whom are women.

At 3.30 pm, Your Secretary of State for Health, Mr Frank Dobson, rose to make a Statement on Health Expenditure about the extra £21 billion to be allocated to the National Health Service under the Comprehensive Spending Review. It was, said Mr Dobson, the biggest cash increase ever announced for the NHS but, he went on to say that it would have to be tightly managed and properly targeted. It is to be used to employ up to 7,000 more doctors and 15,000 more nurses over the next 3 years; also to provide an extra 6,000 nurse training places. Your Government anticipates that, with these extra staff, NHS hospitals will treat an extra 3 million patients.

There is also, Your Majesty, to be extra funding for social services to ensure better help for the elderly and carers, for the mentally ill and children in care. Mr Dobson went on to say that Your Government had resisted calls from 'pointy headed professors' to abandon the principle that care should be provided on the basis of need. He announced that there will be no new NHS patient charges in the lifetime of this Parliament and that, from next April, pensioners will receive free eye tests. That should certainly please the pensioners, as presumably will the Statement from Your Secretary of State for Social Security on pensions tomorrow.

And so, Your Majesty, we are on to the main business of the day: the debate on public expenditure, with speeches restricted to 15 minutes by Madam Speaker (thank goodness), and an Adjournment Debate on the Future of Community hospitals in Powys.

Janet Anderson MP, with humble duty reports
Wednesday 22 July, 1998

Your Majesty,

Just as we thought, Your Majesty, that the days of Welsh business were over, here we are again today with both Welsh Questions and consideration of Lords Amendments to the Government of Wales Bill-all 200 of them. We are assured by the Welsh whip that the debates will not be lengthy but the House has already taken twice as long on the first batch of amendments as he said it would. Surely it cannot be that the Welsh are verbose!

But first today we had this morning's usual Adjournment debates on subjects as diverse as the Future of mutual societies, Radioactive discharges into the marine environment from Sellafield and Dounreay, Government support for clean-coal technology, Teaching of left-handed children, and UK-Argentine relations. Sadly, Your Majesty, I could not witness any of these as I was firstly in the weekly whips' meeting at 12 Downing Street, and then listening to Your Prime Minister at the weekly meeting of the Parliamentary Labour Party. He really is looking very relaxed and confident these days and even the usual suspects could find no criticisms to make.

So, with Welsh questions safely over, without any serious mishap (lots of talk about Welsh farmers and community hospitals), we were, Your Majesty, into Questions to Your Prime Minister. It was not quite as upbeat as last week, but there is no doubt who won. Your Majesty's Official Opposition are in something of a dilemma. They're not quite sure whether they are in favour or against recent spending commitments. When challenged by Your Prime Minister to say whether they want more spent or less, they become greatly agitated. Some nod their heads, some shake them, and the Leader of Your Official Opposition, at one point, resorted to chucking pieces of paper across the dispatch box at Your Prime Minister. Labour MPs liked that a lot, and accused him of petulance.

There were questions about the future of Guys Hospital, the sinking of the Marchioness, the International Criminal Court, healthcare in rural areas (from former GP, Dr Howard Stoate) and the new White Paper on Disabled People's Rights. But, as time wore on, we began to wonder whether Mr Hague was OK. He really looked rather pale and when Your Prime Minister challenged him to get up and say which bit of the Comprehensive Spending Review he agreed with, he just sat tight - to roars of delight from Government backbenchers and shouts of 'get up'.

There were the usual groans as Mr Paddy Ashdown got to his feet. He thanked the House for their good wishes 'if that is what they were'. 'Wrong again,' shouted a Labour wag. Your Prime Minister announced that the annual intake of medical students was to be increased by 1,000 and Vernon Coaker asked Your Government to recognise the difficult job done by many teachers who had to deal with difficult children in the classroom. The ones, he said, who throw pieces of paper around staring at Mr Hague.

Mr Paul Burstow then introduced a Bill to require local authorities to formulate policies to enable people in certain types of accommodation to keep pets. I do hope this is meant to discourage dogs in upstairs flats or it will be deeply unpopular in my constituency. This was followed by Sally Keeble, who wants to introduce a system of advance warnings whereby people who buy or rent homes, stay in hotels, or rent or pitch caravans or tents in flood plains are informed of the risk. I should have thought, Your Majesty, that the risk was pretty obvious.

And then on to Wales (again). This will be followed by more Northern Ireland business where no doubt Mr Paisley and his handful of friends (and it really is just a handful Your Majesty) will attempt to force votes. I just hope I get to count their lobby for even I can manage up to seven late at night.

We shall finish with an Adjournment Debate on Air safety. Glenda is responding for Your Government - let's just hope she turns up on time today.

Janet Anderson MP, with humble duty reports,
Thursday 23 July 1998

Your Majesty,

Questions to Your Chancellor of the Exchequer today were very preoccupied with fat cat pay rises for board room bosses, strength of sterling and the performance of the utilities pre and post privatisation. Geoffrey Clifton Brown alleged that prior to privatisation 9 out of 10 telephone boxes did not work and the roads were always being dug up. I think the former has improved, Your Majesty, but, as was pointed out by Your Chief Secretary to the Treasury, the roads still seem to be dug up on a daily basis.

Your Ministers emphasised that Your Government would continue to resist a return to the boom/bust economic policies of the past and would strive to ensure stable and sustained economic growth. There was much criticism of Your Majesty's previous government for not having properly prepared for the introduction of the single currency and the House was told that the Comprehensive Spending Review would have no direct impact on the United Kingdom's net contributions to the European Community. The Treasury team did a fine job at questions, but I dare say we are all wondering how many of them will still be here next week. We also marvelled at the ability of one backbench member to articulate a question in the Chamber today, given that she had to be carried out of the tea-room last night rather the worse for wear!

Treasury Questions were followed by the usual Business Statement from Your Lord President of the Council telling us what would be the business for our last week before the summer recess. We discovered that Your Majesty's Official Opposition are to stage a debate on Wednesday 29 July on 'The Government's Obsession with Style over Substance'. What can that mean? This is to be followed by another Opposition debate on 'The Government's threat to the quality of life in rural areas'. I would have thought Your Majesty that Your Government's commitment in the Transport White Paper to improving rural transport services could hardly be described as a 'threat'.

The most important announcement in the Business Statement was that we will not be coming back until Monday 19 October. Hurrah!

We are, Your Majesty, again on to Northern Ireland business now, which I suspect will keep us here until around 11 pm. And more of the same tomorrow. But there could hardly be a subject more worthy of our Parliamentary time. Let us hope it delivers the peace for which we all strive eventually.

EPILOGUE

There was sadness when I had to relinquish my post as Vice Chamberlain. I had so much enjoyed penning my daily messages to Her Majesty. I had to report back to Buckingham Palace with my wand of office. Years ago the wand would have been broken in two, but mine was unscrewed in the middle and taken away to have my name inscribed upon it. It stands, to this day, in the hallway of my home, pride of place. The late Sir Sidney Chapman MP, one of my Conservative predecessors as Vice Chamberlain, had a glass fronted cabinet especially made to house his wand of office.

My place was taken by another Government Whip. I am told he found the task of writing to the Queen every day so onerous (it apparently took him five hours on the first day) that the daily message was written by the civil servants in the Government Whips Office. I believe that has remained to the present day. Such a shame. Her Majesty has a great sense of humour and warmth that what she wants is gossip and fun. You can find that in politics and MPs are best placed to record it.

My abiding memory of my time as Vice Chamberlain is the concern of Her Majesty for women MPs. In 1997 there were no fewer than 101 Labour women elected and, of course, we in the Labour Party never lost an opportunity to boast about that for the representation of women in Parliament had been neglected for far too long. It was not just the long hours, as they were in those days, often into the early hours, it was the toll on family life. Several marriages broke up as a result, including mine. Her Majesty often asked me how the women MPs were coping. I guess it was a reflection of what it was like being Head of State and juggling family responsibilities. She understood the difficulties and challenges with which she had to cope for so many years.

And so it was farewell to Queen Elizabeth for me and on to different duties as the Minister for Tourism, Film and Broadcasting at the Department of Culture Media and Sport, under Secretary of State, Chris Smith MP, now Lord Smith of Finsbury. That was a great time too – introducing free entry to museums, free television licences for the over 75's, best ever tax breaks for British films and overseeing the Millennium

Dome (the 02 as it is now) – Peter Mandelson's brainchild which initially looked set to flounder but is now a huge success story.

But I will never forget how much I enjoyed writing to Her Majesty Queen Elizabeth II, reporting with Humble Duty.

APPENDIX

The Vice-Chamberlain is one of three Government Whips in the House of Commons to be a member of Her Majesty's Household. The others are the Treasurer (the Deputy Chief Whip) and the Comptroller. Normally the Comptroller of Her Majesty's Household serves as No 3 Whip in the Commons and the Vice Chamberlain as No 4 Whip.

The Vice-Chamberlain is responsible for acting as a liaison between the Monarch and the House of Commons. According to Erskine May:

'When an Address has been presented in the ordinary way (by a Privy Counsellor or member of the Household) Her Majesty's answer is reported to the House by a member of her household, usually the Vice Chamberlain, who acts in the House as one of the government Whips. This officer presents himself at the bar immediately after prayers and, on being called by the Speaker, announces 'Her Majesty's answer to a loyal and dutiful Address', proceeds to the table with the customary three bows, and, having read the term of the royal answer to the House, presents the document containing them to the Clerk for the purpose of entry in the records of the House and proceeds to make his exit in the same formal manner.' (*i*)

As part of this duty, the Vice-Chamberlain also composes a daily report of the proceedings in the House of Commons for the Queen. Tim Renton, a former Chief Whip, referred to this duty as follows:

'Then, every day, the Vice-Chamberlain writes the Queen's Telegram. This is a summary of the day's proceedings, traditionally written on two sheets of A4 paper, finished by 6 pm, and then delivered by special messenger to Buckingham Palace. A brisk style is appreciated. (*ii*)

The Vice-Chamberlain is famously taken 'hostage' at Buckingham Palace during the State Opening of Parliament to ensure the safe return of the Queen from Parliament.

'should a group of militant anti-monarchists manage to abseil down from the public galleries during the Queen's Speech and snatch Her Majesty from under their Lordships'noses, the hapless Vice-Chamberlain would find him or herself indefinitely detained at the Palace.' *(iii)*

(i)   Erskine May, Treatise on the Law, Privileges, Proceedings and the Usage of Parliament LexisNexis, 23rd ed, 2004, p334

(i)   Tim Renton, Chief Whip: people, power and patronage in Westminster, Politicos, 2004, p18

(ii)   Susan Child, Politico's Guide to Parliament, Politicos, 2nd ed, 2002, p109

The State Opening marks the beginning of the parliamentary session. Its main purpose is for the Monarch formally to open Parliament and, in the Queen's Speech, deliver an outline of the Government's proposed policies, legislation for the coming session and a review of the last session. It takes place on the first day of a new parliamentary session or shortly after a general election. It is the main ceremonial event of the parliamentary calendar, attracting large crowds, both in person and watching on television and the internet. The Queen's procession from Buckingham Palace to Westminster is escorted by the Household Cavalry. The Queen arrives at the Sovereign's Entrance at about 11.15 am, and proceeds to the Robing Room, where she puts on the Imperial State Crown and parliamentary robe. A procession then leads through the Royal Gallery to the Chamber of the House of Lords, where the Queen takes the Throne.

The official known as 'Black Rod' is sent to summon the Commons. In a symbol of the Commons' independence, the door to their chamber is slammed in his face and not opened until he has knocked on the door with his staff of office. The Members of the House of Commons follow Black Rod and the Commons Speaker to the Lords Chamber and stand behind the Bar of the House of Lords (at the opposite end of the

Chamber from the Throne) to hear the Queen's Speech.

The Queen's Speech is delivered by the Queen from the Throne in the House of Lords, in the presence of Members of both Houses. Although the Queen reads the Speech, its content is entirely drawn up by the Government and approved by the Cabinet. Traditions surrounding the State Opening and delivery of a speech by the monarch can be traced back at least to the 16th century. The current ceremony dates from the opening of the rebuilt Palace of Westminster in 1852 after the fire of 1834.

Made in the USA
Charleston, SC
15 April 2016